AN ILLUSTRATED HISTORY OF
WELSH RUGBY

AN ILLUSTRATED HISTORY OF
WELSH RUGBY

JAMES STAFFORD

Illustrated by Raluca Moldovan

With additional art by
Carys Feehan, Josel Nicolas,
Ched De Gala and Anne Cakebread

POLARIS
PUBLISHING

This edition first published in 2021 by

POLARIS PUBLISHING LTD
c/o Aberdein Considine
2nd Floor, Elder House
Multrees Walk
Edinburgh
EH1 3DX

Distributed by
Birlinn Limited

www.polarispublishing.com

2

ISBN: 9781913538231
eBook ISBN: 9781913538248

British Library Cataloguing-in-Publication Data
A catalogue record for this book is available on request from the British Library.

Designed and typeset by Polaris Publishing, Edinburgh
Printed in Great Britain by MBM Print, East Kilbride

Cliff Morgan won 29 caps between 1951 and 1958.

CONTENTS

INTRODUCTION

Every winter Wales do battle with England in the Six Nations. As the white feathers and red roses clash in combat, it seems the whole Welsh nation comes together to roar on the men in scarlet as they fight to get one over on their 'big brother' from across the border.

Every cheer for each thundering tackle and glorious point carries on a tradition that stretches way back into the fog of history. Wales first played England back in 1881. That's an astonishing 140 years before this book was written.

The world was a very different place in 1881. Queen Victoria sat on the British throne and ruled a global empire. Her incredible reign lasted from 1837 to 1901 and her philosophy on winning and losing would have appealed to today's modern rugby coaches.

When fixtures between Wales and England began, outlaws – like the infamous Billy the Kid – still roamed the Wild West of America with their pistols, shooting up saloons, holding up trains and blowing up bank safes.

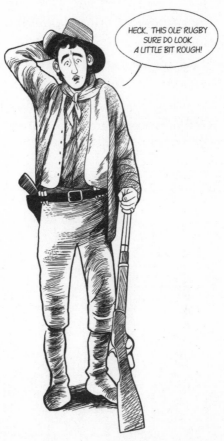

HECK, THIS OLE' RUGBY SURE DO LOOK A LITTLE BIT ROUGH!

The book you hold in your hands will take you on a fun, fascinating and fact-packed journey through the spectacular history of the Welsh national rugby team since 1881.

We can't promise any cowboy stories, but we can tell you about the Welsh international who died from a poisoned arrow and the disallowed try from 1905 that still divides rugby fans (and about which one player supposedly moaned on his deathbed). We'll even explain how Welsh rugby began the tradition of singing the national anthem before international sporting contests.

Plus, we'll have lots of pictures of players from olden days boasting fine moustaches, huge hairy sideburns and wearing ludicrously long shorts. So, jump in and discover the proud, dramatic and sometimes bizarre history of the Welsh rugby team.

1881–99: BEGINNINGS

	PLAYED	WON	DRAWN	LOST
HOME CHAMPIONSHIP	45	15	3	27
TOURISTS	1	1	0	0
TOTAL	46	16	3	27

Championships

1893 (Triple Crown)

Shared Championships

1888

'The life of the toiling thousands is hard and uninteresting enough, the mind of the professional and business man is vexed with the cares of his occupation, and it is good that football should come once a week to take them out of themselves.'

ARTHUR GOULD

HOW RUGBY ARRIVED IN WALES

Everyone likes a ripping yarn. Rugby people's love of somewhat fishy stories is why, when the best international sides from across the planet get together for the World Cup every four years, they compete for a trophy named after William Webb Ellis. William was a pupil of Rugby School in the 19th century. The tale behind why William's name adorns the cup should be taken with a pinch of salt, but here it goes . . .

Back in 1823, William was playing 'foot-ball' at Rugby School with his classmates. In what was either a moment of inspiration or the actions of, well, a cheat, young Bill decided to pick up the ball and run towards his opponents' goal.

At the time there was much tutting of lips and wagging of fingers at this most unsportsmanlike display from Bill. Eventually, however, handling the inflated pig's bladder (which is what balls were made from then) as well as kicking it seemed much more amusing than just recklessly booting it around. Besides, handling meant the chance to make big tackles. This appealed to the bloodlust of these young pupils as it increased the opportunities for school-approved violence. The teachers at Rugby School, meanwhile, were happy for pupils to burn up all of their excess energy as they would be less troublesome through the rest of the school week. Everybody won.

Rugby School eventually realised they were on to something and wrote 'handling' into their 'laws' of football, Rugby the town, of course, inspiring the game's name. From William's rebellious act, so the rather tall and unsubstantiated tale goes, the modern sport we all love slowly developed. Players have been finding new ways to cheat ever since.

RUGBY'S VIOLENT MEDIEVAL ROOTS?

In Wales, some believe rugby really has its roots in a game called *cnapan* (sometimes spelled knapan or criapan). *Cnapan* is best described as an incredibly brutal medieval form of football that was mainly played in areas like Pembrokeshire, Carmarthenshire and Ceredigion. Its origins may even lie as far back as the Ancient Britons over 1,000 years ago.

Television match officials would have been very busy officiating cnapan.

Cnapan essentially involved the entire male population of one village competing against all the menfolk of another village over a ball that – to make it hard to catch – had been boiled in animal fat. The aim of the game was to take the ball to the church of the other village. This meant the 'playing field' could be many miles wide.

Encounters could last an entire day. Frequently no one would win and the chaos would only stop when it got dark. It was often deadly. When you consider that, while poor people played on foot, richer people could ride horses, it isn't surprising players were frequently seriously injured or even killed. Imagine allowing some players today to compete on horseback in rugby matches! While *cnapan* may sound terrifying, you must admit, it must have been brilliant fun to watch.

THE 'BIG FOUR' ARE BORN

Whatever the real roots of the game, rugby as we understand it today arrived in Wales in the 1850s. Reverend Professor Rowland Williams brought the game from Cambridge University to St David's College in Lampeter. Over the coming years the game was mainly spread by students who had played while studying at colleges in both Wales and England.

By the mid-1870s many of the most famous Welsh rugby clubs had been formed. Neath were the first (1871) and by 1876 Wales's 'Big Four' – Swansea, Newport, Cardiff and Llanelli – had all been established.

In the early 1880s, Wales wanted to join in with the likes of England, Scotland and Ireland, who were already contesting international games (also known as 'Tests'). In 1881, Wales got their chance. Sadly, they blew it.

RUGBY IN THE 1870s

- 20 players a side.
- The ball was round and could not be collected from the floor

– it had to be caught from a kick or a bounce.

• Players may have handed the ball to one another but did not throw it to each other.

• There were no line-outs – instead 12 forwards from each side formed a line against each other (heads down) and, in some forms of the game, a spectator was permitted to throw the ball in.

THE FIRST GAME
The massacre upon Mr Richardson's Field

The first rugby game between Wales and England took place so long ago that nobody had yet invented a points system for scoring.

Wales, 1881 – matching kit optional.

The aim of rugby in those days was to register as many goals as possible. A 'goal' is an old-fashioned way of saying a converted try. One converted try beat any number of unconverted tries. A last-minute 'goal' would be enough to deliver victory over a team that had scored 20 unconverted tries!

In fact, that's where the term 'try' came from. Touching the ball down over the try line allowed you to have a 'try' at kicking at the posts to make a goal.

AN OMINOUS START

In 1881, Wales and England agreed to face each other in Blackheath, London. The game took place at a venue known as Mr Richardson's Field. Absolutely nobody expected Wales to win. England had been playing Test rugby since 1871 againt both Scotland and Ireland, winning most of their matches. The English agreed to play Wales so as to 'set a good example to the other nationalities'.

In contrast, Wales didn't even have a proper way of picking a team. The first Welsh side was made up of players selected privately by Mr Richard Mullock – a member of the South Wales Football Union. Mr Mullock had no official permission to pick a side representing Wales. He got in rather a lot of hot water for doing so with many angry letters filling up newspapers.

The match was postponed several times before it was finally played on 19 February. Unfortunately for Mr Mullock, he only had two weeks' notice to assemble a team. Making things worse, Swansea were playing Llanelli in a major cup match that day so many of the best players in the country weren't available.

In the end, most of the players picked had learnt their rugby at the universities of Oxford and Cambridge. In some cases, selection was based on players' reputations from games played many years before. Godfrey Darbishire hadn't played for two years before this match, but he fitted Mullock's idea of having educated 'gentleman' players from different regions of Wales make up the team. Despite this, on the morning of the match, the *South Wales Daily News* optimistically expected '. . . the present fifteen to make a capital fight. The Welsh backs are good drops and sure tacklers, nor are they deficient in pace . . .'

Things started badly for Wales when, according to legend, two players didn't even turn up. A long time after the game, it was claimed by one Welsh player that two spectators – with only the slightest of Welsh links – had to be roped in to make up the numbers.

The story may be a little far-fetched, but Wales did indeed have to make two late changes that day and things didn't get any better as the day progressed.

*Last-minute team preparations were
a little more basic back in the 1880s.*

'LUCKY TO GET NIL'

Echoing Test rugby's humble beginnings, players in 1881 got changed in a local pub and then walked half a mile to the pitch. Coincidentally, the pub on this day was The Princess of Wales and it still stands today. The name didn't bring Wales any luck.

There was no such thing as a neutral referee back then. The home teams supplied the official. Rugby was still such a young sport that different regions or clubs not only used different tactics, they used different law books. For this match England had ten forwards and just five backs. Wales had nine forwards and six backs – but also played two players at full-back.

Full-backs were purely defensive players and, despite having a pair of them, Wales could not hold back England. They lost by seven converted tries (goals), one drop goal and six tries to nil. Today that would be 82-0.

It could have been worse, but one English try was disallowed because the scoring pass was so long and unusual it was deemed 'unsporting'!

Wales's captain for this first match was James Bevan. Born in 1858 in Australia, while still a young boy his parents drowned at sea in a gale and he was sent to live with relatives in Wales. Bevan was playing for Cambridge University when he was selected as captain. He was one of ten players from the 1881 game who never played for Wales again. In later life he became an Anglican clergyman. Since 2007, Wales and Australia have competed for the James Bevan Trophy to honour his memory.

Wales lost two players to injury in the first half. In those days there were no replacements, so Wales played most of the game with just 13 men.

For this historic, if embarrassing match, Wales wore red shirts with long blue shorts (or 'knickers' as they were sometimes described at the time!) and played in ordinary, light walking boots with a bar of leather across the sole to help them swerve. Players wore the famous Prince of Wales feathers on their chests as they do now, but they were much larger and in the centre of the jerseys. Not all the shirts looked exactly the same and it seems, from the team photo of the day, some players played without a crest at all.

It was said Wales were 'lucky to get nil'. England declined to meet Wales the following season as the gulf in quality was simply too great.

WHAT THE PAPERS SAID

The *Daily Telegraph* newspaper described the game as 'utterly devoid of interest' and 'ridiculously easy' for England. *The Field* wrote '. . . it was not possible to congratulate Wales for anything but coming so far with the prospect of "certain defeat" awaiting them'. In contrast, Wales's *Western Mail* said the match was 'well contested'.

The first Welsh XV: (backs) C.H. Newman (Cambridge University/Newport), R.H.B. Summers (Haverfordwest); (threequarters) J.A. Bevan (Cambridge University, captain), E. Peake (Oxford University/Chepstow); (half-backs) L. Watkins

(Oxford University/Llandaff), E.J. Lewis (Cambridge University/Llandovery); (forwards) R.D. Garnons Williams (Cambridge University/Newport), T.A. Rees (Oxford University/Llandovery), F. Purdon (Newport), G.F. Harding (Newport), B.E. Girling (Cardiff), B.B. Mann (Cardiff), W.D. Phillips (Cardiff), G. Darbishire (Bangor), E. Treharne (Pontypridd).

DID YOU KNOW?

• The first Welsh team had players born in Australia (one), Ireland (two), England (four) and Wales (eight) – showing how multicultural international rugby has always been.

• Three of the Welsh team from this game ended up becoming Anglican clergymen.

1881 AT A GLANCE

• William Gladstone of the Liberal Party was the British prime minister.

• The Sunday (Wales) Act prohibited the sale of alcohol on a Sunday.

• Five people froze to death in extreme weather in Wales during January.

• The last amateur FA Cup Final took place. Old Carthusians FC beat Old Etonians 3-0 (no, we've never heard of them either).

• *Treasure Island* by Robert Louis Stevenson was published.

• This was the year fictional heroes Sherlock Holmes and Dr Watson met.

THE MEN IN BLACK

As mentioned earlier, Richard Mullock had been a member of the South Wales Football Club. In December 1875, wearing black shirts with a white leek emblem, they played and beat a Hereford XV. They often played English counties before the creation of the Welsh Football Union (WFU, later the Welsh Rugby Union – WRU) ended their relevance and the men in black became a footnote in football history.

GETTING ORGANISED
The formation of the Welsh Rugby Union

The scale of the embarrassment from the defeat to England forced Wales to get its house in order. The South Wales Football Union made it quite clear that Mr Mullock's severely beaten team was not an official selection. In other words: 'Don't blame us!'

On 12 March 1881, representatives of 11 Welsh clubs gathered at the Castle Hotel in Neath to form the Welsh Football Union (WFU). To avoid confusion, we'll simply refer to it as the Welsh Rugby Union (or WRU) from here on. We can imagine Mr Mullock got quite an earful for his somewhat dubious selection abilities.

The clubs on that historic day were Bangor, Brecon, Cardiff, Lampeter, Llandeilo, Llandovery, Llanelli, Merthyr, Newport, Pontypool and Swansea. Neath, for reasons no one quite understands, were not part of this group. Even though they were the oldest club in Wales and the big meeting was being held in their town, they were not in attendance.

Despite the rather cheeky behaviour of Mr Mullock in picking a team all on his own, he was elected the main man for the brand spanking new WRU and ended up serving as secretary for 11 years. Mullock was a key figure in the history of the Welsh game, but his rather weak grasp of record-keeping did him no favours and his poor accountancy skills (he also served as treasurer) played a major part in him eventually stepping down from a leadership role.

Poor old Neath fail to get invited to their 'own' party.

AN ALTERNATIVE BEGINNING?

As with many things in the history of rugby, there are conflicting stories about how things began. Some believe the roots of the WRU lay in a meeting in Swansea in 1880. Neath were at this one though, as well as Chepstow, Haverfordwest, Llandaff, Llanelli, Newport, Pontypridd and Swansea. Regardless, the official WRU history recognises the 1881 meeting.

Football? In old newspapers and books you'll often see rugby being called football. Rugby – and what we now call football or soccer – were simply seen as different 'codes' of football. Whatever code was most popular in a certain area or region was called football. Thanks to the passion for the oval ball in South Wales in the 1880s, rugby tended to be called football as often as it was called rugby.

Even today, according to where you are in the world, 'football' can refer to soccer, rugby union, rugby league, American football, Gaelic football, Australian rules football and Canadian football. It all depends on what the most popular code is for the people living there. The word 'soccer' comes from the word 'association'. Association football is the full name of the sport most people in the UK call football. Soccer has been used for over 200 years and was a popular term in the UK until the early 1980s.

FIRST VICTORY AND EARLY ENCOUNTERS

A slight disagreement across the Irish Sea

If you think modern rugby has lots of controversy with coaches, players and referees often sniping at each other in post-match interviews, then wait until you read about the disputes they had back in the Victorian era.

Wales played their second international against Ireland, in Dublin, on 28 January 1882 – almost a year after the English loss. Only four Welsh players survived to win their second caps as Wales dispatched the home side by two goals and two tries to nil. Tom Baker Jones, a solicitor from Newport, scored Wales's first ever try.

As always, the result only tells part of the story. The referee that day was Irish, but one of the umpires (what we would think of as touch judges) was none other than WRU honorary secretary, Mr Richard Mullock.

Two Irish players were so incensed at some of Mullock's decisions they walked off the field in disgust. As Ireland also suffered two injuries during the game it meant they finished what the *Irish Times* called a 'wearisome' match with just 11 players. Feelings between the sides became so frosty they would not meet again until 1884. In fact, almost every time these teams were to meet in the late 19th century there seemed to be a bit of a fuss. So much for the Celtic brotherhood.

THE HEATHEN CHINESE OF WALES

Some in Ireland hadn't even wanted to play the Welsh at all. Irish critic Jacques McCarthy had written: 'Wales are most anxious to arrange a match with Ireland this year . . . it is hoped no such proposal will be entertained for an instant. It is bad enough for us to lose internationals with England through the instrumentality of Welsh referees without meeting fifteen of these Heathen Chinese. Once bitten, twice shy.'

What did the papers say about Wales's first win? Not much. The *South Wales Daily News* led with Blue Ribbonites v Non-Abstainers in Swansea as its main football report. That was followed by a write-up of Weston v Cardiff. The Welsh game got just over 50 words dedicated to it, and that included details on scorers. Club rugby was king.

FIRST HOME MATCH

England did not play Wales in the 1881–82 season, after winning so easily in 1881. They changed their mind the following year after a Welsh XV (that means a team for a game where the players were not awarded caps as it was not an official international) did remarkably well against a North of England side, only losing by a goal and a try.

In December 1882, Wales played their first home match in St Helen's, Swansea, against the English. England, playing with nine forwards, won by the smaller margin of two goals and four tries. Impressed, the English placed Wales on their annual fixture list.

If you think modern sport journalists are prone to hype and exaggeration, well, they had nothing on 19th-century ones. One reporter claimed the English passed the ball so fast it 'could not be followed'. The most significant thing about this game historically is that it is considered to be the first match of the Home Championship – which was to eventually become today's Six Nations Championship.

THE HOME CHAMPIONSHIP BEGINS

Check out the full record books for the Six Nations roll of honour (not the half-hearted ones that only go back to the year 2000) and you'll see that the tournament list of winners stretches back to 1883.

That year England, Ireland, Scotland and Wales played a total of five matches among themselves between December 1882 and March 1883. Not all the teams played the same number of games. As the Irish still had a bee in their bonnet about the refereeing of their last match with Wales, the two sides never faced each other. So, England and Scotland played three games each and Wales and Ireland just two.

It's important to note that the official idea of a Championship didn't come into being until several years later. The first time a table of results was published was in 1896 when *The Times* newspaper ran one. It was common for many years for teams to play an uneven number of games. In the late 1880s, England and Scotland had such a big row over a knock-on that they refused to play each other for years (seeing a persistent theme here?) and in the end the International Rugby Board was formed to solve these kinds of law disputes. If you were to make a table for the 1883 Championship, it looks like this.

TEAM	PLAYED	WON	LOST
ENGLAND	3	3	0
SCOTLAND	3	2	1
IRELAND	2	0	2
WALES	2	0	2

Early trophy ceremonies left a lot to be desired.

At least Wales and Ireland can't say they were robbed of the title. Even if they had played each other they would only have been fighting to stay off the bottom. England's win meant they were the first team to win the Triple Crown. Did they like their trophy? Well, no. There wasn't one. Neither was there one for winning the Championship.

Rugby was passionately amateur in those days and many of the ever so highly principled people who ran the game saw trophies as a bit too unsporting or even, whisper it quietly, 'professional'. The first trophy for the Championship wasn't awarded until 1993 and the first Triple Crown trophy wasn't made until 2006. Both came about to please sponsors and help with marketing.

In fact, back in 1883, England didn't even know they had won the 'Triple Crown'. The term was not invented until at least 1894 when an Irish newspaper is said to have first coined it.

WHAT DID EARLY RUGBY LOOK LIKE?

If you travelled back in time to watch an early match of rugby you'd find the sport almost unrecognisable. Firstly, it was a LOT more violent. Until 1871, 'hacking' – tripping a player by kicking their shins – was a legal way to bring a ball carrier to ground. You were also allowed to hack the first player in a ruck. Before the introduction of referees, hacking was a way of discouraging offside players. When it was made illegal in the early 1870s, traditionalists were outraged, saying it would make the game soft and even encourage Frenchmen to play.

As sensible as it seemed to ban hacking, its removal brought fresh problems. The sport slowed down and became incredibly dull to watch. Scrums lasted longer and the ball could get stuck in a maul for as long as ten minutes. Early games could have 20 players a side and it often seemed to just be a bunch of men pushing and shoving a ball you couldn't even see from the sidelines. Well, that's probably because it was a bunch of men pushing and shoving a ball you couldn't see from the sidelines.

The aim of the scrum in early rugby – in which there were no specialist positions and players didn't even have to bind – was to kick the ball towards an opponent's goal line, not heel it back. Passing was unknown, although you could hand it on to another player. Few bothered. In fact, passing was only officially accepted in the 1870s. Punting the ball was seen as very poor form. Full-backs were defensive players and they were expected to kick drop goals to find touch. No full-back scored for Wales until 1934, when Viv Jenkins became the first full-back to score in Home Championship or Five Nations history.

KITTED UP

In primitive club rugby, players often played in their everyday clothes. In an early Cardiff game, some players may have worn bowler hats! Swansea players once wore raincoats to stay dry in the Llandovery weather.

Until 1891, there were no formal laws about the size of the playing field. In 1877, a Newport player is said to have chased a ball for over 500 yards before he scored as there was no dead-ball line. Amazingly, it wasn't until 1930 that all teams, unions and clubs played under the same set of laws.

A BONUS IF THE PLAYERS TURNED UP AT ALL

The Bridie mystery –
Wales and Scotland meet for the first time

Guess what happened in Edinburgh when Wales played Scotland for the first time ever in January 1883? If your guess is that not all the players turned up, well, give yourself a big pat on the back. Four thousand fans did turn up though, bravely enduring a Monday game on a semi-frozen pitch. Wales, however, were one man short. The player who filled in at short notice was a Dr Griffin of Edinburgh University, who some said wasn't Welsh. Mysteriously, the team photo shows just 13 players.

This game was later to give rise to the 'Bridie mystery'. Newspapers of the day say Ron Bridie played, but neither the official record books of Cardiff nor those of Wales list him as playing. Bridie was Scottish by birth and one theory is that the Scots refused to recognise him as having Welsh qualifications (despite the fact he had one cap already for Wales) and he wasn't allowed to play. The truth is we will probably never know now. We do know though that Scotland ran out winners by three goals to one and Wales played with only one full-back – Charles Lewis – for the first time.

QUICK, PASS IT TO CHARLES!

Wales scored their first try against England in Yorkshire in January 1884. The scorer was Charlie Allen from North Wales. The try was turned into a goal by the boot of Charles Lewis – which was Wales's first conversion against England.

In the same game a Charles Chapman won his first and only cap for England. Also winning his first cap that day for Wales was a Charles Taylor. In total, England had four players called Charles and Wales had three with that name and one called Charlie.

There was to be another 'first' for Wales's Charles Taylor. Sadly, he became the first Welsh international player to be killed in the First World War.

PASS IT TO CHARLES!

THE WELSH TRIAL MATCH WHERE
14 PLAYERS DIDN'T EVEN TURN UP

As mentioned, players not turning up to games is a recurring theme of Victorian rugby. Here are a couple more examples.

• In 1884 the WRU organised an East Wales XV v West Wales XV to try and help them select the Welsh team. Angry about selection methods, only one player picked for West Wales bothered to turn up! He did get picked for Wales though.

• When Wales beat Ireland in 1884 at Cardiff Arms Park, the visiting team arrived two players short. Two Welshmen, Harry McDaniel and Charles Jordan, were roped in to play for the men in green.

HERE ARE SOME MORE HIGHLIGHTS
FROM WALES'S EARLY YEARS

1884 – Wales v Scotland (Rodney Parade, Newport)

Wales lost by one drop goal to one try. It could have been different if Wales's Billy Gwynn, after a spectacular run and terrific dummy, hadn't dropped the ball after crossing the Scottish try line. Making it worse, he hadn't even realised he had crossed the line. He was looking for someone to pass to and just dropped it.

Scarlet rage

In 1884 only one Llanelli player was selected to play for Wales against England. One local newspaper begged the player not to turn out for Wales as it was such a disgrace that it was better to 'ignore' the WRU.

1885 – Scotland v Wales (Hamilton Crescent, Glasgow)

Despite holding Scotland to a draw in which neither team scored, Wales were criticised by one Scotsman as not being able to 'grasp the science of passing'. *The Field* magazine was unhappy at Wales's tactics, saying, 'The Welsh method of stopping rushes by lying on the ball is hardly to be commended.'

Lying on the ball against Scotland

1886 – Wales v Scotland (Cardiff Arms Park)

Wales made history by being the first international side to play with four threequarters (two centres and two wings). It was a tactic used by the almost unstoppable Cardiff team of the day, captained by Frank Hancock – who played for Wales in this game. Sometimes an idea is great, but its timing is not. Wales were overwhelmed by Scotland's nine forwards and lost by two goals and one try to nil. The experiment was abandoned until Wales played and beat the New Zealand Native Team in 1888.

1886 saw referees given whistles and umpires provided with 'sticks'. Referees no longer had to worry about losing their voice during games, as the whistles meant they didn't have to yell.

1887 – Wales v England (Stradey Park, Llanelli)

Wales managed a draw with the mighty English. It was their best result yet, even if neither team managed to score. The Welsh forwards were praised as magnificent, but the backs were told off for kicking too much ball away. Sound familiar? Although the match was a draw, some Welsh papers said it was a draw in 'favour of Wales'. In fact, popular journalist 'Old Stager' (sport writers often used made-up names back then) wrote: 'Sound the loud timbrel o'er the muddy waters of the Bristol Channel, the Welshmen have triumphed, or virtually triumphed . . .'

The game was nearly called off due to a frozen pitch. As a result of the cold snap, the match was moved to a back pitch at Stradey Park. The people who had paid good money for nice comfy seats in the grandstand weren't happy as they were forced to stand with everyone else. Adding insult to injury, they didn't even get their money back. This was also the final game for Wales's Charles Newman, the last surviving player from the very first game against England in 1881.

After Wales lost to Scotland in 1887, one Welsh newspaper report wrote: 'It is evident that the **Scotchmen*** are far ahead of the Welsh in football. They are a hardier race, much sterner and played with a dash and determination which awed our men.' Wales had lost by a stunning four goals and eight tries to absolute nil.

*We haven't made this up – this is how Scottish men were often referred to!

1888 – Wales v Scotland (Rodney Parade, Newport)

A year after a record defeat to Scotland, Wales beat them for the first time. Tom Jenkins, making his debut, scored the only try of the game. Scotland suffered five disallowed tries! Welsh centre Arthur Gould was not given the captaincy for the next game against Ireland so, being a somewhat moody man, he refused to travel.

1888 – Ireland v Wales (Lansdowne Road, Dublin)

In Ireland's win over Wales in Dublin, the Irish fielded a full-back, Dolway Walkington, who had such bad eyesight he wore a monocle while he played. He removed it whenever he had to make a tackle! His teammate, Daniel Rambaut, carried the nickname 'the fat little fellow'. Wales complained that seasickness had affected their performance.

1888 – Wales v New Zealand Native Team (Maoris) (St Helen's, Swansea)

Although Wales triumphed by one goal and two tries to nil, it was not a happy day for some of the home players. Local fans were so upset that the Welsh team had so few players from West Wales (just three), many refused to attend and a big chunk of those that did spent more time jeering Wales than cheering them. Poor old Norman Biggs, making his debut, was the target of a lot of the abuse. This was the match where Wales returned to playing eight forwards and seven backs, a move the entire rugby world would later adopt. The New Zealand Native Team played a mind-blowing 107 matches on this tour.

MAKING IT ALL OFFICIAL

The formation of the International Rugby Football Board

Today, rugby around the world is run by an organisation called World Rugby. Founded in 1886 as the International Rugby Football Board (IRFB), it was renamed the International Rugby Board (IRB) in 1998 before becoming World Rugby in 2014.

In 1884, Scotland got rather upset about a try scored by England. Players from both teams, as well as the referee, argued for 30 minutes before the try was finally given and England converted it to win the game. And oh boy, Scotland were upset. A flurry of sharp letters were fired back and forth between Scottish and English officials. England believed that, as they created the original laws, they knew best on such matters and the try should stand. Scotland disagreed and decided, in a huff, not to play England in 1885.

In an attempt to clear up the messy matter of the game's laws, in 1886 Wales, Ireland and Scotland got together to form the IRFB which would set the laws for the sport. This upset England, especially as the Welsh, Irish and Scots said each country should have the same number of representatives on the IRFB. England believed they should have more as they had more clubs and refused to join.

The Celtic unions said no members of the IRFB could play England until they joined the newly created organisation. England were exiled from international rugby. Eventually, in 1890, the matter was resolved when, cheekily, England demanded to have six representatives on the IRFB. The Welsh, Irish and Scots, who only had two representatives each, reluctantly agreed. This meant England, who originally wanted no part of it, had exactly the same amount of officials and voting rights on the IRFB as all the founding members put together.

With everyone on board and finally talking once more, the IRFB became the lawmakers of the game and everyone could get back to arguing on the field again, rather than off it.

POOR OLD (TOM) ENGLAND

Legendary Welsh full-back Billy Bancroft made his debut against Scotland in 1890, but originally Tom England had been selected to win his first cap as full-back for that game. Sadly for Tom, he was injured before his big day and Bancroft replaced him. Even worse, Tom was never capped. Bancroft went on to win an astonishing 33 consecutive caps between 1890 and 1901.

THE REMARKABLE DEATH OF NORMAN BIGGS

Norman Witchell Biggs was born in Cardiff in 1870. He represented Cardiff, Richmond, London Welsh, Barbarians, Bath and Wales as a winger. He also played for Glamorgan in cricket. Sporting prowess flowed in his family's blood. He was one of six brothers to play for Cardiff and his brother Selwyn also represented Wales at rugby and Glamorgan in cricket. Biggs's debut for Wales came in 1888 against the New Zealand Natives, a touring side made up mainly of Maori players. He was just 18 years and 49 days old at the time. Until 2010, when Tom Prydie (18 years and 25 days) played against Italy, he was the youngest Welsh cap. In total, Biggs made eight appearances and was part of the 1893 team that won Wales's first Triple Crown.

Biggs volunteered to fight for the British Army in South Africa in the Second Boer War – fought between 1899 and 1902. His battalion was constantly under attack and he saw enemy action an astonishing 57 times. One day, while patrolling, he was shot in the thigh by a sniper and was sent back home to recover. Biggs wasn't finished and was soon back in South Africa fighting again.

After the war ended he remained in the army and in 1905 he was sent to Nigeria. Tragically, while on patrol in 1908 he was hit by a poisoned arrow. This time, there was to be no recovery.

CLUB OR COUNTRY?

In these early days of international rugby, club rugby was the big attraction. Before Wales played Scotland in 1889, Norman Biggs declined the chance to play for Wales as he wanted to play for Cardiff against rivals Llanelli. In response, three Llanelli players also withdrew from the Welsh team. Some of the replacements called up to replace these Llanelli players in the Welsh team came from Cardiff. As a result, Cardiff said that with a total of six players in the Welsh side, they could not play Llanelli on the proposed date. Llanelli were furious and the sides abandoned fixtures for a while.

THE RED ROSE IS FINALLY ROASTED
1890 – England v Wales (Crown Flatt, Dewsbury)

Nine years on from the massacre of 1881, Wales gained a first ever win over the English. There was so much sleet and snow on the day, it is said players quickly became unrecognisable to the 5,000 spectators.

The men in scarlet's sly thinking was to steal the day as they used a sneaky move to score. The winning try came from half-back 'Buller' Stadden (who had scored Wales's first ever drop goal on his debut against Ireland in 1884). In those days, backs would throw into the line-out. Stadden pretended he was going to throw long and both the Welsh and English forwards edged back to compete for the ball. Instead, the cunning fox bounced the ball near his own feet, picked it up, beat a couple of defenders and went over for the try. Sixteen years later this move was outlawed from the game.

It was to be the only score. Wales, 5-1 outsiders on the day, had a famous victory. They were developing a reputation for quick thinking and smart play. Newspapers of the day often remarked on Welsh teams being smaller than other sides and having to be nimble of foot and sharp of mind to outwit bigger foes.

NAUGHTY BOYS AFTER IRISH DRAW

After securing a late draw with Ireland in Dublin in 1890, one Welsh player ended up in court the next day accused of 'riotous' behaviour. The locals couldn't get too upset: Ireland had eight players arrested. Fortunately for all, the press chose not to publish any names.

MAKING A POINT (OR MORE) IN 1891

By the time the 1891 Championship arrived, a points system had been universally agreed on and implemented by the IRFB. A try was worth just one measly point.

At the start of scoring, as you can see in the table below, you could score three points from a goal from mark. Today, marks can only be called inside your own 22 when catching a ball. Back then, a mark could be called anywhere. Successfully called, a player (or even for a time another nominated player) could then take a drop goal or place kick at goal if they wished. It wasn't as easy as it sounds. You had to be completely static when catching the ball and calling for a mark. Then, when kicking, opposing players could try to charge it down by running up to the point of the mark (meaning the kicker had to retreat to take it). Amazingly, this method of scoring existed until 1977.

HISTORY OF SCORING VALUES IN RUGBY

	TRY	CONVERSION	DROP GOAL	PENALTY	GOAL FROM MARK
1890–91	1	2	3	2	3
1891–92	2	3	3	3	3
1892–93	2	3	4	3	4
1893–94 TO 1904–05	3	2	4	3	4
1905–06 TO 1947–48	3	2	4	3	3
1948–49 TO 1970–71	3	2	3	3	3
1971–72 TO 1976–77	4	2	3	3	3
1977–78 TO 1992	4	2	3	3	NO LONGER POSSIBLE
1992 TO PRESENT	5	2	3	3	NO LONGER POSSIBLE

WHY DO WALES WEAR
THREE OSTRICH FEATHERS?

Since Wales's first game in 1881 they have worn the Prince of Wales feathers on their jerseys. The style, size and positioning has changed over the years, but the symbol has been worn throughout. But what is the association with Wales and why are they ostrich feathers rather than, say, chicken feathers?

Well the answer is a little complicated. They may well be the Prince of Wales's feathers – and the heraldic badge of the Prince of Wales – but the badge has no connection with the native Princes of Wales from days gone by.

Legend – and a small sprinkling of historical detail – seems to trace the symbol back to Edward, the Black Prince (1330–76). He was the eldest son of Edward III, the King of England. His 'Shield of Peace' had three feathers on it. Legend states that the Black Prince took the symbol of the feathers from Blind King John of

Bohemia after he was killed in the Battle of Crecy in 1346. Some say at the end of the fighting, Edward removed the ostrich feathers adorning the dead king and used them as inspiration for his own coat of arms. As an added extra, he also took John's motto, the medieval German phrase 'Ich dien' ('I serve').

The story claims that many of the soldiers fighting for the Black Prince were Welsh and they liked the motto 'Ich dien' as it sounded like the Welsh phrase 'Eich Dyn', which means 'Your Man'. It's no real surprise King John was killed in the battle by the way – he had been blind for ten years by then (hence the name)!

Many historians don't ascribe to this story. Nonetheless, by the late 1400s the symbol of three ostrich feathers and the 'Ich dien' motto were firmly established in British aristocratic and royal families and were being used by those holding the title of Prince of Wales. When it came to choosing a symbol for the Welsh rugby side, the Prince of Wales feathers was a natural choice, having, by then, strong associations with Wales and having been adopted in the Welch Regiment (not a spelling mistake) as early as 1719.

Why ostrich feathers? Ostrich feathers, when they appear on a coat of arms, are said to represent 'obedience and serenity'. But if you've ever been near an upset ostrich, 'obedience and serenity' are probably the last two words you'd associate with the animal.

It's possible the feathers were chosen in rugby to show Wales's loyalty to King and empire (the 1880s was all about love of country and jingoism). When the team started, some argued for a leek to be used as the other Home Unions used national 'floral' symbols such as a rose, thistle and shamrock. Over the years a number of nationalists have argued that Wales should have a more 'Welsh' symbol on the shirts, rather than a coat of arms connected with the British Royal Family.

The 'Ich dien' was removed from the Welsh jerseys in the early 1990s when the WRU trademarked their own stylised version of the famous three feathers which is now worn on all Welsh kit. It was replaced by the slightly less poetic 'WRU'.

OVAL BALLS ALL AROUND

In 1892 the RFU made it compulsory for all rugby balls to be oval, not round!

GLORY AT LAST!
The first Triple Crown

In 1892 there was no indication that Wales were on the verge of making history. In fact, Wales lost every game, including a nasty 17-0 thrashing at the hands of England. Wales took the dreaded (and mythical) 'wooden spoon' for coming last.

There were ugly scenes in the 1892 Scottish match too. Wales fell to defeat at home in Swansea by 7-2 and the match official had to be protected by the players when leaving the pitch. Spectators were so mad that Welsh captain Arthur Gould, defending the referee, got a smack on the chin from one of the 'cowardly blackguards' flooding the pitch in anger.

That was to be the last year Wales lost to all the other home countries until 1923. Yet 1893 was to be the season Wales won its first Triple Crown. How did they do it?

1893 TRIPLE CROWN

MATCH ONE: Wales 12 England 11 (Cardiff Arms Park)

Played in early January, it was so cold that portable fires were used during the night before the game to try and keep the ground from freezing solid and 500 containers of hot coals and tons of straw were used. One writer said the scene the night before was like something from Dante's *Inferno* (a medieval poem about hell). The fires worked but left lots of soft, darkened patches across the field.

In spite of the freeze, 15,000 people packed in to see the match as Wales scored three tries, one conversion and a penalty goal to England's four tries and one conversion.

Arthur Gould grabbed two tries and one report said he glided 'snake-like through the thickest throng' for his second score.

The penalty, by Billy Bancroft, was the first ever in the Championship. In those days players were allowed to drop-kick a penalty kick – it didn't have to be a place kick. And that's how Bancroft did it very late in the game after Wales made an inspired comeback. Some reports said captain Arthur Gould insisted Bancroft took a place kick and Bancroft ignored him and there was a bitter argument on the field. Either way, Bancroft delivered.

Interestingly, international scoring rules were different to the way points were counted in Welsh club games. If the game had been played under the Welsh scoring system, it would have been 14-14. The scoring situation was so confusing that a WRU official had to confirm to the press after the game that Wales had actually won.

When the match ended there was a huge pitch invasion and Gould was carried off on the shoulders of the fans all the way back to the Angel Hotel in Westgate Street. Reports of the day said the players were cheered back to the hotel and girls waved at the players from windows and balconies.

Welsh captain Arthur Gould on the England win: '. . . Welshmen keep themselves in strict training . . . None of us have an ounce of superfluous flesh . . . We practise this in our gymnasium in Newport once a week . . . English individual excellence far exceeds our own. With perhaps one or two exceptions we have no brilliant men; the whole secret of our success lies in our combination.'

MATCH TWO: Scotland 0 Wales 9 (Raeburn Place, Edinburgh)

Newport RFC supplied a whopping nine players to the victorious Welsh team – the first to win on Scottish soil. That wasn't all – captain Arthur Gould of Newport was appearing in his 17th Championship match, a new record not just for Wales, but all nations. Arthur's brother, Bert, scored a try too. He also played for – yep, you guessed it – Newport.

Billy Bancroft, once again, drop-kicked a penalty for Wales. But the major reason for Wales's success was their innovative use of four threequarters. Before the match Wales had never scored a try in Scotland. On this day they grabbed three of them.

After the game, Gould praised the Welsh style as a 'thousand times more interesting for spectators' and said that it would revolutionise the game. He may have been arrogant, but he was right.

MATCH THREE: Wales 2 Ireland 0 (Stradey Park)

Ireland became the last international side to only employ three threequarters in a match. Twenty thousand fans attended this historic occasion and two fans were so hyped for the game they walked 40 miles from Tenby to attend. The winning try came from Bert Gould, who scored after 'typical' Welsh passing led to an overlap. Critical to Welsh glory this year was stability in selection. A core of 13 players were selected for each game. One of the stands at Stradey Park collapsed before kick-off. Luckily, no one was injured.

How the newspapers previewed the 1893 game with Ireland.
'The winning or losing of this our ninth encounter with the sons of Erin has more importance attached to it than is usually the case . . . we have by defeating England and Scotland, put at rest all doubts about our being the champion country, but to win to-day means that Wales will, not only stand pre-eminently at the head of the list of countries, but that she will also establish a record the likes of which she has never approached before . . . Ireland has always been looked upon as a sort of "soft snap".' – *Evening Express*, 11 March 1893

FOR THE LOVE OF THE GAME

Today, Welsh internationals are well paid and can collect extra cash for advertising products or media appearances. But from 1881 to 1995 players were unpaid. Rugby was an amateur sport.

In the Victorian era, many people believed sport should be played purely for the love of the game. In fact, the word amateur comes from the Latin and French word 'amour', which means love. To take money or reward for athletic skill was seen as 'ungentlemanly'.

JOLLY GOOD FUN. HEALTHY EXERCISE AND GLORY ARE MY REWARD!

The Noble Amateur

Those running the game thought that once money was introduced it would lead to cheating, corruption and abuse of officials. These people didn't just prefer amateurism, they were FANATICAL about it. To them, the idea of being paid to play was as horrifying as having your front teeth yanked out while someone pulled off your toenails.

WORKING MEN WANT MORE

As rugby became popular with working men in the north of England and Wales, this commitment to amateurism became a problem. In these areas many players wanted to get what was called 'broken time' payments. Until changes to working laws that gave workers a half day on a Saturday, working men usually worked six days a week and weren't allowed to play sport on a Sunday for religious reasons. They often had to take time off to play rugby.

Many wanted small expenses or match fees to be allowed as a form of compensation for time missed at work. It's worth remembering that if a player picked up an injury and couldn't earn money, he could have trouble feeding his family or paying the bills. Not being paid also made it difficult for working-class players to travel to away games due to cost and time. But those in rugby's corridors of power refused to budge.

'Get these commoners away from me!' There were other reasons some wanted rugby to stay amateur. Gentlemen, who only played once a week, knew they would be no match for full-time professionals. They had seen it happen in football in the 1880s.

An even uglier reason for rugby staying amateur was that some 'gentlemen' simply didn't like working men playing what they saw as 'their game'. Wales was often criticised by other nations for the amount of working men in the team. After another barbed attack in 1909 about this topic, rugby writer 'Forward' wrote: 'Football in Wales is a democratic game, and the dock labourer or collier has an equal chance of playing for his country as the man from either of the great [universities] . . . the supremacy of Wales is not accepted with good grace by the other countries.'

In 1882, WRU finances were in such a mess it was proposed that players paid their own train fare. Horace Lyne (five caps for Wales and president of the WRU from 1906 to 1947) protested, saying: 'If every player had to pay his own train fare, the teams would be teams of gentlemen and not representative teams.'

Some clubs ignored amateur rules and would leave money in players' clothes for them to secretly collect after a game. This became known as 'shamateurism' as it made a sham of amateurism.

Although almost everyone knew lots of Welsh players were getting naughty cash, the English mostly turned a blind eye. The Irish and Scots, however, were particularly sulky about it. Some wanted Wales and Welsh clubs banned. Most English clubs, didn't. In the 1890s, the big four teams of Wales – Cardiff, Llanelli, Newport and Swansea – were huge attractions when they played across the border and nobody wanted to miss out on the money from ticket sales they brought in. Money, you see, wasn't always bad – particularly if it paid for food, drink and travel for greedy committee members.

THE GREAT SPLIT

In 1895, after years of arguments about the issue of players getting money for playing, the matter exploded. Twenty-two clubs in the north of England resigned from the Rugby Football Union (the English version of the WRU) and formed the Northern Union. From this Northern Union the modern game of rugby league was created. Any rugby union player who played professional rugby was, until 1995, not allowed to play, coach, referee or do anything related to rugby union ever again. Just talking to a rugby league official could see you banned from union for life. Sometimes, players who 'went north' for money weren't even allowed into a rugby union clubhouse for a beer with old teammates. In 1899, a rugby league scout who came hunting for Welsh talent in Penarth was taken by locals and thrown in the sea! He lost money in this assault and went to the police in Cardiff. They said he was welcome to return to Penarth to find the money himself or pick out his assaulters. He went home instead.

Bizarrely, you could play any other sport professionally – such as cricket, football, boxing or tennis – and there was nothing stopping you playing rugby union again. But play rugby league once and it was 'goodnight' rugby union for you. Wales was to suffer greatly from these harsh rules and lost countless players to the professional version of rugby.

THE NATIONAL SPORT?
Why did Wales fall in love with rugby?
When people think of the Welsh, they usually also think of rugby. Considered the national game (even though, in truth, more people play and watch soccer these days), the Welsh took to rugby with a passion when it was introduced.

Unlike in places like England, Scotland and Ireland, where it was mainly the game of the middle classes, people of all social backgrounds and occupations played rugby together in Wales.

Why? Well, there are many reasons. In the Victorian era, sport was seen as a way to keep mind and body fit and a method to teach young men (sadly, yes, it was mainly young men)

toughness, discipline, self-control and a sense of fair play. Sport was also seen as an ideal preparation for going to war. Rugby in particular was viewed as shaping strong moral character and was just the thing for moulding good soldiers. Plenty believe the British approach to sport helped build their great empire.

Games like rugby were played in the universities and colleges and considered as a gentleman's game. Former students spread the game in Wales and – because rugby was a fitting thing for gentlemen to do – it was something working-class men could 'aspire' to. Rugby's physical nature appealed to working men. They had to show courage and toughness in the difficult and dangerous jobs they did in places like the coal mines. Rugby was another way of showing their manliness to those in their community.

Many rich men who ran the industries in Wales knew rugby was a way to boost fitness, instil discipline and forge teamwork. They were happy to help build the facilities or supply the equipment for men to play sport. Besides, when local teams won, some of the glory rubbed off on them.

There were other reasons too. Wales, at the time, had a very strong national movement in politics that argued for equality and social unity. Rugby, by mixing men of all social classes, was a fantastic way to build community and unity among the people. By being good at rugby, Wales – which was enjoying a wave of national pride and creativity in its arts, culture and industry – could stand proud on the sporting field too and enhance its sense of national identity. After all, what better way to get one over on England, your 'big brother', than by beating them at their own game?

UPSETTING THE BIG MAN?

While those in the WRU thought that rugby didn't have the 'low status' of soccer, not everyone in Wales loved rugby. Those people making up the strong religious movement of the late 19th century in Wales certainly didn't. They said playing rugby was like 'kicking the head of John the Baptist'! When Swansea played a game in France on a Sunday in 1899, the WRU immediately banned Sunday rugby. It was viewed as a disgraceful thing to do for a team from the 'land of the Bible and the Sunday school'.

THE FALL (BEFORE THE RISE)

The last few years of the 19th century saw little success for Wales. But despite relatively poor results after the first Triple Crown, Wales were slowly, but surely, building a style that would lead to great things. **Here are some notable moments from the end of the century:**

1894: England 24 Wales 3 (Birkenhead)

Wales lost to England as Arthur Gould's instructions to his forwards to quickly 'heel' the ball out of the scrum for the backs to use were ignored by some players (Frank Hill in particular was blasted for his selfish play). The forwards worked against each other to England's advantage. To rub it in, the men in white beat Wales at their own game, introducing four threequarters for the first time. This tactical innovation was once called an 'abortion' by one English writer.

Victorian Twitter? After the Scottish game in 1894, pigeons carrying the score were released to spread the news of the Welsh win all around the country.

In 1895, Wales wanted the match with Scotland in Edinburgh called off as they felt the frozen pitch was dangerous. Eventually it was agreed to tape off the worst section of the field, thereby shortening the pitch by 20 yards. Wales lost 5-4. Frustratingly, Wales had what would have been a winning try disallowed as they crossed the line near the taped-off section and it was unclear if the ball was grounded infield.

THE BIRTH OF THE 'RHONDDA FORWARD'

After another trouncing by England in 1896 (losing 25-0), Welsh selectors decided to pick a new kind of player called the 'Rhondda-type forward'. These were tough men who not only had the ability to scrummage and jump in the line-out, but also were able to take (and crucially dish out) the rough stuff!

The effect was immediate, with Wales surprising everyone by beating the Scots 6-0. The new Rhondda forwards included a very intimidating policeman (Dai Evans), a miner (Jack Evans) and a plasterer (Bill Morris). This combination of rugged forwards and skilful backs was to bring Wales much success.

1897 – Wales 11 England 0 (Rodney Parade)

Wales won in convincing style as the legendary Arthur Gould, on his home ground, played his final game for Wales. The superstar stepped down afterwards so that Wales were not banished from the international game because of what was known as the 'Gould affair' (see page 56).

Dick Hellings made his debut in this match. Originally from Devon, this tough-as-nails forward was so excited to be selected he celebrated by carrying an iron girder from Coed-Ely to Tonyrefail. It is rumoured the secretary of the RFU resented the stamina working-class players brought to the Welsh team!

Wales had plenty of talent coming through though. Just a few games before Gould retired, another Welsh superstar and fellow centre became a regular feature for Wales, the great Gwyn Nicholls.

Dick Hellings carried more than the weight of a nation on his shoulders.

1899 – Wales 26 England 3 (St Helen's)

In front of a record 20,000-plus crowd, Wales grabbed six tries. Willie Llewellyn from Tonypandy scored four on his debut. He was to become a huge threat for Wales and ended up with 16 tries in just 20 games.

Poor old England, beginning to feel the effect of the creation of the Northern Union, were to win only seven of their next 33 Championship games. Indeed, Wales did not lose to England again for 12 years, the longest unbeaten run Wales have ever had against their old enemy.

PRACTICE MAKES PROFESSIONALS?

The *Yorkshire Post* newspaper complained that the Welsh team had got together to practise on the Thursday before the game. The writer, Old Ebor, said it was 'too business-like for amateur sport'.

WALES FALL OFF AS SEASON PROGRESSES

Wales couldn't build on the 1899 English win and lost to both Scotland and Ireland. The Scottish match was postponed an amazing four times due to bad weather, a record for the Championship that still stands. It still snowed when it was eventually played.

The 3-0 defeat to Ireland in Cardiff was watched by a record 40,000 fans. Some spectators sneaked in the ground via the River Taff and hundreds climbed trees or sat on the roof of the grandstand. Fans spilling on to the pitch caused the kick-off to be delayed and the game was frequently stopped as fans leaked on to the field. Half-time was about three times longer than usual (players would stay on the field in those days) as the playing area couldn't be cleared of supporters quickly enough to restart on time due to 'unprecedented scenes of disorder'.

Welsh captain Billy Bancroft was thrown into the spectators by 'rough' Irish players and was so battered he missed threequarters of the game. While the season was a disappointment after a fine start, a very special era was just about to begin for Wales.

1881–99: THE STAR PLAYERS

FRANK HANCOCK

Club: Cardiff
Position: Centre
Caps: 4 (1884–86)
Points: 0

Frank Hancock may only have won four caps for Wales, but his influence lives on. Born in Somerset into a beer-brewing family, Frank moved to Cardiff for business reasons and was soon playing for the 'Blue and Blacks'.

In 1884 he was selected for Cardiff when some regular backs were injured. He was so impressive that Cardiff wanted to keep him in the 1st XV, but also didn't want to leave out the first-choice players returning from injury. In a decision that would change the sport forever, for the next match the selectors only picked eight forwards and included an extra threequarter instead. The tactic was a success and was eventually adopted by the whole rugby world.

Hancock was fanatical about developing good passing and exciting back play – highly unusual at a time when rugby was all about forwards bashing each other about. In 1885–86, as captain of Cardiff, he refused to allow his players to kick at goal. They won all but one of 27 games and scored an astonishing 131 tries – but registered not a single penalty, drop kick or goal from mark. In one game, a teammate tried a drop goal and was lectured fiercely by Hancock, who threatened to send off the next player that tried it! He retired aged 26.

ARTHUR 'MONKEY' GOULD

Clubs: Newport, London Welsh, Richmond
Position: Centre, full-back
Caps: 27 (1885–97)
Points: 13 (4 tries, 1 conversion, 2 drop goals)

Arthur Joseph 'Monkey' Gould was rugby's first true superstar and responsible for Wales becoming a respected sporting nation. Gould got his 'Monkey' nickname due to his skill at climbing trees when a boy. A natural athlete – known for his ability to kick with both feet and his mean sidestep – Gould trained fanatically and loved to be the centre of attention.

A centre and full-back, Gould led Wales to their first ever Triple Crown and Championship in 1893. He made his debut for Newport as a teenager, ignoring the captain's pleas to kick the ball and ran in two tries (for which his skipper called him a 'devil'). He was never dropped by his club.

Gould didn't like the four-man threequarter system Frank Hancock introduced to Wales in 1886 and made the selectors abandon it for a few years. Why? Some say it left him less able to shine as an individual. Despite this, he was still a key player in developing a more exciting way of playing rugby.

Gould won 27 caps for Wales (18 as captain) in a period where Wales would usually only play an average of three games a year. Despite missing a season of games in 1891 by moving to the West Indies with his brother to build bridges as an engineer, no Welsh player won more caps at centre than Gould until 1980 and no player was captain more often until 1994 (when Ieuan Evans took the record). The great Welsh captain Gwyn Nicholls said that trying to mark Gould was like trying to 'catch a butterfly in flight with a hat-pin'.

Gould even got to use his famous climbing skills in a game once. In the 1887 draw with England at Stradey Park, he climbed up one of the goalposts to replace the crossbar which had fallen off due to sleet and snow. A huge show-off, Gould delighted in greeting Welsh fans with the famous words 'Cymru am byth' (Wales is forever), even though he admitted he didn't know what it meant! He was described as having the 'pomp of an emperor'.

Gould retired just before the First Golden Era of Welsh rugby, but he is credited with laying the foundations of its success. After he retired his image was used to sell everything from matches to cigarettes to Belgian chocolates. Outside of rugby he won over £1,000 through his skills in running and hurdling.

The 'Gould affair'

Arthur Gould was so popular among rugby fans that in 1896 the Welsh public raised hundreds of pounds as a 'testimonial' to his service to the game. The Welsh Rugby Union also made a contribution. In the amateur days of old this was a major scandal. The IRFB was not impressed. Wales, by sticking by Gould, were in major danger of being banned from Test rugby.

Eventually, after a complaint from the Rugby Football Union, the WRU backed down. But such was the anger of the Welsh public that the WRU eventually withdrew from membership of the IRFB, held a massive public dinner for Gould and presented him with the deeds to a house. Unsurprisingly, the other unions huffed and puffed even more.

Scotland and Ireland were so furious they refused to play Wales in 1897. It was only after Gould – not wishing to spoil everyone else's fun – offered to retire from international rugby that Wales avoided being kicked out and were able to resume all fixtures.

JIM HANNAN

Club: Newport
Position: Forward (Front row)
Caps: 19 (1888–95)
Points: 2 (2 tries)

A Newport boilerman, Hannan was one of early rugby's greatest scrummagers and considered an intelligent tactician. Part of the feared Newport pack of the day, Hannan came from a period where there were not the same specialist positions in the pack as today, so he is listed merely as a front row in the record books. But what a forward he was.

It was said he could wheel an entire scrum on his own. This was particularly useful as for much of his career Wales played only eight forwards to their opponents' nine. Another crucial skill for forwards in those days was dribbling the ball. Forwards would dribble together in a huge pack and charge upfield like a stampede of buffalo! Hannan could hold his own here as well.

He scored on his debut against the New Zealand Native Team in 1888 and his try against Scotland in 1892 was Wales's only score of a miserable season. He played a central role in Wales's famous 1893 Triple Crown, where his silky ball skills helped set up a crucial try for Arthur Gould against England.

BILLY BANCROFT

Club: Swansea
Position: Full-back
Caps: 33 (1890–1901)
Points: 60 (4 penalties, 20
conversions, 1 drop goal, 1 goal
from mark)

William Bancroft, or 'Billy', was an incredibly confident athlete. The Swansea man made his debut for Wales aged just 19 and went on to make an astonishing 33 consecutive appearances. It was a record that stood until Ken Jones beat it in 1954. In all that time, Bancroft only faced Ireland, England and Scotland as there were no other opponents on the fixture list.

He claimed to have spent two hours a day practising his ball skills since he was a boy. During his 11 years with Wales, he took every single place kick Wales were offered and made many game-winning scores. A bit of a showman, one of his tricks was to catch a long kick, wait for opponents to chase him and then dart to the other side of the field. Then he would once more wait for opponents to catch up with him and then do it all again until the crowd burst out laughing. Not everyone liked these shenanigans.

Bancroft captained Wales 11 times, winning on seven occasions. He led Wales to its second Triple Crown. His brother Jack also played for Wales. Billy was also a dab hand at cricket, scoring over 8,000 runs for Glamorgan.

THE JAMES BROTHERS

Club: Swansea

Positions: Half-backs

Caps: Evan James – 5 (1890–99),
David James – 4 (1891–99)

Points: 0

The James brothers may not have played often for Wales, but their place in Welsh rugby folklore is unique. Some rugby historians credit them with creating specialist half-back play as one played as an 'inside' half-back and one as an 'outside' half-back.

Massive fan favourites at Swansea, they apparently used to enter the field performing somersaults! Brave defenders, their reputations were made via their inventive and cunning attacking play. Rugby writer W.J. Townsend Collins described them as geniuses both as individuals and in combination. Skilful and deceptive, the Irish team once took the field under instruction to '. . . go for the Jameses; never mind whether the varmints have got the ball or not. By the time you reach them one of 'em's sure to have it . . .'

Despite their extraordinary abilities, they only played four times together for Wales. This was in part due to the fact they were banned for being professionals for a period, having taken generous 'expenses' when playing for Broughton.

They were briefly reinstated and their finest hour was helping Wales obliterate England by 26-3 in 1899. One report said: 'No international team England put in the field has ever been more routed. The English captain wasted a good deal of his energy in empty protests when he found the brothers James too good for him.'

Sadly, the 'curly-haired marmosets' – as they were nicknamed (a marmoset is a type of monkey) – left for professional rugby at Broughton when England complained about their previous breach of amateur regulations. There was such sadness when the brothers turned professional, one newspaper published a cartoon depicting Dame Wales weeping as the pair flew away in a hot-air balloon.

1881–99 NOTABLE EVENTS IN WELSH HISTORY

- 1881: Alcohol is no longer permitted to be sold in Wales on a Sunday.

- 1882: Thirty-two people die when the steamer *Clan Macduff* sinks off Holyhead.

- 1883: Cardiff University opens.

- 1884: After a legal battle, Welsh doctor William Price cremates his son. It was the first cremation to take place in the modern era.

- 1885: Frances Hoggan becomes Wales's first registered female doctor.

- 1890: Eighty-six miners are killed in an accident at the Morfa Colliery in Port Talbot.

- 1891: The UK census lists 1,685,614 Welsh speakers in the country (54.5% of the population).

- 1893: World-famous composer and actor Ivor Novello is born in Cardiff.

- 1894: A total of 290 miners and 123 horses are killed in an accident at Albion Colliery in Cilfynydd. The youngest victim was 13.

- 1896: The Snowdon Mountain Railway opens and a passenger is killed jumping from the first train that travels down the mountain.

- 1899: Cardiff City FC is founded (under the name Riverside AFC).

1900–14: THE FIRST GOLDEN ERA

	PLAYED	WON	DRAWN	LOST
HOME CHAMPIONSHIP	52	41	1	10
TOURISTS	4	2	0	2
TOTAL	56	43	1	12

Championships

1900 (Triple Crown), 1902 (Triple Crown), 1905 (Triple Crown), 1908 (Grand Slam), 1909 (Grand Slam), 1911 (Grand Slam)

Shared Championships

1906

'The one thing necessary is a love for the game – to realise that it is the grandest, most glorious and most scientific of all games, and that if one cannot play it with all one's heart . . . and for its own sake one had better devote one's energies to croquet.'

GWYN NICHOLLS

'GALLANT LITTLE WALES' RULES THE WORLD

The period from 1900 to 1911 is considered the 'First Golden Era' of Welsh rugby. 'Gallant Little Wales' came, saw and conquered everyone they faced (well, apart from some pesky South Africans, but we'll get to that).

How good were Wales? They played 43 matches between 1900 and 1911 and won 36 of them. Scotland, Ireland and England lost every game on Welsh soil from 1899 to 1913. Wales averaged 3.6 tries a game between 1900 and 1911 – extraordinary for the time. Here's how Wales's traditional rivals performed in Wales around the start of the 20th century:

- *England – no wins in Wales between 1895 and 1913*
- *Ireland – no wins in Wales between 1899 and 1924*
- *Scotland – no wins in Wales between 1892 and 1921*
- *France – no wins in Wales between 1908 (first game) and 1948*

But the game that defined this amazing period – and secured rugby as the cultural game of Wales – was the historic win against the 1905 All Blacks. Considered by many students of the sport as the greatest international ever played, it shaped the history of both nations in surprising ways.

Wales, captained by Gwyn Nicholls, the 'Prince of Centres', led the world.

WALES AT THE START OF A NEW CENTURY

At the dawn of this golden period, Queen Victoria was in the final days of her 63 years upon the throne. After her death in 1901, Edward VII become monarch. The Edwardian age was to be one of success for Wales not only on the field, but also in many ways as a nation.

Wales was experiencing an economic boom thanks to the 'black gold' of the South Wales coalfields. By 1911 Wales had a population of almost 2.5 million, exploding from 1.5 million in 1871. Over a century later, Wales's population has only grown to 3.1 million. The industrial revolution was changing the make-up of society and more people were living in towns and cities, rather than in rural areas. South Wales was growing faster than any other part of the UK.

Cardiff, not yet capital of Wales, was gaining wealth and power thanks to its geographical location making it the perfect place for exporting Welsh coal to the world. It was nicknamed the 'Chicago of Wales'. In 1841, Cardiff had a population of fewer than 10,000 people. By 1901 it had over 172,000 and in 1905 it was granted city status.

This economic strength was accompanied by a flourishing of Welsh arts and literature and a growing taste among many for Wales to have 'Home Rule' and not be governed by Westminster. Against this backdrop, Welsh rugby was also transforming. Fans had money to attend matches, newspapers covered the game extensively and there was an explosion of new clubs. Welsh success on the sporting field further reinforced Welsh nationalism and national confidence.

THE CROWN IS RECAPTURED

Wales welcomed in the 20th century by winning a second Triple Crown in 1900. The title came in style too, with five of the seven tries in the Championship originating from 'attractive bouts of threequarter passing' according to rugby historian John Griffiths. It was to be the first of six titles in the next 12 years.

1900 TRIPLE CROWN

MATCH ONE: England 3 Wales 13 (Kingsholm, Gloucester)

The only Home Championship match ever played at Kingsholm saw Wales dispatch England comfortably. The home side gave debuts to an astonishing 13 players – one for every Welsh point! Fifteen thousand attended and they were allowed to mingle with the players on the field at half-time. Wales scored two converted tries and kicked a penalty goal. One Welsh try came from debutant W.J. 'Billy' Trew. Playing on the wing this day (he was also a centre and fly-half), the slight and 'frail' Trew was said to have had a poor game, but he was to go on to become a Welsh great. Forward Dick Hellings played almost the whole game with a fractured arm. He still scored a try!

Wales before the 1900 England game.

MATCH TWO: Wales 12 Scotland 3 (St Helen's)

After the win over England, an unimpressed Arthur Gould, now a selector, expressed doubt that Wales would be able to beat Scotland. In fact, as Billy Bancroft later said, Wales 'whacked' them by four tries to one.

It was a key turning point in the fixture. Wales had won four of the previous 15 clashes with Scotland, but Scotland only managed to win three of the next 15. During the match, the crowd burst into a rendition of 'God Save the Queen'. The singing was a patriotic reaction to news that British forces had suffered a major defeat in the Boer War in South Africa.

MATCH THREE: Ireland 0 Wales 3 (Balmoral, Belfast)

The scorer of the winning try for Wales on this famous day had to be informed later of his feat. Centre George Davies was knocked out by a stray foot while scoring.

Captain Bancroft was praised for changing tactics during the game to overcome brutal Irish defence. He became the first Welshman to win two Triple Crowns. The Irish press were generally happy with the home performance, with one publication writing: '. . . the fact the Taffies won by the lowest score possible when compared with their big totals ran up by them against England and Scotland speaks well for the losers.'

INJURED? HURRY UP, WE'VE A GAME TO PLAY

In the early 20th century there was concern about how much time was being taken up treating injured players during games.

In 1901 it was decided that injury treatments could last a maximum of three minutes. Sometimes, lack of replacements led to bizarre outcomes. Against England in 1903, forward Jehoida Hodges was forced into the backs due to an injury to winger Tom Pearson. He scored three tries!

FAREWELL TO BILLY
1901 – Wales 10 Ireland 9 (St Helen's)

This narrow win was the last game of the great Billy Bancroft. It was his 33rd consecutive cap and during that time he had taken every place kick for Wales. Fittingly, his kicking was the difference on this day as two converted Welsh tries beat Ireland's three tries. While Billy said goodbye, new legends arrived. Rhys Gabe, Dicky Owen and Dick Jones came into the side for their first caps. The Irish were unhappy with the referee and said after the game that officials should be required to be as fit as the players.

THE THIRD TRIPLE CROWN

After losing the Championship and Triple Crown to Scotland in 1901, Wales took it back the following year.

1902 TRIPLE CROWN

MATCH ONE: England 8 Wales 9 (Rectory Field, Blackheath)

Wales, risking seven new caps, squeaked past England. Gwyn Nicholls was the new captain and would go on to become one of the most celebrated players in the history of not just Wales, but the sport. The victory was Wales's first at Blackheath, the site of the 1881 massacre.

Wales won in part thanks to a sneaky bit of play by scrum-half Dicky Owen, who pretended to remove the ball from the scrum and fooled England's Bernard Oughtred who jumped offside and gave Wales the winning penalty shot.

MATCH TWO: Wales 14 Scotland 5 (Cardiff Arms Park)

Often during the Golden Era, this match was the key one in deciding the title. Considered one of the finest Scottish sides ever, this was an epic Welsh win and largely down to an excellent forward display. The WRU were doubly happy as the crowd paid a record £2,178 to attend.

MATCH THREE: Ireland 0 Wales 15 (Lansdowne Road)

This was a record defeat at home for Ireland. It was also the first ever all-ticket rugby international as there was so much public interest in the clash. In the end, 12,000 saw Wales take Ireland apart. Captain Nicholls even managed a left-footed drop goal

EYE DON'T UNDERSTAND WHY EYE FEEL SICK

The sea voyage to the Irish game was rough and several WRU officials tried to combat seasickness by covering one eye with a bandage. Amazingly, it seemed to work. However, during the trip, one official noticed that one sick passenger had an artificial eye. It occurred to them that their ruse wasn't particularly scientific. Immediately, they began to feel ill.

WORKING-CLASS WOES?

At this point in international rugby, Wales were still the only national side fielding a significant number of 'working men'. In 1903, Scottish referee and union official Crawford Findlay expressed in a post-match dinner that he was 'surprised that Wales selected miners, steelworkers and policemen' and that they would be more suited to rugby league in the north of England. When Findlay refereed Wales, he always seemed to be against the men in red. It wasn't just the Welsh feeling paranoid, even opponents were bamboozled by his decisions against Wales. In Ireland, meanwhile, some felt the tough working men in 'hardy occupations' gave Wales an unfair advantage.

In 1904, when Wales drew with England, Findlay penalised Welsh scrum-half Dicky Owen so much at scrum time that Owen refused to place the ball in the scrum after a while as he expected to be penalised. Instead, he gave it to his opponent to place in the tunnel.

Later that season, Findlay refereed Wales's narrow defeat to Ireland. Even Irish players were surprised to see him allow one dubious Irish try and disallow another seemingly fine Welsh one. Alfred Brice, a Welsh forward who played in the loss, called Findlay a 'thundering idiot'. He never played for Wales again. In response to his performances, one Welsh critic said: 'It is futile to waste words on Mr Crawford Findlay . . . he must be pachydermatous.' We don't know what that means either.

AN IRISH FUNERAL?

After Wales demolished Ireland by 18 points to nil in Cardiff in 1903 (despite only having 14 men for most of the match), enterprising young boys went around the city selling 'memorial' cards for the 'Death of poor old Ireland'. An unrecognised Irish captain was even approached by one of the sellers to buy. The captain politely declined, saying he had already been to the funeral.

1905 AND ALL THAT

Barring a World Cup win, it's unlikely 1905 will ever be surpassed in Welsh rugby history. Wales won a fourth Triple Crown and defeated the mighty All Blacks.

THE FOURTH TRIPLE CROWN

MATCH ONE: Wales 25 England 0 (Cardiff Arms Park)

Until 1972, this was the biggest defeat England had suffered in the Championship. Wales, inspired by fly-half Richard 'Dick' Jones, racked up seven tries and the backs ran rings around an England side still unable to master the four three-quarter system.

MATCH TWO: Scotland 3 Wales 6 (Inverleith, Edinburgh)

This was Wales's first win at Inverleith and wasn't secured until a late score from winger Willie Llewellyn who crashed over with a head-down charge (his second score of the match). Wales's Rhys Gabe was booted so hard on the backside it was said he could not sit down properly for six months and had to teach his schoolchildren while standing up. The Scottish press claimed Wales had been 'downright dirty' and full of 'caddish tricks'.

MATCH THREE: Wales 10 Ireland 3 (St Helen's)

For the first time ever, these sides clashed with the Triple Crown on the line for both sides. Scrum-half Wyndham Jones became a one-cap wonder, scoring a debut try and having a key hand in the other try by Teddy Morgan.

A ROTTEN SHOW

'Prince of Centres', Gwyn Nicholls, is one of the most celebrated players in history. But when he came out of retirement to play in the 1905 Triple Crown match against Ireland in Swansea he was pelted with fruit. Swansea's Dan Rees had been selected for the game, but on match day he told the selectors he was injured. The official reserve for the day on standby was Swansea's Frank Gordon, a teammate of Rees. Some selectors, probably unfairly, thought Rees was feigning injury to give his buddy a first cap so they asked Nicholls to play.

Reluctant at first, he was eventually persuaded when selectors said they would not pick Gordon even if Nicholls refused to play. When Nicholls came out on the field before the game for the team photo, mud and oranges were flung at him by several angry local fans. He later said it was one of the most unpleasant experiences of his life.

THE TERRIFYING INVASION OF THE COLONIES AND THE GREATEST MATCH OF ALL TIME

The New Zealand rugby team are one of the most successful teams in the history of sport. Since their first game in 1903, they have either been at the top of the rugby tree, or just one or two branches below it.

Their greatness was established from the off. After easily defeating Australia in their first Test in 1903, they went on to beat a British Isles team in 1904 and Oz again before travelling to Europe and North America for their now almost mythical tour of 1905. It was this trip that built the fierce reputation today's All Blacks still carry.

How good were they? They played 35 games and won 34 of them. Most matches were massacres. They conceded just 59 points and scored an incredible 976, with 23 opponents failing to score against them at all.

ARE WE NEARLY THERE YET?

The 1905 All Blacks left on 30 July by boat and, after two short stops, arrived in England on 8 September! Before they left, New Zealand's prime minister's last words to the team were to make sure they beat Wales.

SHAPING NATIONS

The 1905 tour shaped the identity of New Zealand. In the early years of the 20th century some British people considered places like New Zealand and Australia as mere colonies of the British Empire, rather than unique, vibrant countries in their own right. Yet the All Blacks were so dominant over the teams of the 'Mother Country' – and the visiting players seemed so athletic, healthy and muscular compared to the Home Union ones – that many feared it showed a decline in the masculinity of men of all classes in Britain.

At the start of the tour plenty of folk in Britain and Ireland, full of smug superiority, thought the visitors would struggle. When Devon lost 55-4 in the opening game, some newspapers ran the score the other way around, unable to believe the reported score was correct.

WHAT MADE THE NEW ZEALANDERS SO GOOD?

Apart from their size and fitness, New Zealand brought a style of rugby with them that no one had ever seen before. In the scrum, the New Zealanders specialised with each player having a specific role. This was in contrast to British and Irish teams, who had a system where players packed down at scrums in the order they arrived. The All Blacks used a 2-3-2 formation in the scrum: two hookers, three in the middle row and two in the back. The other forward, the wing-forward or 'rover', placed the ball in the scrum and the scrum-half awaited it at the back, ready to whip it away quickly. This rover, usually superhuman tour captain Dave Gallaher, was accused of obstructing defenders and the role caused home teams all sorts of problems.

Other ways they excelled was in line-out play, where they practised obsessively, and a different back formation – they played what they called two five-eighths. One reason the Kiwis were fitter was they used to play 45 minutes a half back home but in the UK games were 35 minutes a half. Some even thought the 'silk' shirts the All Blacks wore made them hard to grab.

THE BUILD-UP TO THE 'GAME OF THE CENTURY'

When New Zealand arrived for their game against Wales, a Hollywood scriptwriter couldn't have set things up more dramatically. New Zealand had won all their 27 previous games, including the battles with Scotland, Ireland and England. No side had scored against them (including Ireland and England) for seven games. In total they had scored 801 points to 22. Wales, meanwhile, were holders of the Triple Crown. In an age before World Cups, this was seen as a match to decide the champions of the world.

Some said Wales were the best in the world after 1905.
South Africa, however, soon had something to say about that.

On 16 December 1905, the visitors were met by the largest crowd of the tour at Cardiff's main train station and needed a police escort to avoid what was described by the New Zealand manager as a 'dense mass of humanity'. Most of Cardiff Docks had closed early so workers could attend the game and 50 special trains had been put on to help people from all corners of the land attend. Programme sellers wore special dragon badges to show they were offering the genuine article.

A record 47,000 fans packed Cardiff Arms Park on a bright, spring-like day. Cardiff Market ran out of leeks for fans to wear, so some wore onions! The crowd included hundreds of ladies wearing 'multi-coloured garments'. Before the game, the packed stadium rang out to the sound of songs and hymns such as 'Boys of the Old Brigade', 'Ton-y-Botel', 'Men of Harlech', and 'Lead Kindly Light'. One writer said the tension was so great before some could 'hardly speak or write'.

THE CREATION OF A GREAT SPORTING TRADITION

The tradition of singing national anthems before international sporting occasions can be traced back to this game. Wales wanted a way to combat the haka. WRU man, Tom Williams (who played against Ireland in 1882), wrote to the *Western Mail* suggesting Wales respond to the Maori war cry by singing 'Hen Wlad Fy Nhadau'. Written by father and son Evan James and James James of Pontypridd in 1856, it was fast becoming the 'unofficial anthem' of Wales.

The letter worked. As the haka finished, Welsh winger Teddy Morgan led his team in singing, and the crowd soon joined in. All Blacks captain Dave Gallaher said he had never been more impressed in his life than on hearing the singing that day. One paper in New Zealand said the anthem gave a 'semi-religious' feel to the contest. The *Western Mail*, meanwhile, described the haka as 'not very musical but it is very impressive'.

While Wales established the tradition of singing anthems before international sporting fixtures, it wasn't until 1975 that 'Hen Wlad Fy Nhadau' was the sole song the team sang. Until then, 'God Save the Queen' or even 'God Bless the Prince of Wales' were sung as well.

THE IMMORTAL TEST

Welsh rugby in the First Golden Era was built on smart thinking and innovation. Choosing to fight fire with fire, Wales mirrored the eight backs and seven forwards of the All Blacks and employed Cliff Pritchard as a 'rover'. Captaining the side that day was the great Gwyn Nicholls. Nicholls had, once again, been tempted out of retirement to pull on the national shirt. He played a blinder.

Wales adjusted their scrummaging too and matched the 2-3-2 formation they were facing. But 'cunning' Wales went one better. To the confusion of the All Blacks, Wales placed four men in the front row as the teams went to pack down. Once the two Kiwis settled down, Wales removed one player and sent him to shove in the back row. The extra Welsh man left was always in today's loose-head position, giving Wales a scrum advantage.

Wales played aggressively. One observer said they chased the ball like terriers after a rat! For most of this titanic struggle, the two sides were evenly matched. But ten minutes before half-time came the most celebrated try in Welsh history.

Winger Willie Llewellyn, in later life, said that there was usually little preparation for matches but for this game they made an exception and had a practice. Based on an idea from scrum-half Dicky Owen, Wales had rehearsed a move in which Percy Bush, Gwyn Nicholls and Llewellyn ran a decoy move to the right from a scrum. Owen would then throw a reverse pass to Cliff Pritchard who, taking advantage of what would hopefully be a confused defence, would have space to work with Rhys Gabe and winger Teddy Morgan. It paid off. The plan worked and Morgan scored in the corner of the city end. The crowd roared so loudly a carthorse bolted down Westgate Street. Retired Welsh legend Arthur Gould danced on the tables of the press box.

There was to be no more scoring. Well, no more scoring was recognised (see page 80). Bob Deans believed he had scored in the second half, but to the crowd's immense relief it was not allowed. 'Gallant Little Wales' heroically held on, despite the size, strength and stamina of the All Blacks. Dicky Owen exemplified the Welsh effort. Around 25kg lighter than his opposite number, he was battered and bruised for his brave resistance, displacing a cartilage in his chest and getting briefly knocked out. The 'Mother Country' had had her pride restored.

RACIST ATTITUDES

Writers back at the start of the 20th century had what we would see as rather shocking views on race. One described the crowd for this famous match as follows: 'I had heard about crowds so huge they could not be counted. I saw one today in Cardiff . . . I have no particular desire to see another like it. Every nation under the sun was represented . . . black, white, yellow – the clean-living, rustic Welshman, the self-confident Englishman, the dark-skinned negro, the yellow-complexioned Jap [sic] and Chinese – all assembled to watch thirty strong, rugged men play rugby football . . . Who said the Revival has killed off football?'

Some cartoonists in national papers even depicted the New Zealanders symbolically as black-skinned savages.

THE AFTERMATH

Wales were labelled unofficial world champions. The victory was seized upon by nationalists as an example of the kind of country Wales was as the team showed courage, strength and intelligence. One newspaper wrote: 'We all know the racial qualities that made Wales supreme on Saturday . . . It is admitted that she is the most poetic of nations. It is amazing that in the greatest of all popular pastimes she should be equally distinguished.'

New Zealand writer Terry McLean argued the game was the greatest moment in his nation's rugby history and shaped Kiwi rugby forever.

THE MOST FAMOUS DISALLOWED TRY

Even today, no Wales–New Zealand match takes place without journalists raising the disallowed Deans try of 1905. Yet, after the game, some claim the players themselves seemed to have said nothing at the post-match dinner, and the controversy only started the following morning when a *Daily Mail* reporter, looking for a juicy story, suggested to Deans he may have scored. Deans laughed and said: 'I thought I did!' The journalist seized on it, got Deans to wire a telegram to their offices, and the paper ran the story: 'Deans says he scored'. Rugby's longest debate had begun.

The legend grew. The shock of the Kiwis' defeat and the loss being the only blemish on their otherwise perfect record made the story of the 1905 All Blacks even more appealing.

Rhys Gabe, the man who to his 'immortal glory' tackled Deans, was in no doubt there was no try. He later said that '. . . as [Deans] kept struggling to go forward, I knew he had not reached his objective. Other players joined the maul from outside the Welsh line . . .' Different New Zealanders and officials put forward their own thoughts on the matter. Later, the match official John Dallas, who was criticised for being unfit and behind play by the losers, was even moved to publish a letter defending his decision.

Did he or didn't he score?

Fifteen years later, Teddy Morgan admitted he believed Deans had scored. He also thought the Welsh touch judge, who was not consulted by Dallas, agreed. Fuelling the story, it was claimed that even on his deathbed, Deans claimed to have scored. It's a romantic story, but likely untrue. He was in a coma for a considerable time before he died, so it is probably a legend. We'll never know what happened for sure. Which makes it even more beautiful.

WHAT THE PAPERS SAID

***Evening Express*, 18 December 1905**

• 'In Cowbridge-road people waited at street corners and as cyclists and runners shouted 'Wales won' they ran cheering up side streets to communicate the welcome news.'

• 'Scores of men from the Western Valleys of Monmouth who are on strike walked over fifteen miles to see the match.'

• 'A foreign seaman standing in St John's-square was seized by a group of enthusiastic young people and, in spite of his protests, rushed into a public-house to drink the health of the victors.'

• 'A conspicuous feature were the crowds of women waiting about the streets for their better halves coming from the match. Scores of them gave vent to their feelings and shouted "Good old Wales" . . .'

• By columnist 'Forward': 'Wales can rightly claim the absolute supremacy of the British Empire in Rugby football . . . it is only right, also, that those English critics who have never missed a single opportunity of belittling the prowess of Wales should be reminded at this hour of their asinine folly and other stupendous lack of knowledge of the subject which they profess to handle with all the wisdom of the ancients . . . we can smile, gird, and laugh while they pose as men who have knowledge of the game . . .'

1905 ALL BLACKS

Played: 35
Won: 34
Lost: 1
Points for: 976
Points against: 59
Combined points scored against NZ by Wales, Glamorgan, Newport, Cardiff and Swansea: 17
Combined points scored against NZ by other 30 teams: 42
Average tour score: NZ 28 Opponents 2
Average score in Wales: NZ 6 Welsh Teams 4
Players known to have worn hats while playing: George Gillett

THE REVIVAL THREATENS RUGBY

The Welsh Revival of 1904–05 was a Christian movement in Wales that saw a major rise in those attending church and chapel. For those leading the movement, rugby was deserving of condemnation. In fact, international tickets were sometimes torn up in public by those wishing to show their newly found devotion. Others burnt jerseys as church attendance was boosted by the previously lost souls of football and rugby players. The captain of Treorchy RFC renounced rugby for ever and at

Ynysybwl the entire team was baptised and for three years all sporting activities were abandoned. One ex-rugby man, inspired by Welsh religious leader Evan Roberts, said: 'I used to play full-back for the Devil, but now I'm forward for God.'

A NEW NEMESIS ARRIVES FROM AFRICA

The 1905 All Blacks tour shook up the Home Unions and in the following seasons Wales, England, Ireland and Scotland all made some attempts to transform how they played the game and keep pace with the astonishing skills and strategies of the Kiwis. Until a frustrating loss to Scotland in 1907, Wales often played the same seven forwards and eight backs that had helped them defeat New Zealand.

Championship defeats to Ireland in 1906 and to Scotland in 1907 stopped Wales collecting more Triple Crowns, but Wales still played some fantastic rugby when the mood took them. In 1907 they smashed England 22-0 and Ireland 29-0. But between those seasons a new opponent and rival came on to the scene. It would take Wales an astonishing 92 years to overcome them.

THE FIRST SPRINGBOKS

A year after the All Blacks left most of British rugby quaking in its boots, the South Africans arrived. Like their New Zealand counterparts, they changed the sport with their strategy and tactics. They were the first Test team to use today's 3-4-1 scrum formation.

Not quite as dominant as the All Blacks, they still won 26 of their 29 games, with one draw and only two defeats. Scotland overcame them by 6-0 and England were the team that managed the tied game. Their only other loss was a crushing defeat to Cardiff. The Welsh match, however, was one of woe for many of the home team and marked the end for some of the nation's greatest servants.

Wales's unofficial world title crown was brutally stolen by the Springboks.

1906 – Wales 0 South Africa 11 (St Helen's)

This result shook the rugby world. The unofficial world champs were truly humbled, their forwards completely played off the park. It was the first defeat at Swansea for 11 years and the only time Wales lost at home during the First Golden Era.

Adding to the humiliation was that South Africa had even implemented the extra loose-head forward trick Wales had used against New Zealand the year before, something they had learnt when playing Newport (the tactic was explained by a Welsh player!). It was claimed that the home forwards quarrelled among themselves before the match and four of the ageing Welsh pack never again wore the famous red shirt.

Springbok skipper Paul Roos was carried off the field on the shoulders of the home fans, so impressive had the visitors been in victory. In contrast, Welsh captain Gwyn Nicholls, who had AGAIN been persuaded to come out of retirement, was unable to repeat his heroics of 1905. Battered and injured, he was not even able to attend the post-match function. It was a sad end to a glorious international career.

Nicholls, though, restored some pride. A few weeks later his Cardiff side dismantled the Springboks by 17-0, with the great man himself scoring a superb individual try in a standout performance.

'WHEN I'M CLEANING WINDOWS'

In the early 20th century, the Welsh selectors still preferred to use club pairings at half back. Before Wales played Ireland in 1907, R.J. 'Dickie' David was in a panic. He had been selected for his first cap at scrum-half with his Cardiff club partner Percy Bush. Unfortunately, on the Thursday before the game Bush was bedridden with flu.

David worked as a window cleaner. Worried about missing his chance to play for Wales, David used his ladder to climb up to Bush's window, knock on it and beg Bush to play or he would be dropped. Thankfully for him, Bush rose out of bed. Not only did he beat the flu to help Wales win 29-0, but Bush scored a try in which it is said he beat the entire Irish backline, helped set up five others and even kicked a drop goal. Despite a fine game, David never won another cap.

POPULAR PONTY PLAYER

For the 1907 Scotland v Wales match, Pontypridd's captain, Duncan MacGregor, was selected for both teams! Wales named him as a reserve in case anyone was injured before the game, but Scotland picked him in the centre. Welsh-born, he chose the country of his father's birth and lined up for Scotland, who won 6-3 as they went on to win a Triple Crown.

THE FIRST GRAND SLAM

In 1908 France joined the Championship. Kind of. It wasn't official until 1910. This meant that a team winning all of its games would claim a 'Grand Slam' (although the term was not used at the time). Wales won it at the first attempt.

1908 GRAND SLAM

MATCH ONE: England 18 Wales 28 (Ashton Gate, Bristol)

The fog was so thick this was dubbed the 'Phantom Match' as most of the time, fans could only see outlines of the players. Wales won through two tries from Rhys Gabe and others from Percy Bush, Billy Trew and Reggie Gibbs. Welsh legend and Newport scrum-half Tommy Vile made his debut. Vile was in tears before the game as he thought the fog would see the game cancelled and he wouldn't win his cap. At one point the mist was so thick the English backs chased Bush, not realising that Gabe had already scored under the posts. At half-time, Bush mingled with fans.

MATCH TWO: Wales 6 Scotland 5 (St Helen's)

Scotland were furious to be denied a last-minute try as the referee felt that it had been a double movement. Billy Trew and Johnnie Williams scored for Wales.

MATCH THREE: Wales 36 France 4 (Cardiff Arms Park)

Before this first match with France, played on a Monday, the French players were treated to trips around Cardiff in horse-drawn carts, taken around the city's docks, climbed huge cranes, visited the Coal Exchange and even drank wine. Already underdogs, the festivities probably didn't help. Wales ran in nine tries, four from Reggie Gibbs. His four tries are still a record jointly held with seven other players. It should have been five though, but in trying to go under the posts to make the conversion easier, he was tackled by a hard-working French defender who hadn't given up the chase.

MATCH FOUR: Ireland 5 Wales 11 (Balmoral Showgrounds, Belfast)

With ten minutes remaining, Wales's victory looked in doubt. But with the scores tied at 5-5, Dick Jones, Billy Trew and Rhys Gabe worked some magic to send Reggie Gibbs over. Just two minutes later, Johnnie Williams added to his earlier score and Wales were safe. Newspapers celebrated the 'Triple Crown', rather than the not yet established concept of a Grand Slam. In fact, it wasn't until 1910 that all the Home Union teams played France in one season.

The game kicked off at 3.15 p.m. Irish time and 3.40 p.m. Welsh time! Irish and British time was not the same until new regulations in 1916. One reporter commented on the impressive size of the leeks the Welsh fans wore, dwarfing the locals' shamrocks.

THE WALLABIES ARRIVE

In 1908 it was the turn of the Australians to visit Britain for the first time. Scotland and Ireland didn't want to play them, but Wales and England did. Wales battled to a narrow victory, while England fell. Australia won 25 games, lost five and drew one. Underappreciated before they came (the novelty of visitors from far-off places was apparently wearing off), they impressed everyone with their innovative approach to the game.

Thirty thousand came to watch Wales triumph 9-6. The Australians, to their embarrassment, were often forced by the Australian Rugby Union to perform a war dance before the game.

A DOUBLE DOSE OF THE GRAND SLAM

Wales followed up the 1908 Grand Slam with another as they marched to 11 consecutive wins, a national record that lasted until 2019.

The 1909 Grand Slam was almost halted at the second step, but Scotland missed a late penalty goal by inches. It would have been a cruel loss. Jack Bancroft, brother of Billy, was penalised for lying on the ball. While the referee was technically correct, Bancroft had been kicked in the head and was unconscious!

THE TOUCH

Before autographs and selfies were the norm, young fans would often want to touch players' jerseys instead, almost as if they had magical properties.

HERE ARE SOME NOTABLE MOMENTS
FROM THE FINAL PRE-WAR YEARS:

Crowds calm down? By 1911 there were complaints that crowds were less enthusiastic and singing had declined. In the 1911 win over England, some claimed the most interesting bit of crowd interaction was when a 'well-known' acrobatic performer entered the arena with a bicycle and chairs. It took seven police officers to remove him and, for their troubles, the officers were bombarded with fruit.

An impressive record. Between 1900 and 1911, Wales played 43 games, lost seven, and the only home defeat was against South Africa in Swansea. They did not lose in Cardiff. Here are the combined Championship scores from the period:

- Wales 190 England 73
- Wales 130 Scotland 65
- Wales 167 Ireland 50
- Wales 147 France 23 (first game 1908)

Writer W.J. Townsend Collins wrote of the Welsh forward play as key to the Welsh way: 'Welsh forwards in the early years had been the anvil, now they became the hammer.'

HQ opens. In 1910 Twickenham (nicknamed in later years as 'HQ' as it was the 'headquarters of rugby') opened and Wales fell to England for the first time in 12 years. Wales got stuck in traffic on the way and arrived shortly before kick-off. The game was delayed by 15 minutes and England scored from the opening play! It was not to be a happy hunting ground for Wales until 1933.

A THIRD GRAND SLAM
(WITH A LONG WAIT TO FOLLOW)

Wales again claimed a clean sweep in 1911. It was Wales's seventh Triple Crown. Unbelievably, Wales would not claim either again until 1950. The Grand Slam was still not seen as important as the Triple Crown. In fact, for the game in Paris, Billy Trew gave the captaincy to Cardiff's Johnnie Williams as he had never had the honour to lead Wales before (and he also spoke French).

An era ends. The 1912 loss to England is seen as the end of the First Golden Era. Results started to drop off and, for the Irish game that year, Dicky Owen and Billy Trew refused to play for Wales, opting for a Swansea tour of Devon instead. The match against France in 1912 was also the last time Newport's Rodney Parade was used for a Welsh match, and that year saw the Springboks humble Wales again, this time by 3-0 in Cardiff. It was followed in 1913 by England winning for the first time at the Arms Park.

HQ horrors! Before the 1912 Twickenham game, one Welsh person said: 'There is an indefinable something in the atmosphere and the surroundings at Twickenham which is not congenial to the Celtic temperament.'

Just in time. In 1913 Wales scored in the last five minutes in Paris to win 11-8 and avoid a shock defeat to France. Even Welsh fans, though, admitted the referee added 17 minutes to the game at the end!

A SOUR-TASTING ROSE

In 1913, Pembrokeshire-born William John Abbott Davies played at fly-half against Wales for England. A true great, he was only once on the losing side in 22 matches for England. Some in Wales were upset about his choice of team, as a poem in the 1913 programme notes confirmed:

'Hurrah for the Leek, the succulent Leek, That hall-marks our lads as true metal!
Hurrah for the Rose, the real English Rose – Except for the Pembrokeshire petal.'

THE TERRIBLE EIGHT

In 1914, Wales appointed forward Reverend Alban Davies of Llanelli as captain. Despite being a man of the church, he was said to be as fierce and tough on the field as he was in the pulpit. His forwards 'worshipped him'. He was once asked if he ever found the rich language of the other seven players in his pack offensive. Smartly, Davies said he wore a scrum cap and never heard such things.

The Terrible Eight played their most famous role in the 1914 Irish clash. The two packs had met the night before and promised each other a 'hard time'. The match was horrifically violent. The referee let them get on with it as they were all as bad as each other. Afterwards, the packs drank together and became friends.

REVD. ALBAN DAVIES'S WELSH PACK OF 1914

The Reverend Davies died in California in his eighties. The other infamous members of the pack were: David Watts (Maesteg), Jack 'Bedwellty' Jones (Abertillery), Thomas Lloyd (Neath), Percy Jones (Pontypool), Harry Uzzell (Newport), Tom Williams and Edgar Morgan (both Swansea). That season was the first time the Welsh pack had remained the same for each game. Sadly, due to the First World War, the pack never played together again.

THE FALLEN OF THE FIRST WORLD WAR

With war on the horizon in 1914, the WRU's appeal to the rugby community to join the war effort reflected the patriotic mood of the times. They wrote: '. . . we feel we shall not appeal in vain . . . If only every man in every First XV in Wales were to enlist, what a magnificent body there would be at the service of our country, and even then there would still be plenty of players left to enable the game to be played as usual . . .' Wales lost an estimated 40,000 men and women in the war.

13 WELSH INTERNATIONALS DIED IN THE FIRST WORLD WAR:

- Billy Green (3 caps)
- Bryn Lewis (2 caps)
- Fred Perrett (5 caps)
- Lou Phillips (4 caps)
- Charlie Pritchard (14 caps)
- Charles Taylor (9 caps)
- Edward Thomas (4 caps)

- Horace Thomas (2 caps)
- Phil Waller (6 caps)
- David Watts (4 caps)
- Dai Westacott (1 cap)
- Johnnie L. Williams (17 caps)
- Richard Garnons Williams (1 cap)

1900–14: THE STAR PLAYERS

GWYN NICHOLLS

Clubs: Cardiff, Newport
Position: Centre
Caps: 24 (1896–1906)
(British Isles, 4 caps)
Points: 13 (3 tries, 1 drop goal)

Called the 'Prince of Centres', Erith Gwyn Nicholls was born in Westbury-on-Severn in 1874 and moved to Wales as a child. His place in rugby history is carved not just from his power, agility, sensational swerve, pretty pass, positional brain or kicking skills, but his strategic brain and ability to lead and shape a team.

Nicholls saw his role as making space for the players around him. It was said for every try he scored, he created three for others. A great captain, he once stated that 'if any player [is] head and shoulders over his fellows . . . he is the weak point of his team'. He guided Wales to a Triple Crown, but his finest moment was coming out of retirement to lead Wales to glory over the All Blacks.

Early in his career, Nicholls was partner to the other 'Prince of Centres' Arthur Gould. The two played together successfully for Wales, but were chalk and cheese in terms of personality. Nicholls argued that in an ideal Welsh game, the players were like 'great chess masters' working together intuitively. A hero off the field, he suffered poor health in retirement after he tried to save some young girls from drowning. He died in 1938.

JACK BANCROFT

Club: Swansea
Position: Full-back
Caps: 18 (1909–14)
Points: 88 (4 penalties, 38 conversions)

Jack Bancroft was one of the great players of his era. Unfortunately for him, his brother Billy hogged all the limelight. Whereas his brother was all razzle and dazzle, Jack had no time for his sibling's fancy ways.

His 88 points for Wales over 18 caps were a tremendous amount for the period and it wasn't until the 1970s that the legendary Barry John surpassed them. A hefty chunk of Jack's points came against France in 1910 on New Year's Day (Jack kicked eight conversions and one penalty). His 19 points that day were only equalled in 1967 by debutant Keith Jarrett against England. In fact, Bancroft's record was almost forgotten by the 1960s and many thought Jarrett had set a new record. How quickly heroes are forgotten!

A brave defender, it was once written after a heroic rearguard action against overwhelming English dominance that Jack had as many arms and legs as a 'Hindu deity'.

A good cricketer, like his brother, Jack was the first paid professional for Glamorgan. His dad was groundsman at St Helen's rugby and cricket ground in his native Swansea, giving him and his brother a head start on the playing fields.

BILLY TREW

Club: Swansea
Position: Fly-half, centre and wing
Caps: 29 (1900–13)
Points: 39 (11 tries, 1 conversion, 1 drop goal)

William James Trew, affectionately known as Billy, weighed just 67kg (10st 7lb). Small even by the standards of the era, he suffered countless injuries. Despite the bumps, and the fact he is said to have retired ten times, he played first-class rugby for 16 years. He was both a world-class finisher and a marvellous creator of space and time for others.

Making his debut for the great Swansea side of the period aged just 17 in 1897, he quickly became the deadliest try scorer in Welsh club rugby. While he made a try-scoring arrival in a Welsh shirt against England as a winger aged 20, he didn't secure his place in the national side until 1907. A celebrated strategist, he led Wales 14 times.

Trew was captain for most of the three Grand Slams of 1908, 1909 and 1911, playing as fly-half, centre and wing across all 12 matches. In fact, he played four complete seasons for Wales in which they never lost a contest.

In 1912 he cleverly captained Swansea to victory over South Africa. To hold on to a narrow lead in the second half, Trew removed several forwards from the pack and placed them with the backs. Swansea finished with just five forwards! Not only was he a great leader of men, he was a principled one too. In 1907 he refused to play against Ireland in support of a club teammate he felt had been unfairly suspended by the WRU (Fred Scrine was accused of using naughty language with the referee).

The legendary Rhys Gabe called him 'the most complete footballer who ever played for Wales'. Trew tragically died aged 48. Some believe the injuries he suffered on the playing field contributed to his early death.

RHYS GABE

Clubs: Llanelli, London Welsh, Cardiff
Position: Centre
Caps: 24 (1901–08)
(British Isles, 4 caps)
Points: 33 (11 tries)

Born in Llangennech in 1880, Rhys Gabe made his debut for Llanelli at 17 and Wales at 20. He proved his greatness with a stunning series of performances in attack and defence in the 1902 Triple Crown and he frequently partnered Gwyn Nicholls for Cardiff and Wales.

Gabe, Nicholls, Teddy Morgan and Willie Llewellyn formed the threequarters unit for the victory over New Zealand, one of the greatest combinations to play together for Wales.

A canny operator, in 1907 he ran rings around Ireland, playing a part in all six Welsh tries. Better yet, against England in 1908 he scored a remarkable and crucial try in the heavy Bristol fog. Gabe and Percy Bush arrived at a loose ball at the same time. Taking advantage of the murky weather, the pair split off in opposite directions, with Bush shouting loudly to draw attention to himself. It worked. The home team had no idea where the ball was. Eventually, it was realised Gabe was standing alone on the try line waiting for the referee to spot him and award the try.

DICKY OWEN
Clubs: Swansea, Glamorgan
Position: Scrum-half
Caps: 35 (1901–12)
Points: 6 (2 tries)

Richard Morgan Owen was born in Landore in 1876. He is considered one of the greatest Welsh scrum-halves. Just 163cm (5ft 2in) and 60kg (9st 7lb), Dicky was as tough as nails and earned the nickname the 'Pocket Hercules'. He played a critical role in the famous win over New Zealand, despite having a damaged rib from the battering he took early on. His surprising sturdiness was combined with an innovative mind. A rugby nut, he never stopped dreaming up moves, tactics and new strategies. He was credited with pioneering the tactic of 'feint attacks' as well as revolutionising the way scrum-halves teamed up with back-row forwards.

Owen captained Wales three times and played in five Triple Crown teams (including three Grand Slams). His 35 caps were a record until 1955 when Ken Jones overtook his tally. Owen hated playing with another Welsh legend, Percy Bush, as he felt the fly-half was too unpredictable and flash and they were rarely paired by selectors.

After his final game for Wales, at the remarkable age of 34, he was carried aloft from the field of play by fans. Tragically, he took his own life at 55.

CHARLIE PRITCHARD

Clubs: Newport
Position: Forward (back row)
Caps: 14 (1904–10)
Points: 3 (1 try)

As tough as they come, Charlie Pritchard's finest moment was his performance against the 1905 All Blacks. Considered the best forward in the magnificent Welsh pack, he both gave and took a beating that day. Pritchard died a war hero fighting in France in 1916 and was mentioned in dispatches. Dying of his wounds after bravely leading a trench raid and capturing a prisoner, his last words were: 'Well, I have done my bit.'

PERCY BUSH

Club: Cardiff
Position: Fly-half
Caps: 8 (1905–10)
 (British Isles 4 caps, 20 points)
Points: 20 (2 tries, 1 conversion,
3 drop goals)

Despite only winning eight caps, Percy Bush is one of the key players in Welsh history. He was a dazzling, controversial, mesmerising, confident and often infuriating player. His ability to sidestep, swerve, dummy and move at pace terrified defenders, even the mighty All Blacks (whom he had troubled in 1904 with the Lions).

The 1905 All Blacks tour summed up the good and bad of Bush as a player. A week after leading Wales to its most famous win, he cost Cardiff a victory against the same opposition. Instead of kicking a harmless ball dead near the Cardiff try line, Bush nonchalantly waited until a hopeful All Black got near. As he casually tried to kick the ball dead, he sliced it and the attacker only had to fall on the ball to claim the decisive score.

He once played for Cardiff after enjoying a champagne lunch. He left the field after 20 minutes having already scored 17 points. His departing words were: 'That's enough, boys. I'll leave the rest to you.'

1900–14 NOTABLE EVENTS IN WELSH HISTORY

• 1900: The United States census records 93,744 Welsh immigrants living there, the highest ever.

• 1901: 15% of the population, according to the UK census, speak Welsh.

• 1904: The first ever Royal Welsh Show takes place.

• 1905: Cardiff is granted city status.

• 1906: For the first time ever, not one Conservative MP is elected in Wales.

• 1907: The National Library of Wales and the National Museum receive their charters.

• 1908: The Coal Mines Regulation Act 1908 restricts the number of hours (eight) that miners can spend underground.

• 1910: Riots and strikes across South Wales lead to violent clashes between miners and police.

• 1911: Two men are killed in Llanelli by soldiers during demonstrations supporting a national railway strike.

• 1913: At the peak of Welsh coal production, 439 men die in a mining accident in Senghenydd, the worst ever British mining disaster.

1919–29: THE DEPRESSING TWENTIES

	PLAYED	WON	DRAWN	LOST
HOME CHAMPIONSHIP	40	17	3	20
TOURISTS	3	0	0	3
TOTAL	43	17	3	23

Championships

1922

Shared Championships

1920

'. . . the Welsh forwards in the 1920s [never mastered] the quick heel from the loose. They still relied on the foot rush to make ground and it was foreign to their temperament to heel the ball back rather than kick anything higher than a daisy.'

ROWE HARDING

GRIM TIMES ON AND OFF THE FIELD

After the feast comes the famine. Between 1919 and 1929, Wales won just 17 from 43 games. Nine of those wins came against the lowly French and Wales won only one outright Championship during these grim days.

But sporting misery was nothing to how things were off the field. The 1920s were a time of great economic hardship in Wales. Coal, once thought of as 'Welsh gold', lost its worth due to cheap foreign coal and other alternatives. Making it worse, new naval technology meant the British Navy was no longer so hungry for coal to fuel its ships. In around a decade, the number of miners in South Wales fell by over 100,000. By the end of the twenties, nearly a third of Welsh adults were unemployed. At one point, Pontypridd had a 76% unemployment rate.

This was devastating for Welsh communities and around one in five people from South Wales moved away due to economic circumstances. The population did not recover until the 1960s. The knock-on effects of this exodus affected every aspect of Welsh life. Chapels closed, choirs lost members, sporting clubs ran out of players, countless cultural events were cancelled and entire communities were ravaged. Many rugby clubs were reduced to sending begging letters to the WRU and a great deal ceased to exist at all.

Taking advantage of this, rugby league scouts came to South Wales and snapped up swarms of players who needed to provide for their families and took the fees and wages on offer to turn professional. An astonishing 48 capped players went north between 1919 and 1939. Soccer took advantage too, with the sport booming in popularity as the national rugby side floundered. The rugby writer J.B.G. Thomas said that Welsh rugby reflected the spirit and economic 'prosperity of the Principality'. In other words: sorrowful.

THE TORTUROUS TWENTIES

• From 1920 to 1929 Wales won just eight games from 30 against the Home Unions.

• In 1924 and 1925, the selectors picked a different captain for each Championship match.

• In 1924, Ireland had a first win in Wales since 1899, and in 1925 beat Wales three times on the bounce for the first time.

• Between 1920 and 1934, every time Wales faced England they had a different player at fly-half.

CLINGING TO OLD GLORIES

When empires fall, it is common that the generals and emperors who led in the glory days refuse to accept the world has moved on. In Welsh rugby, the generals were the players and the emperors were the WRU. Too many wanted to stick to the style that had led to success in the First Golden Era.

Leading the complaints about the old guard was Rowe Harding, who won 17 Welsh and three Lions caps in the 1920s. The Swansea wing blasted the WRU and clubs for sticking to old methods of play, especially in the back row and among the pack, where England were light years ahead. In a spiky 1929 book he wrote: 'Welsh rugby traditions are no longer abreast of the scientific thinking of modern theorists, Welsh village rugby is fastbound in the rusty fetters of obsolete tradition, and it is to the public schools that Welshmen must look for the revival of Welsh rugby.'

He added that the WRU was full of 'portly elderly gentlemen wearing Rugby blazers and tasteless red ties with life-size ostrich feathers'.

LOSING A BATTLE WITH THE ARMY

Wales played their first capped match after the war against the New Zealand Army, losing 6-3 in Cardiff. Originally, like other unions, the WRU refused to play the Army team as there were concerns about them having professionals in the team. One outraged army officer wrote to the press saying: '. . . as though it matters a damn whether they are amateur or professionals when they have come all this way to fight and die for us'. Only two players in the Welsh team – Glyn Stephens and Walter Martin – had been capped before the war.

THE FALSE HOPE OF 1920

Despite the gloom to come, Wales should have won the Grand Slam in 1920. Instead, they had to settle for sharing the Five Nations with England and Scotland (points difference favoured Wales, but titles were decided on outright win totals only back then).

History was made in Swansea against England when centre Jerry Shea, on his Championship debut, became the first Test player to score a 'full house' of a try, conversion, penalty and drop goal. With drop goals worth four points, he grabbed 16 of his team's points in the 19-5 win. Not everyone was happy. Plenty blasted his selfish play and his hogging of the ball. In victory he was forgiven, but his fortunes soon changed.

Harry Uzzell (of Terrible Eight fame) along with Jack Wetter were the only two players in the England game to have played for Wales in the Championship before the war. Harry, who was captain for the match, was an impressive 37 years old – the oldest Welsh international ever.

ANOTHER SCOTTISH TANTRUM

Scotland's obsession with professionalism reached a new high (or rather low), when they threatened to cancel the 1920 game in Edinburgh with Wales because Wales's Jerry Shea had boxed professionally. The *Daily Telegraph*'s Colonel Philip Trevor dared the SRU to make good on their threat: 'Do it! Do it! And I'll make you the laughing stock of two continents!'

Ironically, Shea was blasted for costing Wales the game as he repeatedly tried to drop goals instead of passing to his wings. His side blew a five-point lead to lose 9-5 as Scotland ended a seven-match losing streak to Wales. Shea ended up with just four caps and in 1921 turned professional with Wigan. As a boxer he fought 69 bouts in the ring, winning 52 of them and facing some of the big names of the era.

PROACTIVE REFEREEING

After the Scottish loss, Wales scraped home in Paris. A Welsh touch judge controversially disallowed a potential match-winning French try and the referee got so frustrated with the scrums he ended up putting the ball into them himself! Wales won 6-5.

Wales wiped Ireland off a waterlogged Cardiff Arms Park by 28-4 in the final game of the season. But it was not the sign of things to come.

AT THE COALFACE TOGETHER
AT WORK AND PLAY

In the 1920 French win, scrum-half Fred Reeves of Cross Keys made his debut. In the second row that day was his clubmate Steve Morris. Amazingly, the two also worked side by side in the Risca Colliery!

WHEN THE CROWD 'BEAT' WALES
1921 – Wales 8 Scotland 14 (St Helen's)

This match was a major embarrassment for Wales. The ground was overflowing with spectators and many of the 50,000 fans kept encroaching on to the field, stopping play. Mounted police had to repeatedly push fans back and at one point the teams left the field until order was briefly restored. The Scottish threatened to march off when things continued to unravel. The pitch invasions ruined plenty of chances for Wales. But even a win would have likely been overturned afterwards by the IRFB. At 37, this was a sad final game for Tommy Vile and Scotland's first win in Wales for 29 years.

A (FALSE) FLICKER OF PROMISE

Only the second ever draw with Scotland prevented a Grand Slam for Wales in 1922 as they won their last Championship until 1931. Key to the title was a rare bit of selection consistency: the forwards were the same for every game. Wales were led by forward Tom Parker, who won six of his seven games as captain in 1922 and 1923. The stalemate with Scotland was his only blemish.

1922 CHAMPIONSHIP WIN
MATCH ONE: Wales 28 England 6 (Cardiff Arms Park)

This was the first time both sides wore numbers in a Championship game. Wales scored eight tries, including one from 32-year-old new cap Dai Hiddlestone. No team had scored so many against the English before. Wales picked two flankers (or wing-forwards) instead of one, as was the style at the time. While England slipped and fell in the mud, Wales wore illegally long studs and kept a firm footing. Naughty, but smart.

Rugby was now a numbers game, with Wales and England both numbering players in the 1922 clash.

MATCH TWO: Scotland 9 Wales 9 (Inverleith)

Thanks to a four-point drop goal two minutes from time by centre Islwyn Evans, Wales grabbed a shock draw.

MATCH THREE: Wales 11 Ireland 5 (St Helen's)

Wales ran up their fifth win over Ireland on the bounce, with two tries from hooker Jack Whitfield and one from Islwyn Evans.

MATCH FOUR: France 3 Wales 11 (Stade Colombes, Paris)

For this Thursday contest with France, the Welsh selectors cruelly dropped Frank Palmer and Harold Davies shortly before kick-off, believing the travelling replacements were better suited to the dry and hard conditions. Poor Davies had to wait two years for his first (and only) cap.

TRAGEDY OF YOUNG WILLIAMS

In 1922, Wales and Swansea scrum-half Tudor Williams, aged 23, was electrocuted and died working in a colliery. He had been capped against France in 1921 and holds the sad record of being the youngest Welsh international to die.

HIGHLIGHTS AND (PLENTY OF) LOWLIGHTS OF THE 1920s

1923 – England 7 Wales 3 (Twickenham)

The 'curse' of HQ continued for Wales. As in 1910, England scored from the kick-off without Wales touching the ball. The home side kicked off, regained the ball and tried a drop goal. It missed. Wales relaxed, but the wind didn't. It kept the ball in play and England's Leo Price scored just ten seconds after kick-off.

Triple woes. The 1923 loss to England was the start of three grim seasons in which Wales would not beat anyone other than France. The next win against one of the Home Unions was against Ireland in the third match of 1926.

Kick in the teeth. It wasn't just the Welsh team getting a good kicking; one poor boy lost several teeth in the 1923 Scottish match in Cardiff. The unfortunate young spectator was hit by a stray foot as Archie Gracie scored late for the visitors. However, the boy, who was Scottish, apparently didn't mind. Gracie was carried off in triumph by the home fans who appreciated his play.

Scrum changes. From 1923 only three men were allowed to make up the front row.

1924 – Scotland 35 Wales 10 (Inverleith)

This was humiliation on a grand scale and the worst defeat Wales had suffered since points had been introduced. At half-time, Wales were 22-0 down. Wales's Jack Whitfield asked his teammate Tom Jones what they should do. Jones replied: 'Stick a pin in the ball and let's go home.' Scotland's Ian Smith so outsmarted his opposite number Harold Davies, he cheekily introduced himself afterwards, saying they had not met on the field. After the game, the Welsh party visited Scotland's famous Forth Bridge. One wag said they should take a good look at it as the WRU would not be paying for them to visit it again!

THE BIG FIVE ARRIVE

In 1924 it was finally decided the archaic way the WRU selected the national team be modernised. Wales still had 13 district representatives picking the side, all trying to push their own local men forward so they would get re-elected on the committee by the clubs they represented.

It wasn't just poor results that forced the WRU to act. The 'Ossie Male incident' in 1924 increased public anger at the Welsh selection process. En route from Wales to Paris, full-back Ossie Male was suddenly dropped for playing for Cardiff six days before (players were not supposed to play within a week of a Test match). To the fury of the Welsh rugby community, he was taken off the train in London and sent home. Shortly after, the WRU introduced a smaller selection panel of five, known as the 'Big Five'. This format would survive until the 1990s when it too had grown archaic and selection was left to team management.

1924 – Wales 0 New Zealand 19 (St Helen's)

The All Blacks had waited 19 years to get revenge for the 1905 loss. They scored a point for each year as they took the home side apart. Dai Hiddlestone of Wales mocked the haka with his own war dance, but he wasn't laughing by the end. The great George Nepia of New Zealand was so nervous before the game he couldn't stop his knees knocking together. The *Daily Telegraph* criticised the home fans, even those in the expensive grandstand seats, for booing the referee. New Zealand won all 32 of their games. Scotland, still upset about perceived injustices in 1905, refused to meet them.

New Zealand had waited a long time for revenge over Wales.

LACK OF 'SCHOOL' HOLDING WALES BACK

Many people, including respected players like Harry Bowcott (eight caps for Wales and five for the Lions), argued that Wales were at a disadvantage to their Scottish and English counterparts as few Welsh players had the chance to develop their skills and tactical ability in public schools. Bowcott said Welsh players had 'little to offer beyond courage, national enthusiasm and the ability to create openings (which tended at times to confuse their teammates)'.

'YES! WE HAVE NO BANANAS'

The match-day experience in the 1920s offered many types of experiences and refreshments that today's fan may not be so familiar with. Cardiff rugby historian Danny Davies said that fans were on occasion known to eat the leeks they wore on match day to show off. Other more tasty nibbles available on match day include potatoes, hot chestnuts, brandy snaps, pastries, peppermints, bulls-eyes and pepsin chewing gum.

Singing was more varied too. Before the England clash in 1924, the fans sang a song called 'Yes! We Have No Bananas' (a popular novelty song from 1923). After Wales slunk off the pitch defeated, the crowd adapted the lyrics to: 'Yes! We Have No Threequarters'.

LAND OF WHOSE FATHER?

Arguably the greatest Welsh player of this era was William John

Abbott Davies. But he played for England (see page 92). The WRU complained that the RFU were stealing players. There were fierce arguments over whether birth, parentage or where a player lived should be the key factor. The RFU sarcastically said that the WRU should sever its links with Newport, as Newport had joined the RFU first. Some even suggested the father's parentage was most important, not where the player had been born.

'WHAT'S THIS FLAG FOR?'

Before the 1924 game with England, the Welsh official due to be touch judge was removed as he didn't know what the duties of the position were. In those days being nominated as a touch judge was a reward or a perk! They were even encouraged to offer the team advice during the game.

1926 – Wales 11 Ireland 8 (St Helen's)

Nineteen-year-old fly-half Windsor Lewis starred as Wales came back from 8-3 down to inflict on Ireland their only defeat that season. A crowd of 55,000 saw Wales win their first game over another Home Union side for four years (and the last until the second game of 1928).

THE CLASH WITH A NEWER WALES

In 1927 Wales lost 18-8 to New South Wales from Australia (known as the Waratahs). The match is now recognised as a full Australian Test match by both countries.

FOOTBALL NO MORE

In 1927, the WRU officially ceased being named the Welsh Football Union (WFU), bowing to popular usage.

DUBLIN A BIT TOO FANCY

Wales's trip to Dublin in 1927 was their last game in the city until 1952. Although up to 3,000 fans travelled for these trips, the IRFU did not think enough Welsh fans bought stand tickets, so the terraces of Ravenhill in Belfast were deemed more suitable for the kind of supporter Wales brought over.

Blunt weapons. After another loss to Ireland in 1927, *The Times* wrote: 'The Welsh forwards are like cavemen in the age of machine guns.'

WALES ARE ATTACKING IN GRID THREE!

The 1927 Scottish game in Cardiff was the first live international match radio broadcast in Wales. In those days, people followed using a grid from a newspaper or magazine that illustrated the field of play and split it into numbered squares. The commentator would then relate to the audience where on the grid the action they were describing was taking place.

1928 – France 8 Wales 3 (Stade Colombes)

Two games after shocking Scotland at Murrayfield, Wales finally fell to France on Easter Monday, ending a 15-game winning record in the series. France had now beaten all of the Home Unions and were on the way to becoming a major force.

A GENTLEMAN NEVER REVEALS . . . ANYTHING

In 1928, the Home Unions stopped the increasingly common features of players and officials publishing articles or giving special insight to newspapers and magazines. Such gossip and chatter simply wasn't the done thing!

THE LONG ARM OF THE LAW
(AND THE WELSH LINE-OUT)

Between the two world wars, more police officers played for Wales than miners. In the 1920s, Welsh teams were packed with police officers. When Wales drew with England in Cardiff in 1926, six of the home pack were policemen. They were: Tom Lewis, Sydney

Hinam (both Cardiff), Howell John (Swansea), Ron Herrera (Cross Keys), Dai Jenkins (Treorchy) and Bryn Phillips (Aberavon).

Unsurprisingly, the press had a field day with this sort of thing and loved to talk about the 'arresting' Welsh team and cartoons on the topic filled newspapers. Between 1923 and 1939, Cardiff averaged ten coppers in their match-day side.

One of the reasons there were so many police players was that high unemployment made it a popular job option. With sky-high jobless rates in the South Wales valleys, political activism and frequent strikes led to repeated clashes between striking miners and the police. Authorities in Wales were keen to have as many officers at their disposal as possible, even if the Home Office in London argued they were overstaffed!

J.B.G. Thomas claimed that a 'big fellow with average intelligence joined the police force or the services'. These were tense times for law and order. In this period, one match official took charge of a club game in Glyncorrwg with a gun strapped to his waist for his own protection!

1919–29: THE STAR PLAYERS

TOM PARKER

Club: Swansea
Position: Forward (Prop, second row, flanker)
Caps: 15 (1919–23)
Points: 6 (2 tries)

Tom Parker may be little known today, but he has one of the best captaincy records. He led Wales seven times and never lost (winning six and drawing one) and was as likeable off the field as he was tough on it.

A smart, calm captain, it was his decision to ensure Wales were re-studded (with studs that were technically illegal) before a rainy clash with England in 1922 and Wales thrashed the slipping Englishmen. Coming off the back of the Golden Era, his success wasn't appreciated at the time, but the rest of the dark 1920s showed how good a leader he really was. His younger brother, Dai, was capped ten times, but the two never played together.

ALBERT JENKINS

Club: Llanelli
Position: Centre
Caps: 14 (1920–28)
Points: 47 (4 tries, 7 conversions, 3 penalties, 3 drop goals)

A war hero who fought through the horrors of the Battle of the Somme, Ypres and Epehy, Jenkins is considered one of the all-time great Scarlet players. The handsome centre was like royalty in his native Llanelli and sometimes got fed up with all the attention he received. It was claimed he would sometimes drink up to five beers before a game.

If he was injured before a Llanelli game, hundreds would turn away from Stradey Park and head home. A prolific scorer with both hands and feet, Jenkins had perhaps his finest moment in a Welsh shirt away against Scotland in 1928 when he helped Wales shock the home side 13-0. Jenkins and his fellow Llanelli players were treated to a civic reception when they returned home. Jenkins was even kissed six times by an admiring fan on the train back. Poor selection by the WRU in the 1920s meant he was limited to just 14 caps. When he died in 1953, Llanelli gave him a civic burial.

ROWE HARDING

Clubs: Swansea, Cambridge
University, London Welsh
Position: Wing
Caps: 17 (1923–28)
(British Isles, 3 caps)
Points: 15 (5 tries)

Rowe Harding was extremely unfortunate to play in the grim 1920s. Wales only won six of the 17 games he played in. Five of them came against France.

Harding had speed to burn and he was champion sprinter in Wales. Alongside his natural skill he had a sharp mind and wasn't afraid to speak hard truths and blasted the WRU for allowing the game in Wales to remain stuck in the past by clinging to old-fashioned ways of doing things. Harding retired from rugby aged 28 to dedicate himself to his legal career and went on to become a judge.

1919–29 NOTABLE EVENTS IN WELSH HISTORY

• 1919: Race riots break out in Newport, Barry and Cardiff, leaving four dead.

• 1920: The Church in Wales is established and the first Archbishop of Wales appointed.

• 1921: The group Byddin Ymreolaeth Cymry (Home Rule Army) is founded, laying the roots for Plaid Cymru.

• 1922: David Lloyd George, the first and only prime minister to have spoken Welsh as his first language, is replaced in office. He came to power in 1916.

• 1924: The world's first radio play, set in a Welsh coal mine, is broadcast by the BBC. It also includes the first spoken Welsh to be aired.

• 1925: The first Welsh-made cartoon, *Jerry the Tyke*, is shown in cinemas.

• 1927: Kathleen Thomas of Penarth becomes the first person to ever swim across the Bristol Channel.

• 1927: Cardiff City win the FA Cup (the only non-English team to win it).

• 1929: Megan Lloyd George becomes the first female MP in Wales.

1930–39: POTENTIAL AND PROMISE

	PLAYED	WON	DRAWN	LOST
HOME CHAMPIONSHIP	32	17	3	12
TOURISTS	2	1	0	1
TOTAL	34	18	3	13

Championships

1931, 1936

Shared Championships

1932, 1939

Two shillings and eleven pence for a packet of twenty cigarettes.
THE EXPENSES THAT WELSH PLAYERS COULD
CLAIM IN THIS PERIOD ACCORDING TO
WILLIAM JAMES 'BOBBY' DELAHAY

TOUGH TIMES CONTINUE,
BUT GLIMMERS OF HOPE TWINKLE

On the field, the 1930s, compared to the 1920s, were positively joyous for Welsh fans. Although economic and social circumstances were still incredibly tough, things improved a little off the pitch too. This period is often called the 'Hungry Thirties'. Rickets, a medical condition that results in soft or weak bones in children and can stunt growth or cause bowed legs and curved spines, was common in South Wales. This was attributed to the poor diets of Welsh children.

Tragically, official government reports and records showed that deaths during childbirth, and women's illnesses overall, were higher in Wales than the rest of the country. Many families couldn't afford such basic goods as nappies and milk and had to replace these key items with newspapers and sugar water. In 1939, it was found that seven of the 13 Welsh counties had the worst occurrences of tuberculosis in the whole of Wales and England.

People were still leaving Wales in droves to find a better life. Ten thousand people left Merthyr Tydfil alone in the 1930s. Making things harder, 1931 saw the introduction of the Means Test by the government. To qualify for benefits of financial aid, families or workers were visited by officials. These tests could be incredibly unfair and something as simple as having an elderly relative living with your family, or a mother or child having a part-time job, could see a family disqualified from getting any aid.

On the plus side, the late 1930s finally saw the first increase in wages since 1917. Thanks to mass production and lower costs, half of households in Wales now owned radios, giving them access to news, entertainment, culture, sports and educational programmes. There was even significant Welsh language content. The change such a device made to daily life is hard to imagine for those of us living in today's digital age.

SCHOOLMEN RUGBY

Welsh historian Gareth Williams has written about the changing nature of the national team in this period. When Wales went to Twickenham in 1924, the team at HQ included 'a colliery foreman, ship's painter, electrician, civil engineer, carpenter, six policemen, miner and fitter's labourer'. Williams notes that when Wales finally broke the HQ curse in 1933, all seven of the backs 'were products' of secondary school and college rugby and the captain and forward Watcyn Thomas was a university graduate.

A FLYING START TO THE DECADE

Amazingly, 1930 was the first year that IRFB rules were applied to all rugby games around the world. Until then, variations had existed regionally. Wales, meanwhile, began the decade with a home loss to England in Cardiff. The visitors had a late injury and so flew in a replacement, Sam Tucker, by light aeroplane so he could make the game in time. He played a blinder.

SNAPSHOT OF WELSH LIFE

On the morning of the English game, Welsh writer 'Old Stager' published the following: 'A Rugby international penetrates and permeates Welsh life to an extent that nothing else is capable of doing . . . Welsh life in all its many facets is never so truly represented at any national event as at a Rugby international match in Wales. Creeds, political opinions and social distinctions are all forgotten.'

BATTLE OF COLOMBES
1930

1930 – France 0 Wales 11 (Stade Colombes)

This clash has gone down as the 'Battle of Colombes'. Wales had only beaten Ireland this season, but a hyped-up France were in position to claim their first ever Championship. Wales took the field with Ned Jenkins as the old man of the team at just 25 years old! With two teenagers playing in Edgar Jones (prop) and Norman Fender (back row), the average age of this baby team was 22 years and 109 days. Seven Welsh players were unavailable as they were travelling with the Lions.

Hooker Hubert Day of Newport needed nine stiches in his lip (that was apparently all but hanging off) after getting whacked. Neath's Tom Arthur, seeing the offending punch, threw one back, hitting the wrong man (who unfortunately for him was a boxer). Boots and fists never stopped flying and Wales gave as good as they got. Amazingly, after one fight, the referee was about to ping a Welsh forward when a top official from the French Rugby Federation (FFR) entered the field of play to explain to the match official that the home side had in fact started the dust-up! One home player was told after the 11-0 defeat that he would never play for France again. In total, nine of the French never gained another cap. Wales were bombarded by rubber cushions as they left the field.

CHAMPIONSHIP GLORY,
BUT HQ CURSE COSTS WALES DEARLY

Wales went undefeated in 1931 to win their first title since 1922. They were hugely inspired by the great centre Claude Davey, who battered opponents with his tackling. Sadly, a bizarre opening draw cost them the Grand Slam. Interestingly, this season was the first time Wales had the same captain for an entire Championship since 1922.

1931 CHAMPIONSHIP WIN
MATCH ONE: England 11 Wales 11 (Twickenham)
Wales's bad luck at Twickenham continued. England failed to win a single match in the Championship, but still thwarted

the Welsh. Two cruel moments made it even harder to swallow. Firstly, both touch judges ruled an English conversion in the first half as a miss. However, at half-time the referee told those operating the scoreboard to add the points. Despite this, Wales still led 11-8 with three minutes left on the clock. With a first win at the ground looking likely, Wales conceded a penalty. From five yards inside the visitors' half, Brian Black of England kicked a monster and levelled the game. The result meant it was nine games without a win for Wales in this fixture.

The final mark. In the draw at Twickers, Wales's Wick Powell marked himself, quite literally, in Welsh rugby history. He scored Wales's third and last goal from a mark. Even more bizarrely, he did so by kicking it off the ground. When he placed it on the ground after calling a mark, the home players were utterly confused and did not try to charge, giving him plenty of time to slot the kick over!

MATCH TWO: Wales 13 Scotland 8 (Cardiff Arms Park)
Wales's Watcyn Thomas (Swansea), operating at number eight, played 70 minutes with a broken collarbone and still grabbed a vital try.

The 'bigoted five'. No players from Llanelli made the Welsh team for the opening two games of the 1931 Championship. This prompted a local paper to relabel the Big Five selectors as the 'bigoted five'.

MATCH THREE: Wales 35 France 3 (St Helen's)
MATCH FOUR: Ireland 3 Wales 15 (Ravenhill, Belfast)

This was another brutal match as Ireland were aiming to win the Triple Crown and Wales the Championship. In one sequence of play, two consecutive tackles from Welsh captain Jack Bassett and Claude Davey left two Irish players unconscious. Ireland didn't finish the game with a full team, due to injuries, and Wales had several players barely able to move properly due to neck, head and ankle injuries. The visitors clung on to claim the title.

FAREWELL TO THE FRENCH

After the 1931 Championship, the tournament again returned to just four teams as France were exiled for 16 years. There was dismay among the Home Unions at blatant player payment in French rugby. The FFR was unable to stop what their clubs were doing, and so it was *au revoir*.

WALES UNABLE TO BAG A SPRINGBOK
1931 – Wales 3 South Africa 8 (St Helen's)

As in 1906, this was seen as an unofficial world title bout. Playing on what was more a lake than a field, captain Jack Bassett gave an epic performance at full-back, but a poor one as a captain. Wales were criticised for trying to play dry-weather rugby on a day when it was so wet that the anthems were not even played beforehand. South Africa's Danie Craven praised the Welsh forward effort, saying: '[our] pack met its equal . . .

after the match our locks had no skin on their shoulders and the props suffered the same fate'.

CORNER FLAGGING

The 1930s were a very defensive era and it was hard for backs to find space. Ex-international Rowe Harding wrote of the new defensive style: 'In the late twenties, the blind side wing-forward in the 3-2-3 formation stopped the scrum-half moving around the blind side . . . while the open side wing-forward drove the opposing outside-half across field. The [number eight] broke from the scrum and moved across behind his backs as an extra defender . . . kicking [out on the] full was allowed.'

BASSETT BLAMED AS CROWN SLIPS AWAY

In 1932, after a first win over England for a decade and a hard-earned win away to Scotland, Wales faced Ireland for the Triple Crown. For the first time ever, Wales were unchanged in selection for all three Championship games. In Cardiff, against the men from the Emerald Isle, captain Jack Bassett had a game he was (sadly) never to be allowed to forget.

Bassett was at fault for two tries – one of which saw him watch in a 'trance' as his dropped ball allowed Shaun Waide to run in from 80 metres. Then, a try at the death from Dicky Ralph gave Bassett a chance at redemption. Kick it and Wales would draw and win the Championship. Sadly, it was nowhere near and Wales had to share the title with England and Ireland.

It was Bassett's last game after a fine career for Wales, but he was never allowed to forget this dreadful day.

LAND OF SONG

Welsh fans in the mid-1930s had a little more to cheer than in the previous decade and, after a drop-off in attendance, games began selling out again. E.D.H. Sewell wrote: 'Those unhappy people who have never heard the Welsh mass of anything from 30,000 to 50,000 singing 'Land of my Fathers' and 'God Save the King' have heard very little music . . . there is no community singing elsewhere to equal it.'

THE CHAIN OF MISFORTUNE IS BROKEN
1933 – England 3 Wales 7 (Twickenham)

When Pontarddulais-born Welsh-speaking Arthur Vaughan-Jones played in the back row at Twickenham in 1933, Wales were still trying to break the HQ curse which stretched back to 1910. Sadly for him his side lost. Wales celebrated! Why? Vaughan-Jones was in the English, not the Welsh back row!

It was Wales's tenth game at Twickenham. When the selectors announced a new captain in Watcyn Thomas and seven new caps, plenty felt this was not to be the year the duck would be broken. In fact, famous Welsh poet Sir (Albert) Cynan Evans-Jones had even penned a poem asking why Wales could not break 'her' long chain of misfortune at Twickenham!

Yet 'cheeky chappie' Ronnie Boon, with a drop goal and a try, earned his place in rugby folklore as Wales won 7-3. Two of

the debutants on that day were Wilf Wooller and Vivian Jenkins, both of whom would become key players. The scoreboard on the day said Wales had won 9-3, but after the game the referee said he had disallowed the conversion of winger Boon's try. Bizarrely, it was Wales's only win of the Championship. Four of this Welsh team went on to play cricket for Glamorgan.

HOLDING BACK THE TIDE OF PROGRESS

The IRFB tried to stop the progress of forward play in 1933. Disliking the specialisation that had developed in forward play, it was decided that once again (as had been the norm decades before) the first forwards to arrive at a scrum would be the first to pack down. Former international Horace Lyne agreed, saying specialist forwards 'distressed him for they were spoiling football in all the countries'. The idea lasted two seasons and was thrown away.

THE LONG TYRANNY OF CAPTAIN REES

Captain Walter Rees served as secretary of the WRU from 1896 to 1948 (no, that is not a typo!). A non-rugby man, he ran matters with an iron fist. Journalist Peter Jackson later wrote that Rees sounded like a man who had 'graduated from the Joseph Stalin school of administration'.

Rees was incredibly tight with expenses for players, even over a mere few shillings. However, hypocritically, if a player had attended Oxford or Cambridge University, he would suddenly become extremely generous. He expected other WRU committeemen to be sycophants and cosy up to him. Failure to do so could see them lose their precious allocation of match tickets. It is said he kept a 'black book' listing the favoured and unfavoured.

The 'tyranny' of Walter Rees.

Tight-fingered with expenses to working-class players, he was kind to himself. For away games two special coaches would be attached to trains for the Welsh party, one of which was known as 'Walter's saloon'. Sycophants were expected to pay tribute here. In 1948 he turned up at HQ with a police escort and in a Rolls-Royce saloon.

There is one delightful story about Captain Rees we can relate. After an away defeat in the 1930s, the Welsh party were travelling back via train. Tyrant Rees upset a few players and, for once, they had had enough. They dumped Rees in one of the skip baskets containing the playing kit and parked it in the corridor.

THE NIGHTSHIFT MAN

Cross Keys hooker Frank 'Lonza' Bowdler won 15 caps for Wales. A hooker, he was famous for working a night shift underground in his local colliery before playing for Wales in the afternoon. After the game he would head back to do another shift!

UNLUCKY 13

Wales selected a ridiculous 13 new caps against England in 1934. Unsurprisingly, they lost 9-0. Played in front of a fancy new grandstand in Cardiff, Wales were lucky the slippery pitch kept the score down. Tactically, the forwards had been told to leave a tunnel in the scrum for the ball to emerge. Afterwards, Wales's Arthur Rees said they had done that and 'the whole England pack came through it!'

TAKE THE BUS NEXT TIME

Eight Welsh miners chartered a flight up to Scotland to see the game in 1934. Thanks to a faulty compass, the plane landed in Portsmouth, not Edinburgh.

FULL MARKS FOR EFFORT AT THE BACK

Vivian Jenkins scored Wales's first ever try from full-back in the 1934 win over Ireland in Swansea. Remarkably, it was also the first ever Championship try for a full-back. It would be 33 years before a Welsh full-back grabbed another one.

THE LOVELY POINT

1935 – Wales 13 New Zealand 12 (Cardiff Arms Park)

For only the second time since the epic 1905 match, Wales met New Zealand. This was extra special as the bruising Kiwi win of 1924 had been in Swansea and the visitors were keen to lay the ghost of the Arms Park. In 1905, 1924 and before they reached Cardiff in 1935, the All Blacks had played 85 games in the UK and Ireland. Their only losses were Wales (1905) and Swansea (1935).

Wales picked a schoolboy at scrum-half for this game! Despite being just 18 years old, Haydn Tanner had already defeated the All Blacks three weeks earlier, playing with his cousin Willie Davies (also a schoolboy) in Swansea's 11-3 win over the tourists. Afterwards, New Zealand captain Jack Manchester said to the press: 'Don't tell them at home we were beaten by a pair of schoolboys.'

*Hadyn Tanner was still a schoolboy
when he helped defeat New Zealand.*

The match took place during a cold spell, and seven tons of straw had been laid on the field to keep the pitch playable. The All Blacks almost scored from the kick-off when Wales full-back Vivian Jenkins slipped on a frozen patch and nearly conceded a try. Wales recovered to lead 10-3 thanks to two quick tries from Geoffrey Rees-Jones and captain Claude Davey. Then, things started to go badly wrong. The Kiwis rallied through two tries, a conversion and a four-point drop goal to lead 12-10 with minutes remaining. If that wasn't bad enough, Welsh hooker Don Tarr was almost killed when he broke his neck. He was placed on a stretcher face down when he was removed from the field, an act that saved his life.

With no replacements, Wales were down to 14, trailing by two, with just six minutes remaining. From a scrum, Tanner fed Cliff Jones who popped a short pass to Wilf Wooller. The Cambridge back ran a decoy move using captain Claude Davey as a shield and slid through a gap. Knowing he was going to be tackled, he kicked to the line and hoped for a kind bounce. It wasn't kind and flew over his head . . . and into the arms of winger Rees-Jones who scored his second try. Amazingly, Wales only won four scrums all game, but had scored from three of them. Minutes later the crowd invaded the pitch, mobbed the players and sang the national anthem. Apparently, some of the players were even kissed by happy female fans! Welsh pack leader Arthur Rees said Wales had won by a 'lovely point'. It would be 1953 before the All Blacks returned.

Prior to the All Blacks game, Haydn Tanner and Cliff Jones met up to get to know each other as they would be playing together as half-backs for the first time. Meeting in Swansea, Tanner brought some cockles and Jones some bananas. On such food and friendship was history made.

CHAMPIONS AGAIN AS WIN ALMOST ENDS IN TRAGEDY

In 1936, Wales drew 0-0 with England at St Helen's, but beat Scotland (13-3) and Ireland (3-0) to claim the Championship. The final game in Cardiff against the Irish was huge as Wales were going for the title and Ireland the Triple Crown. Spectators started queuing five hours before the game and, when the gates were closed two hours prior to kick-off, fans rushed the stadium. Fire hoses were turned on the crowd to try and break up the danger and drive people away. In the end 70,000 still packed into a stadium built for 56,000. Several people were injured and trampled in the melee and needed serious medical treatment. Wales followed their Championship win by losing all three games in 1937 for the first time since 1892.

NEW SCRUM STYLE

The 1938 season saw Wales pack down 3-4-1 in the scrum for the first time ever, although 3-2-3 was still preferred by traditionalists.

INVISIBLE AEROPLANES FILL
THE SKY IN CRUEL LOSS

In the 1938 match with Scotland, referee Cyril Gadney gave a controversial penalty against Welsh forward Harry Rees for lying on the ball. He may well have been right, but poor old Rees had an unconscious Haydn Tanner lying on him at the time. Rees was also concussed and began blathering about aeroplanes in the sky (not a common sight in 1938).

Afterwards, reflecting on the decision, Gadney said: 'It was a horrible thing to do at that time of the game. To me it was almost as bad as taking a man's life.' Wales had been reduced to 13 men effectively before this with prop Eddie Morgan off injured and Wooller a wounded passenger. It was Wales's only defeat that season and Scotland went on to win the Triple Crown.

THE WORLD DARKENS AGAIN

The arrival of the Second World War saw Wales cease official internationals until 1947. Only four players from the last game in 1939 would play again for Wales (Howard Davies,

Haydn Tanner, Bunner Travers and Les Manfield). It is believed around 15,000 Welshmen were killed during the war.

THREE WELSH INTERNATIONALS DIED IN THE SECOND WORLD WAR

• Cecil Rhys Davies (1 cap) failed to return after piloting his aircraft on patrol in Cornwall and was 'presumed killed in action'.
• John R. Evans (1 cap) was killed in 1943 in the Middle East.
• Maurice Turnbull (2 caps) was killed in Normandy in 1944.

THE SHOW MUST GO ON

Unlike during the First World War, sport was encouraged as it kept up the morale of soldiers and citizens. International and club sides played many unofficial games throughout the war. For instance, 20,000 watched a Wales XV face their English counterparts in 1942. Union and league players often played together in a wartime amnesty too (except in Scotland). The match programme for one army services match said: 'It must stagger our enemies to think that while Britain is engaged in the most momentous struggle of our existence, in the sterner game of war, the sporting community in its midst find time and facilities for participation in its favourite games and pastimes . . . [it is hoped spectators] . . . follow their rugby idols into khaki, in which outfit more undying glory can be won than in an international jersey.'

ARMS PARK DISARMED

In January 1941, a German bomb destroyed the Arms Park's North Stand and West Terrace. It also damaged drainage pipes, causing severe pitch problems in later years.

1930–39: THE STAR PLAYERS

RONNIE BOON

Clubs: Cardiff, Dunfermline,
London Welsh, New Brighton
Position: Wing
Caps: 12 (1930–33)
Points: 20 (4 tries, 2 drop goals)

Barry-born Boon will forever be associated with Wales's first win at Twickenham in 1933. 'Have no fear, Boon is here,' he would often say when arriving for games. Cocky, but sure, he had a lot going for him: exceptional speed (he represented Wales in athletics), great hands (he played cricket for Glamorgan) and an exceptional kicking foot. He contributed all seven of Wales's points in the famous Twickenham win through a try and a remarkably 'calm' drop goal. The year before, in Swansea, he scored a try and kicked a 'freak' drop goal that gave Wales their first win over the auld enemy for a decade.

WILFRED WOOLLER

Clubs: Sale, Cardiff, Cambridge
University
Position: Centre
Caps: 18 (1933–39)
Points: 26 (6 tries, 1 conversion,
2 penalties)

You know that friend you have who is annoyingly amazing at everything they do? That was Wilfred Wooller. Not only did he win 18 caps for Wales, but he also captained Glamorgan in cricket (he would have played for England but for business commitments) and played for Cardiff City in soccer. Not impressed? He also represented Wales at squash and played bowls for Cardiff Athletic Club.

At 1.88m (6ft 2in) and 89kg (14st), Wooller was a big centre for the 1930s. Yet he also had pace and a great swerve. He was respected for his ability to kick the ball far and accurately. He once kicked a 50-metre drop goal, an astonishing feat with the heavy leather balls of the 1930s. Wooller played in the famous 1933 Twickenham win and the 1935 All Blacks victory. In an era of often dull, forward-based rugby, his skills and flair were a delight for romantics.

During the Second World War, Wooller spent over three years as a prisoner of war in Singapore. He survived and went on to become a successful sports administrator, journalist and broadcaster.

HAYDN TANNER

Clubs: Swansea, Cardiff
Position: Scrum-half
Caps: 25 (1935–49)
(British Isles, 1 cap)
Points: 0

Haydn Tanner is one of just 45 Welshmen to have played in a winning side against New Zealand while representing Wales. Yet he wasn't really a Welshman when he did so, but a Welsh schoolboy. He was just 18 when he played his first game for Wales and helped fell the mighty All Blacks. Even more remarkably, he had also beaten them with Swansea just a few weeks before. On the day of his Welsh debut, his gym mistress from school accompanied him to Cardiff from Penclawdd to make sure that he did not get lost.

Tanner played in an era when not only was he often behind a beaten pack, but scrum-halves were subject to laws and tactics that allowed back-row forwards to smother and disrupt them. Despite this, he still emerged as one of the greats in the position. His pass was a thing of wonder, honed by dedicated practices as a young boy where he spent long hours passing the ball against a goalpost.

It was claimed he never tried to make more than three breaks a game and believed a scrum-half should only try to break to score. In 1947, against France in Paris, he so dominated his opposite number, Yves Bergougnan (known as the 'Idol of Paris'), that the Frenchman was reduced to tears. Tanner was never dropped by Wales in a career spanning over 14 years.

CLAUDE DAVEY

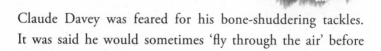

Clubs: Swansea, Sale and London Welsh
Position: Centre
Caps: 23 (1930–38)
Points: 15 (5 tries)

Claude Davey was feared for his bone-shuddering tackles. It was said he would sometimes 'fly through the air' before making contact. His arrival on the scene for Wales was resented by the press in Llanelli, angry their players were getting overlooked unfairly. One paper wrote: '. . . he can do nothing except emulate a battering ram, and too often forgets to take the ball with him'.

In 1931 he led the way in Belfast as Wales denied Ireland a Triple Crown. His fierce tackling knocked out both his opposite number and the forward who was shifted to centre to replace him. Claude captained Wales on eight occasions, losing just two games. In 23 caps he only saw defeat seven times. He is one of only three Welsh captains, all centres, who have led Wales to victory against New Zealand. His triumph over the All Blacks was one of two occasions he beat the men in black on that tour as he also played in the victorious Swansea side (scoring in both matches).

Welsh international Viv Jenkins said Claude 'had the smile of an angel, but tackled like an avenging Fury'. His tackling style later inspired the tough-as-teak Jack Matthews.

CLIFF JONES

Clubs: Cardiff, Pontypridd, Cambridge University, London Welsh
Position: Fly-half
Caps: 13 (1934–38)
Points: 6 (2 tries)

At school, Cliff Jones had originally refused to play rugby (the only sport on offer) as the shape of the ball upset him!

A rugby 'alchemist', his footballing abilities established him in the pantheon of great outside-halves. Despite his late start, he appeared for Pontypridd and Cardiff before he was even 18. He was instrumental in Wales's win over New Zealand in 1935 and captained Wales on three occasions. He suffered many injuries in his career, often due to the ball being 'heeled' back slowly by his pack, allowing back-row forwards to rough him up. He suffered four broken bones before he was 20.

Bizarrely for the era he played in, he never mastered the drop goal. His influential coach at Llandovery College forbade him to kick them! A true innovator, while injured once he wrote a book on the game with many ground-breaking opinions and ideas. After retiring, he became a Welsh selector and was also key in introducing and establishing coaching into the Welsh game.

WATCYN THOMAS

Clubs: Llanelli, Swansea, Waterloo
Position: Number eight
Caps: 14 (1927–33)
Points: 6 (2 tries)

Watcyn Thomas once played 70 minutes against Scotland with a broken collarbone and still managed to score a vital try to help win the game. A beast in the loose, Thomas also excelled in the line-out. He was able to win and provide clean ball, even when several opponents marked him. Respected as a great thinker and good leader by his teammates, he was known to perform a 'fire dance' after games! He captained the first

Welsh team ever to win at Twickenham.

He regularly spoke his mind to the selectors when he disagreed with them, which was not the done thing. In 1933, unhappy that the selectors had picked two players out of position, he swapped them around during the game to where he felt, as captain, they should play. He was never selected again. Despite being ignored by Wales, the 1935 All Blacks considered him the best line-out forward they faced during their tour.

He once knocked a policeman's helmet off and kicked it down the street. He wasn't arrested, but instead ended up having some beers with the officer! Years after he retired he wrote one of the shortest and most bizarre rugby autobiographies ever.

1930–39 NOTABLE EVENTS IN WELSH HISTORY

- 1931: A meteorite lands on a small farm in Pontllyfni near Caernarfon.

- 1932: On St. David's Day, members of Plaid Cymru twice replace the Union Flag flying over Caernarfon Castle with the Welsh flag. The following year both fly officially.

- 1933: Dylan Thomas publishes his poem 'And death shall have no dominion'.

- 1934: 266 people are killed in an accident at Gresford Colliery in Wrexham. Only 11 bodies are recovered.

- 1935: Swansea are the first British club to defeat the All Blacks and the first Home Union club or international team to defeat New Zealand, South Africa and Australia.

- 1936: 118 men from South Wales join the International Brigade to fight fascism in the Spanish Civil War – 34 are killed.

- 1939: The Second World War begins and the first batch of children removed from cities to avoid enemy bombing arrive in Wales.

1947–57: THE POST-WAR REVIVAL

	PLAYED	WON	DRAWN	LOST
FIVE NATIONS	44	28	2	14
TOURISTS	3	2	0	1
TOTAL	47	30	2	15

Championships

1950 (Grand Slam), 1952 (Grand Slam), 1956

Shared Championships

1947, 1954, 1955

'The first requirement of captaincy, is a team to captain.'

JOHN GWILLIAM

A BOOM AFTER THE WAR

After the Allies emerged victorious from the horrors of the Second World War, a series of 'Victory Internationals' were played in 1945 and 1946. These games meant enough to some fans that when a Welsh XV fell to a New Zealand XV at Cardiff in 1946, Kiwi fans listening live on the other side of the world ran out into the streets in the early hours of the morning to celebrate. Official capped matches resumed in 1947. The decade that followed was to be a positive one for the national side, with some of the greatest names in rugby history gracing the scarlet shirt and the end of a long quest for a Grand Slam.

Off the field, Wales and the rest of Britain were to undergo several years of hardship after the shock of war, before experiencing a post-war boom. Some thought the sense of 'togetherness' Britain had experienced during the war was going to lead to major shifts in the social and class make-up of society. Alas, no such changes came. However, Wales benefited greatly from the shock general election result of 1945, when wartime hero Winston Churchill was voted out of office. The elected Labour government created the modern welfare state. Revolutionary for the time, it created a system of benefits which provided social security from 'cradle to grave' for all. In 1948, Aneurin Bevan, a Welsh MP for the British Labour Party, led the founding of the National Health Service, so that all, regardless of wealth, would have access to medical care.

COLD BEGINNINGS SPOIL BLAZERS' FUN

The start of official Tests coincided with one of the coldest European winters of the century. Parts of Wales saw the thermometer hit −21°C in 1947. For a country low on energy and resources after the war, this was devastating. Many died from the cold and, when the weather thawed, flooding caused severe damage. The cold affected the 'blazers' (committee men) of the WRU in slightly less dramatic ways too. The special extra dining carriage the WRU wanted to add to the train to Scotland was refused by the Ministry of Transport due to coal shortages.

1947 – Wales 6 England 9 (Cardiff Arms Park)

Wales's return to a bomb-damaged Arms Park (only 43,000 could attend) ended in defeat. Haydn Tanner (captain) and Howard Davies were the only previously capped players in the team. A new generation was arriving though: future legends such as Bleddyn Williams, Jack Matthews, Rees Stephens, Billy Cleaver and Ken Jones. Wales and England would share the 1947 Championship.

1947 – France 0 Wales 3 (Stade Colombes)

Wales won a bruising encounter by a single penalty goal. The victory included some rather sneaky Welsh tactics. At line-outs, Cardiff prop Cliff Davies would often bend over and a teammate would shove a French player so they fell over the crouching Welshman! Davies also admitted to nibbling on a French ear.

CRUEL CAPTAIN REES STRIKES AGAIN

When Wales travelled by train to play France for the 1947 clash, WRU secretary Captain Walter Rees (see page 133) had Newport second row George Parsons thrown off the train en route. The WRU had heard he had spoken with rugby league scouts and refused to listen to his protestations of innocence. He was never selected again and didn't even get presented with his Welsh cap, won several weeks before against England, for almost 30 years.

LEAKS IN THE ROOF

In the 1940s and 1950s, Cardiff Arms Park was not a comfortable place for radio broadcasters. The stadium was also used for greyhound racing at the time and the rugby commentators used the judges' box that hung above one of the stands. It was reached via a trapdoor and removable ladder. The commentators had to climb up 45 minutes early to get into position and stay there until long after the game ended. A bucket was sent up with them so they could answer the call of nature.

BLACK AND BLUE ALL OVER

Cardiff supplied a Championship record ten players to the 1948 side that drew 3-3 with England and beat Scotland 14-0. The latter win was to be the first of seven consecutive wins over the Scots. The capital side also supplied another ten against France.

A WHITE MESS

When Wales lined up to face England in 1949 in Cardiff, they did so playing in white shorts for the first time. After the practice session the week before the game, WRU secretary Eric Evans presented them to the team. The players were horrified. The 'shorts' reached the knee and resembled equipment from the 19th century. Captain Haydn Tanner was furious and asked how the WRU expected the players to be able to run in them. Evans suggested that perhaps the players' wives or mothers could amend them. In disgust, Tanner threw them back onto the dressing-room table and said that was the job of the union and it was not the 19th century any more!

'I'M BACK!'

When hooker William 'Bunner' Travers was selected for the 1949 England win, he was making quite the comeback. His last match had been ten years earlier!

A STEP TOWARDS A NEW WORLD

May 1949 saw seeds of change planted in the Welsh rugby landscape. At a meeting of the clubs in Porthcawl, the WRU gave a series of presentations on training, refereeing and coaching. Hugely controversial, it was the start of what was to become the coaching revolution and would help Wales forge the celebrated team of the 1970s. It soon became possible to obtain a WRU-approved coaching certificate. However, there was little demand at first. In the late 1950s the WRU were pleading for more clubs to take an interest.

1950 – FROM WOODEN SPOON TO GRAND SLAM

Between 1911 and 1949, Wales had won the Championship outright just three times: 1922, 1931 and 1936. They had also shared four titles (1920, 1932, 1939 and 1947). But there had been no Triple Crown or Grand Slam for an incredible 39 years. Following a 1949 Wooden Spoon, Wales finally got their act together. Built on the power and smartness of a fierce pack, Wales wore sides down and allowed their classy backs to finish off tired opponents. The men in red conceded just eight points all Championship. Some of the forwards, like Roy John and Dai Davies, were described as 'gambolling like gazelles with disturbed hormones'!

1950 GRAND SLAM

MATCH ONE: England 5 Wales 11 (Twickenham)

A then record 75,532 packed into Twickenham to see Wales win there for just the second time in 15 attempts since 1910. Thousands were locked outside. Bleddyn Williams pulled out late due to injury and his captaincy was taken by the great John Gwilliam at number eight. The star of the show was 18-year-old full-back Lewis Jones who kept running balls that players of his position were simply not meant to do back then. His mazy and risky galloping paid off, no more so than when it created a score for prop Cliff Davies. Journalists were surprised by the win and many blasted the home team as a foreign legion for having three New Zealanders and a South African in a side 'officially labelled England'.

MATCH TWO: Wales 12 Scotland 0 (St Helen's)
MATCH THREE: Ireland 3 Wales 6 (Ravenhill)

Ireland had won the Grand Slam in 1948 and the Triple Crown in 1949. Wales, trying to claim their first Triple Crown since 1911, were stuck at 3-3 with just three minutes left on the clock. In the dying moments, winger Malcolm Thomas burst for the line from 15 metres out after a long ball from Lewis Jones. Thomas went in at the left corner and glory came to the men in scarlet after nearly four decades.

J.B.G. Thomas wrote: 'Many a Welsh eye was moist that afternoon at Ravenhill Park; even hardened second-row forwards were moved . . . there was special pride that day in being Welsh and the fifteen tired heroes had restored the national game to its proper place in the . . . hearts of Welsh people.' On the ferry back, the players partied hard. Leslie Spence (future WRU president) saw all the belongings in his cabin thrown overboard. Even the mattress had gone through the porthole. Detectives met the boat when it docked and no one was allowed off until all damage was paid for.

THE LLANDOW AIR DISASTER

The importance of the Triple Crown was soon put into horrifying context. The next day a plane returning from Ireland, chartered especially for Welsh supporters, crashed. Eighty people were killed and only three survived. At the time it was the worst civil aviation disaster the world had ever seen. One survivor of this terrible tragedy was

Handel Rogers. He later became WRU president and returned to Ireland in 1976 to see Wales win another Triple Crown.

MATCH FOUR: Wales 21 France 0 (Cardiff Arms Park)
For the final game against France later that month, a packed Arms Park stood in silence as five uniformed buglers played the 'Last Post' in tribute to the dead. Wales won 21-0 and claimed the Grand Slam.

MISERABLE MURRAYFIELD MYSTERY
After dismissing England 23-5 in Cardiff in 1951, Wales looked on course to retain the title. But against Scotland they lost 19-0 in one of the biggest shocks in Championship history. The Scottish team went on to lose their next 17 matches, including a mind-bending 44-0 home loss to South Africa just three matches later. The Welsh selectors responded by leaving five spaces blank when they announced the team for the next game as they had no idea what to do to fix whatever had happened in Edinburgh.

SELECTION HEADACHE
When the great fly-half Cliff Morgan was picked for his first cap it caused a nasty injury to his mother. Hearing her son's name announced on the radio when the final team was revealed for the Irish game of 1951, she jumped up in delight, banged her head on a boiler and knocked herself out.

DRESSING ROOMS OF SONG

In the 1950s the Welsh team would open the dressing-room door before a game and, led by prop Cliff Davies, sing 'Calon Lân'. The idea belonged to John Gwilliam who wanted to show opponents how unified the team were. Welsh fans, meanwhile, would roar out music like Handel's *Messiah*!

John Gwilliam is considered one of the great Welsh captains.

BOKS TRIUMPH AGAIN

Cliff Morgan had perhaps his worst game in a Welsh shirt as he wasted ample possession with poor kicking at Cardiff against the superb South African team of 1951–52. Wales failed to take advantage of strong forward play and fell 6-3 to the Boks. It was the closest any Five Nations side came to beating the Springboks, who won 30 of their 31 tour matches.

Winning in Cardiff meant a lot to the South Africans. Legendary Springbok Danie Craven later wrote: 'Cardiff Arms Park is all-inspiring. It is as if, to us outsiders, the whole Welsh spirit is embodied in it, and that no one who is a Welshman is excluded from it. Just to pass through the gates which bear the name of one of the nation's famous players [Gwyn Nicholls] starts this feeling which cannot be described in rugby terms. It is akin to trembling and/or fear; and yet one which wakes the responsibility of every player who has to feel the soft surface under his feet . . . we sneaked into the ground at night so that we could be by ourselves and take in that spirit in such a way that we could use it to motivate our team.'

CELTIC LOVE

Andrew Mulligan, who played 22 times for Ireland between 1956 and 1961, said of Wales: 'I used to hate the Welsh. I suppose it was because I had a sneaking regard for them, especially as it was the Welsh . . . who were responsible . . . for occasionally robbing Ireland of the Triple Crown . . . In Wales rugby is a game of the people. It is imbued with a democracy that does not exist elsewhere, it positively pulsates with proletarian passion that spreads upwards and outwards embracing everyone of whatever class or creed in a warm Celtic embrace . . . I hate the Welsh no longer even when they beat the Irish, for there's always the All Blacks to keep them in their place . . . when Ireland beat them they say in the Irish pubs: "Begod we beat the cream of the world." But, alas, it does not happen very often.'

1952 GRAND SLAM

After ending a 39-year wait for a Grand Slam in 1950, Wales grabbed another in 1952. Again led by John Gwilliam, Wales were consistent, if not brilliant, and deserved winners.

MATCH ONE: England 6 Wales 8 (Twickenham)

After so many years struggling at HQ, Wales won two on the bounce here, and including the 1948 draw made it three games without a loss in London. The win was particularly impressive as Wales conceded two tries while winger Lewis Jones was off injured. With no subs in those days, Jones returned to hobble through. In the second half, limping heavily, Jones still managed to send the British Olympian Ken Jones away for his second try.

Once again, the gates had to be closed early due to overcrowding. Many fans were invited into local homes to watch the game on the newfangled technology known as television! The mighty Roy John ruled the line-out and other forwards like props Don Hayward and Billy Williams bossed the home team around the park.

MATCH TWO: Wales 11 Scotland 0 (Cardiff Arms Park)
A Welsh record of 56,000 saw Wales earn payback for the Murrayfield massacre of 1951. Scrum-half Rex Willis played most of the second half with a fractured jaw!

MATCH THREE: Ireland 3 Wales 14 (Lansdowne Road)
During the Triple Crown match, Welsh fans kept a ball that had been kicked into the crowd. The game was held up to retrieve it, but to no avail. On return to Wales the WRU secretary, Eric Evans, launched an appeal for the return of the ball, promising no action would be taken against whomever had stolen it. He soon received an anonymous note saying that his wife should meet the letter writer with a shopping basket in a designated spot in Cardiff. Mrs Evans arrived, the ball was placed in it and the mysterious 'criminal' left. It was then sent back, deflated, to Dublin.

MATCH FOUR: Wales 9 France 5 (St Helen's)
Lewis Jones, like many others on this day, had a poor game. Sadly, it was to be his final game for Wales. The former teenage sensation turned professional not long after and went on to be one of the biggest ever Welsh league stars.

THE THREAT OF LEAGUE

Rugby league was still a thorn in Welsh rugby's side as many players continued to go north to cash in on their skills. When, in the late forties and early fifties, league began setting up teams in Wales, former international Rowe Harding said: 'The Rugby League is only an infant, but it wants strangling!'

FAREWELL TO THE WEST

In 1953, a vote of 136 to 110 among the WRU confirmed all future internationals were to be held in Cardiff and no games marked for Swansea. The decision was logical (Cardiff was bigger, had better facilities and, crucially, brought in more money), but West Walians were very upset. One newspaper letter said it was 'one of the greatest sporting tragedies of our time'. Some even demanded a boycott of future games as they felt it was a betrayal of the turf that the likes of Billy Bancroft and Billy Trew had graced so finely.

Ken Jones scored a dramatic winner over the 1953 All Blacks.

THE FINAL BLACKOUT

1953 – Wales 13 New Zealand 8 (Cardiff Arms Park)

Wales's third victory over the All Blacks was greeted by many newspapers as a formality. This was the first time a Welsh game was televised live in Wales and there was much debate about whether it was the right thing to do as clubs often still played on international weekends and attendance would be affected.

Despite being favourites (Cardiff had beaten the Kiwis a few games before), Wales were fortunate to win as the All Blacks dominated up front. Things looked bad for Wales when Gareth Griffiths left the field with a dislocated shoulder. He bravely returned and helped inspire his team to rally. With five minutes remaining and the score tied at 8-8, Swansea back-rower Clem Thomas found himself on the right wing, with a loose ball at his feet. He skilfully gathered, shrugged off a tackler, half threw a dummy and then made the most famous cross kick in Welsh rugby history. The ball landed near the posts and bounced beautifully for Ken Jones who timed his run to perfection, gathered the ball, stepped Ron Jarden of New Zealand and scored. Captain Bleddyn Williams admitted he wasn't sure how Wales had won.

In 1954 New Zealand invited Wales to their turf, but the IRFB overruled it, as the Lions were going to South Africa the year after!

REVENGE IS A DISH BEST
SERVED COLD . . . 33 TIMES

After defeating the All Blacks, Wales had truly earned their spot as the Kiwis' most difficult opponents. The men in red now led the series three wins to one – the only loss had been in Swansea in 1924. Wales had won every clash in Cardiff. New Zealand were determined to get revenge and, by the end of 2021, the All Blacks were leading the series 33 wins to three. That's pretty good payback.

BUYING BACK IN

In 1954, Wales selected Glyn John as a centre against England. Remarkably, John had played several games of rugby league after signing for £400 for Leigh. However, as he was 17 at the time and still in school, he was allowed to return to union after repaying his signing-on fee!

REX, TARZAN AND THE
WILD WOMEN OF WONGO

Rex Richards of Cross Keys RFC won one cap as a prop for Wales, in the 1956 win over France. Not long after, he headed to Hollywood to try his luck as a movie star. He succeeded too, landing roles in films such as *The Wild Women of Wongo* (considered among the worst films ever made). As a child, he ran away five times with travelling aqua performers! He eventually became a professional diver himself. It is said that when he was named in the team for Cross Keys, groupies would turn up to watch him play, so besotted were they with his good looks. In Hollywood, he almost got the role of Tarzan. From 1,000 applicants, he got down to the final two candidates. Coincidentally, Rex's nickname back in Wales had been Tarzan. He died aged just 55 of a heart attack. Despite having to sleep rough and hunt for food when he first moved to the USA, he left behind cash and belongings worth £750,000.

A CLEAN START

Cardiff Arms Park was a notorious mudbath in this era. In the 1957 win over Ireland, it was so muddy that the entire Welsh team were ordered to change into fresh jerseys during the second half as the referee could no longer tell players apart.

1947–57: THE STAR PLAYERS

JOHN GWILLIAM

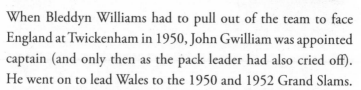

Clubs (include): Edinburgh Wanderers, Gloucester, Newport, London Welsh, Cambridge University
Position: Number eight, second row
Caps: 23 (1947–54)
Points: 0

When Bleddyn Williams had to pull out of the team to face England at Twickenham in 1950, John Gwilliam was appointed captain (and only then as the pack leader had also cried off). He went on to lead Wales to the 1950 and 1952 Grand Slams.

A strategic thinker and student of the game's history, many felt his calm and schoolmaster-like talks and leadership style were not very Welsh. He won over his doubters in the end. On captaincy he said: 'I am the captain and accept the responsibility of failure. The players under me win the matches and the glory is theirs . . . I am just the general as the other fourteen do the work.' Once during one of his two Twickenham wins, he lost his voice and could only whisper. The player next to him in the line-out assumed Gwilliam was only speaking to him for the whole match, blaming him for each mistake. He sometimes 'inspired' players by irritating them. In 1951, he took the great Bleddyn Williams and Jack Matthews aside to show them how to pass!

At 190.5cm (6ft 3in) and 96kg (15st 2lb), the Pontypridd-born forward was big for the time and famed for his line-out ability. He missed out on touring with the Lions due to teaching commitments.

CLIFF MORGAN

Clubs (include): Cardiff, Bective Rangers
Position: Fly-half
Caps: 29 (1951–58)
(British Lions, 4 caps, 3 points)
Points: 9 (3 tries)

One of the greatest men to grace the fly-half shirt (he usually wore six, not ten), he was known as both 'Morgan the Mighty' and, after his exploits with the Lions in South Africa, 'The General'. His ability to burst past or jink through defenders was all the more impressive as he played primarily in a defensive era with little room for poetry and skill.

He directed the Cardiff and Wales teams that defeated the 1953 All Blacks. After he hung up his boots he became just as celebrated for his television work. His commentary on the famous Gareth Edwards try for the Barbarians against New Zealand is as well loved as anything he did with his boots on.

JACK MATTHEWS

Club: Cardiff
Position: Centre, wing
Caps: 17 (1947–51)
(British Lions, 6 caps)
Points: 12 (4 tries)

Dr Jack formed a dream centre partnership with his Cardiff clubmate Bleddyn Williams (the pair were friends for life off the field too). A Welsh schools' sprint champion, he was known as a brutal tackler and was famous for breaking ribs. Tough as nails, during the Second World War he went three rounds with the great heavyweight boxer Rocky Marciano. After smashing the English midfield for a try in 1951 (one of two that day), it is claimed one of the unfortunate defenders remarked he was made of iron. He was then christened the 'Iron Man'.

BLEDDYN WILLIAMS

Club: Cardiff
Position: Centre, fly-half
Caps: 22 (1947–55)
(British Lions, 5 caps, 3 points)
Points: 21 (7 tries)

Following Arthur Gould and Gwyn Nicholls, Bleddyn Williams also became known as the 'Prince of Centres'. Despite playing in the cluttered, defensive 1940s and 1950s, he was a lethal scorer, making the most of his size and sidestep. For Cardiff he once scored an astonishing 41 tries in a single season. Born in Taff's Well, his seven brothers all played for Cardiff too. Bleddyn was just 16 when he made his debut for Cardiff Athletic.

Despite his fame in the game, he was desperately unlucky with injury and only played once in the two Grand Slam teams of that era. He twice captained the British Lions and led Wales to five wins. In 1953, in the space of a few weeks, he captained Cardiff and Wales to wins over the All Blacks. He served with the RAF in the Second World War, flying on dangerous missions behind enemy lines. He once spent almost a week sleeping under a parachute in Germany on a vital mission, before being hurried back to the UK to play for the British Army in a special game!

DON HAYWARD

Club: Newbridge
Position: Second row, prop
Caps: 15 (1949–52)
(British Lions, 3 caps)
Points: 0

Don Hayward's strength and toughness was a key part of Welsh success in the 1950 and 1952 Grand Slams. Originally a second row, he was pushed up to prop to counter the huge South African pack of 1951. While Wales lost, he caused the Boks all sorts of trouble. Along with Billy Williams, he tormented the English at Twickenham in 1952. He turned professional in 1954.

KEN JONES

Clubs: Newport, Leicester
Position: Wing
Caps: 44 (1947–57)
(British Lions 3 caps, 6 points)
Points: 51 (17 tries)

Ken Jones ranks among Wales's greatest athletes. Outside of the muddy rugby fields of Wales, he was a Welsh sprinting champion who reached the semi-final of the 100 metres in the 1948 Olympics and won silver as part of the relay team.

For Wales he won a then record 44 caps, 43 of them being

consecutive (a world record). His 17 tries were also a marvel for the defensive era he played in (as well as the awful pitches). Despite his ability, he was often starved of possession and one writer suggested he wear a sign reminding others to pass to him. He grabbed 17 tries in 17 games with the 1950 Lions in Australia and New Zealand, including one of the greatest of all time in the fourth Test against the All Blacks, when he almost travelled the length of the field.

For all his stunning rugby achievements, the man himself ranked his performance in the 1948 Olympics as his most treasured moment. Cruelly, the silver he won in the relay had originally been gold. But an appeal by the US team, disputing a decision on the handover of a baton, saw them knocked down to silver the following day.

1947–57 NOTABLE EVENTS IN WELSH HISTORY

- 1947: The coal mining industry is nationalised (run by the newly created National Coal Board).
- 1948: The Welsh Folk Museum at St Fagans opens and is the first open-air museum in the United Kingdom.
- 1951: Snowdonia is granted National Park status.
- 1953: The first ever entirely Welsh language television broadcast is made (a service from the Tabernacle Baptist Chapel, Cardiff).
- 1955: Cardiff becomes Wales's official capital.

1958–68: GLORY AND FAILURE

	PLAYED	WON	DRAWN	LOST
FIVE NATIONS	44	20	6	18
TOURISTS/TOURS	6	1	0	5
TOTAL	50	21	6	23

Championships

1965 (Triple Crown), 1966

Shared Championships

1964

'He had six different signals and they all meant kick.'

SCOTTISH FAN ON CLIVE ROWLANDS

A NEW WORLD OPENS UP

The 'Swinging Sixties' were transformative years for the UK and Wales. Compulsory military service had ended and for many teenagers there was a choice and freedom that hadn't existed for previous generations. The end of rationing in the mid-1950s and easing of austerity measures implemented after the Second World War drove up the quality of life. Rock and roll music and fashion transformed youth culture and the increasing affordability of technology such as television was changing the way people spent their leisure time. For younger people, attending chapel or church seemed old-fashioned or of less importance than other activities on offer. Despite this, Wales in many ways was still very conservative. Many regions voted to retain 'dry' Sundays, forbidding the sale of alcohol on the Sabbath.

Wales's economy was transforming too and traditional industries such as steel, coal and slate were in decline. Fifty coal mines closed between 1957 and 1964. Women, however, were slowly seeing the workplace open up as more and more types of jobs became available, presenting opportunities that their mothers had never had. On the downside, it was still legal to pay women less.

For Welsh rugby, the world was opening up too. Wales finally embarked on tours to faraway places like South Africa and Argentina, no longer just waiting for the non-European world to come to them. In terms of results, Wales flipped between brilliant and bumbling. It was hard to know when they would claim a Championship and when they would end up clutching a wooden spoon.

FEATHERLESS WALES HAVE A CROSS TO BEAR

In 1958 against England, Wales wore scarlet shirts without the famous three feathers. A mix-up between the WRU and the kit manufacturers meant Wales had travelled to Twickenham with shirts intended for a trial match.

Wales drew against a good England side thanks to a 50-metre penalty in the opening minutes from full-back Terry Davies. The game finished 3-3, but another late shot at goal by Davies hit the upright and then the crossbar and was blown back infield. Afterwards, Welsh fans sneaked back into Twickenham, took down the crossbar Davies had struck and took it home as a souvenir. Travelling back the next day the supporters stopped in a cafe and, by coincidence, Davies himself walked in! They cheekily got Davies to sign a piece of the crossbar (today it hangs in a pub). The RFU were not amused. Davies, a timber merchant, offered to replace it and the thief behind the operation had to send a letter of apology.

1958 – Wales 6 France 16 (Cardiff Arms Park)

After half a century of trying, France won in Cardiff, to give Cliff Morgan a miserable send-off in his last game for Wales. The French had lost 24 of 28 matches with Wales, but would now emerge as one of the strongest rugby nations. This was the first of four consecutive wins over Wales and in 1959 they would win their first Championship.

THE BROWN, BROWN MUD OF HOME

Wales often had a world-class team, but the home field at Cardiff (with the proximity of the River Taff an eternal problem) was a global embarrassment. Often it made matches a lottery. It got even worse after the 1958 Commonwealth Games. The groundworkers failed to break up the subsoil which had been laid especially for the racetracks. This prevented proper drainage of rain and river water. It got so bad that other national unions were openly critical of conditions. But the WRU didn't own the ground – it was Cardiff RFC's and the union only had the right to it for six games a year. Meanwhile, rugby sides trained and played on it multiple times a week and there was even greyhound racing held there.

WIND OF FATE

1960 – Wales 0 South Africa 3 (Cardiff Arms Park)

It was so dark, wet and windy in Cardiff that both sides wore tracksuits during the anthems. It is believed that this was the first time it had ever happened. Welsh captain Terry Davies (full-back) chose to play against the fierce wind and rain when he won the toss, figuring his side could make hay when the Boks tired in the second half. When Wales turned around just three points down after bravely defending and limiting their opponents to a penalty goal, it seemed that after 54 years and five matches the dragon would finally slay the springbok. Alas, the South Africans' superior fitness saw them through. The weather got so bad that the referee offered to end the game early, but the captains wished to play on. *The Times* suggested that when Davies had a shot at goal in the second half, he must have 'felt like an old-time convict trying to kick an iron ball off his chain'. Players had to use towels to clean the mud from their eyes and spectators could barely see through the heavy rain. Despite winning praise for effort from the press, Wales again fell short.

The next day, the River Taff burst its banks and the pitch was submerged under two feet of water. The 1960–61 Springbok team lost only one of their 34 games in Europe (a 6-0 loss to the Barbarians).

COACH CALL

After another loss to the Boks, and with the French reimagining the way rugby could be played (their use of forwards as skilful, fast, powerful attackers saw them win three Championships and share one between 1959 and 1962), there began to be calls in Wales for the introduction of a coach for the national side. Traditionalists sniffed at the idea, but support for such thinking was growing.

TEAM SELECTION . . . A MATTER OF LIFE AND DEATH

The Welsh selectors, or the 'Big Five', took so long to finish their selection meeting for the game against England in 1961 that several people waiting for the team news got impatient enough to go and see what was happening. Wilfred Wooller and J.B.G. Thomas entered the meeting room to be greeted by the smell of gas and the selectors 'lolling about the table, half-conscious'. A gas leak had almost killed them! They recovered enough to select a team that beat England. When their next selection failed against Scotland, several fans suggested gassing them again.

FAMINE

In the 1962 Championship Wales scored just nine points and not a single try. However, they beat champions France (their only loss) and drew with England and Ireland. The Irish game was played in November and nicknamed the 'hangover' match as a result. It had been postponed due to an outbreak of smallpox in the Rhondda.

1963 – Wales 6 England 13 (Cardiff Arms Park)

Wales fell to their old rivals, despite the special underwear they had been given to combat the chill. This was England's last win in Cardiff until 1991. While Wales lost, some remarkable players began their Test careers. Fly-half David Watkins made his debut. He played 21 times before turning pro and is considered one of the greats in both league and union. Scrum-half Clive Rowlands also won his first cap. He would go on to be a key player, coach and WRU member. In the pack, the ferocious Brian Thomas and Denzil Williams also made their debuts.

1963 – Scotland 0 Wales 6 (Murrayfield)

Wales's Clive Rowlands took full advantage of the kicking rules of the day. There was no problem with kicking out on the full outside your 22 back then. Wanting to win, not entertain, he kicked to touch almost every time he got the ball. It is claimed there were 111 line-outs as Wales ended a ten-year drought. Fly-half Watkins got his hands on the ball on just five occasions.

Clive the Kick.

THE WELCOMING SPIRIT OF THE
INTERNATIONAL RUGBY FOOTBALL BOARD

In February 1963, the WRU decided to invite Fiji to tour Wales. The IRFB did not back this attempt to spread the game, make new friends and enrich the sport. They refused to sanction an official tour and Wales had to meet all costs. The WRU hoped that rugby fans would 'appreciate the efforts . . . to introduce a breath of fresh air into the Welsh rugby scene'. The tour was only saved when the French, who did far more to build new international relationships than the insular IRFB, also invited Fiji to connect with them on the trip.

FORTRESS ARMS PARK FINALLY
FALLS TO THE DARKNESS

1963 – Wales 0 New Zealand 6 (Cardiff Arms Park)

It is claimed that a million New Zealanders listened to this match live in the middle of the night back home, so keen were they to see if their heroes could finally defeat the Dragons on Cardiff soil. They were not disappointed as legendary full-back Don Clarke kicked them into an early lead they never relinquished. Unlike the famous 1905 clash when Wales were kings of Europe, the home side came clutching the Wooden Spoon after a dismal Five Nations which saw Ireland win in Wales for the first time since 1949.

There was an ugly end to the game when Colin Meads kneed Clive Rowlands in the back after the Welsh captain had called for a mark. Rowlands was temporarily paralysed and had to be carried off. Meads would later end the career of Australian scrum-half Ken Catchpole, but luckily Rowlands recovered. Afterwards, Meads said: '. . . I got the little b******. Ran right over the bloody top of him. He put on a good act, 80,000 people booed me and all I did was knee him up the a*** . . . the memories are good.' Video footage shows otherwise.

The only game the All Blacks lost during their 36-match tour was 3-0 to Newport.

New laws were brought into rugby in 1964 to open up a game that was increasingly becoming cluttered and dull. It was now required that any player not involved with the line-out had to retreat ten metres from the throw-in and offside at the scrum was marked by the hindmost foot. It transformed the sport and served Wales well.

THE SPRINGBOKS GET A TASTY WELSH BIRTHDAY CAKE

Before 1964, away games for Wales had been no more exotic than France. But in 1964 the WRU accepted an invitation from South Africa to undertake a tour to celebrate 75 years of organised rugby in the country. Wales beat East Africa, Boland and Orange Free State, but were soundly beaten by Northern Transvaal and humiliated by South Africa. The tour was called a 'trek to disaster'.

1964 – South Africa 24 Wales 3 (Kings Park, Durban)

Wales's most faraway Test to date wasn't going too badly at the halfway point, with the score 3-3. But in the last 40, Wales collapsed. At one point they conceded 13 points in seven minutes. *The Times* described the Welsh backs trying to stop rampaging forwards as 'pygmies trying to stop giants'. It was Wales's worst result for 40 years and increased calls to appoint a coach for the national side. Meanwhile, Clive Rowlands was teased by home fans for his extremely white legs.

JUST A GAME!

WRU president Nathan Rocyn-Jones was against the idea of bringing a national coach on board, saying the game should be about enjoyment, and too much 'emphasis could be placed on technical and tactical skill'. He wasn't the one trying to tackle giant Springboks though.

FIJIANS MAKE MOCKERY OF MISERABLE IRFB

Despite the IRFB not approving, the Fijian tour of Wales was a major success and over 100,000 fans attended the five matches they played. The WRU even made a profit.

Fiji were a breath of fresh air, but sadly resented by the likes of the IRFB.

1964 – Wales XV 28 Fiji 22 (uncapped match) (Cardiff Arms Park)

Fifty thousand fans packed the famous old stadium to see rugby like they had never seen before. Down to 14 men after losing a second row in the opening ten minutes, Fiji were losing 28-9 with just 12 minutes remaining. Then, chaos of the like only Fiji can produce. Fans in 1964 didn't know what had hit them. The tourists snagged 13 points and gave their hosts a real scare. During the match, prop Sevaro Walisoliso grabbed three tries! To their eternal shame, the IRFB would not permit caps to be awarded for the game. Wales bagged seven tries in all, including strikes from legends such as winger Dewi Bebb and the mighty number eight Alun Pask. One newspaper wrote that the game was so enjoyable that using a scoreboard to make sense of it was as 'inadequate as trying to express Wagner on a penny whistle'.

The IRFB may not have liked them, but Welsh fans adored them and after the match, fans and players had a sing-song on the field.

TWO YEARS OF GLORY

Thankfully, Wales bounced back from their African disaster by winning the Five Nations in 1965 and 1966 (after sharing it in 1964). Here are some highlights:

Rowlands lacks bite – In the 1965 win over England in Cardiff (14-3), the referee stopped the game to investigate an alleged bite on an English player. The referee asked Welsh captain Clive Rowlands about it. The scrum-half smiled and, after revealing his missing teeth, said, 'I don't know, ref, but it wasn't me – my dentures are in the dressing room.'

1965 – Wales 14 Ireland 8 (Cardiff Arms Park)

Wales claimed their tenth Triple Crown, despite losing centre John Dawes early on. To compensate for being down to 14 men until Dawes was able to return later, Wales moved full-back Terry Price to centre and number eight Alun Pask to full-back! Ireland, also going for the Triple Crown, conceded critical tries to the magnificent David Watkins and Dewi Bebb and had to watch Price nail a humongous drop goal. Despite the subsequent 22-13 loss in Paris, Wales claimed the Championship.

1966 – Wales 9 France 8 (Cardiff Arms Park)

France had smashed Wales's Grand Slam dreams in the final game of 1965, but this year Wales took the spoils, denying France a chance of the title. Wales had named a squad, rather than a team, for this match. They only revealed their hand a few hours before. France were 8-0 up after 12 minutes and few felt Wales would be able to pull back. But a spectacular interception try from winger Stuart Watkins from his own 22-metre line set up a famous win. Wales's shock 9-6 loss in Dublin the match before had cost them the Grand Slam.

WEEPING WALLABIES

When the 1966 Wallabies came to Europe on tour, the game they really wanted to win was Wales at Cardiff. All the other

THE EVOLUTION OF THE WELSH JERSEY

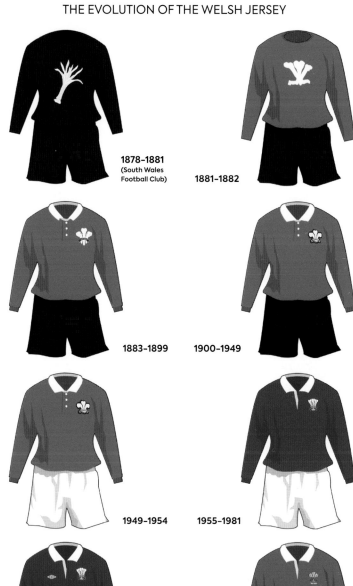

1878–1881
(South Wales
Football Club)

1881–1882

1883–1899

1900–1949

1949–1954

1955–1981

1975
(v Australia)

1980–1981
(Centenary kit)

1982–1991

1987
(Change kit)

1991
World Cup

1992–1993

1993
(Change kit)

1994–1995

1995
World Cup

1995
World Cup
(Change kit)

1995–1996

1996–1998

1997
(Change kit)

1999
(Change kit)

1998–2000

1999
World Cup

2000–2002

2000–2001
(Change kit)

2002–2004

2002
(Change kit)

2003
World Cup

2003
World Cup
(Change kit)

2004–2006

2004–2005
(Change kit)

2005
(v France)

2005
(125th anniversary)

2006–2008

2006
(Change kit)

2007
(v France)

2007
World Cup

2007
World Cup
(Change kit)

2008–2010

2008–2009
(Change kit)

2010–2011

2010
(v Fiji)

2011–2013

2011–2013
(Change kit)

2011
(World Cup)

2011
World Cup
(Change kit)

2013–2015

2013
(v Tonga)

2015–2017

2015–2017
(Change kit)

2015
(World Cup)

2015
World Cup
(Change kit)

2017–2019

2017–2018
(Change kit)

2019–2020

2019–2020
(Change kit
- not worn)

2019
(World Cup)

2019
World Cup
(Change kit
– not worn)

2020–

2020–
(Change kit)

Five Nations teams had lost multiple times to them in the previous 58 years, but the Dragons had never fallen. With Wales coming off the back of a Triple Crown and Australia having lost seven times on tour (including games to Newport, Cardiff and a combined Pontypool, Cross Keys & Newbridge), few expected the tourists to fare well at the Arms Park.

Yet, in a thriller of a game (in which the greats Barry John and Gerald Davies made their debuts), Australia pulled off a historic win. After the game some Aussies openly wept with joy.

THE JARRETT MATCH
1967 – Wales 34 England 21 (Cardiff Arms Park)
Wales had to beat England in the final game of the season to avoid a first ever Five Nations whitewash.

England were up for the Triple Crown and possible title. The Big Five prepared for this crucial game by picking uncapped 18-year-old Keith Jarrett at full-back. Brave? Reckless may be a better description. Jarrett had NEVER played there. He was a centre. The weekend before, Newport wanted to help the teenager out so they picked him there against Newbridge. He was so poor he was switched back to centre at half-time!

The following week Jarrett scored an epic try, kicked five conversions and two penalty goals to score 19 points as Wales ran up their highest ever total against England. His personal points tally equalled a record Jack Bancroft had set in 1910. The try? It was only the second ever by a Welsh full-back (the last coming in 1934 by Vivian Jenkins) and he ran in alone from 80 metres out. His kicks? Three came off the posts and still went over.

Legend has it that that night the young Jarrett missed his last bus home. A bus driver, seeing it was Jarrett, sneaked back to the depot to get a bus to drive him home. As they were leaving they were caught by a supervisor. The driver was told that he should return the bus to the depot and get a double-decker so Jarrett could sit upstairs if he wanted a cigarette.

WRU SHOCK THE RUGBY WORLD WITH PROGRESSIVE THINKING

In 1967 the WRU appointed Ray Williams as the national coaching organiser. It was the first such position in world rugby. On his appointment at the WRU annual general meeting he declared: 'I am not naïve enough to think that everyone in this gathering is 100 per cent in favour of coaching. There are those among you who are not certain what it involves . . .' In 1968, amazingly, he had to make a formal request through the committee to be able to attend away Welsh games. The same year Wales appointed ex-international David Nash as coach. Traditionalists tutted, but rare forward thinking by the WRU played a huge role in the golden era that was shortly to arrive.

1967 – Wales 6 New Zealand 13 (Cardiff Arms Park)

New Zealand levelled the series between the two sides at three games each. Norman Gale became the only Welsh hooker to ever kick a penalty goal.

A FAREWELL LETTER

When the divinely talented David Watkins broke the hearts of romantic Welsh fans by turning professional, something rather unusual happened: the WRU wrote a letter thanking him for his service!

DUBLIN DRAMA

Irish fans were so incensed that a wide drop goal by scrum-half Gareth Edwards was given in 1968 in Dublin, they stormed the field and even threw food and bottles towards the referee. They had not done the same though when a Mike Gibson drop goal had been allowed that should have been refused due to a technicality. Ireland won deep in injury time, probably to the referee's relief as he needed police protection after the game.

CRY FOR WALES, ARGENTINA

Wales headed on another tour to a distant land in 1968, this time to Argentina. The two matches with the Pumas were uncapped as Wales did not pick any of the 11 players who travelled with the Lions to South Africa that year. The WRU originally did not appoint a coach for the tour. It took the resignation of a selector to change their minds and Clive Rowlands was given the role. Wales lost the first 'Test' 9-5 and drew the second 9-9. Full-back J.P.R. Williams (simply known as 'J.P.R.') was nicknamed 'Canasta' (basket) by the locals, who threw beer bottles at him.

1958–68: THE STAR PLAYERS

BRYN MEREDITH

Clubs (include): Newport, St Luke's College, London Welsh
Position: Hooker
Caps: 34 (1954–62)
(British Lions, 8 caps, 3 points)
Points: 9 (3 tries)

Abersychan-born Bryn Meredith is among the finest Welsh hookers. A three-time Lions tourist, Meredith won 34 caps for Wales, then a national record for the position. He captained Newport, Wales and the Lions. In a period when hookers of both sides had a genuine chance to compete for the ball at scrum time, he won countless critical strikes against the head. A quick thinker, nifty handler, smart supporter and solid defender, his retirement was much mourned and many begged him to come back.

CLIVE ROWLANDS

Club: Pontypool
Position: Scrum-half
Caps: 14 (1963–65)
Points: 3 (1 drop goal)

Top Cat, Dai Ding-Dong or Clive the Kick, was born in Cwmtwrch in the upper Swansea Valley. As an eight-year-old, while staying in hospital, he kicked a rugby ball through a window and was placed in a straitjacket for days! He captained Wales on his debut in the 1963 loss to England. Amazingly, he led Wales for each of his 14 caps, winning a Triple Crown and always partnered with David Watkins. He approached his role as captain like the 'mother of a typical Welsh family' and was famous for his inspiring team speeches. A passionate Welsh language speaker, he went on to become the youngest Welsh coach, a selector, WRU president and Lions team manager.

DAI MORRIS

Club: Neath
Position: Flanker, number eight
Caps: 34 (1967–74)
Points: 19 (6 tries)

Dai Morris was nicknamed 'The Shadow' for his ability to always be close in support of key players like Barry John. He could do this thanks to his incredible fitness. A miner at Tower

Colliery, Hirwaun, he kept fit running up coal heaps. In the same year as Morris played in the victorious Welsh team at Twickenham in 1972, he was on the picket lines as part of that year's major miners' strike. He was known to work morning shifts down the pit before playing in the afternoon. A tough man on the field, he was a true gentleman off it. He became a folk hero in Wales and inspired several poems and songs by Welsh comedian Max Boyce.

DEWI BEBB

Clubs: Carmarthen T.C, Swansea
Position: Wing
Caps: 34 (1959–67)
(British Lions, 8 caps, 3 points)
Points: 33 (11 tries)

'Should do well' were the words written about Dewi Bebb in the match programme for his debut game against England in 1959. He was just 20 and had only played five first-class games. He scored the winning try. Bebb made a habit of scoring against England and fans named the patch he often scored on at the Arms Park 'Bebb's Corner'. He played in an era when he could get just one pass a game. Lightning fast, in another time he would have scored bucketloads more.

DAVID WATKINS

Club: Newport
Position: Fly-half
Caps: 21 (1963–67)
(British Lions, 6 caps, 12 points)
Points: 15 (2 tries, 3 drop goals)

David Watkins is always in the mix in arguments about the greatest Welsh fly-half. In a stifling defensive era, his outside break and sidestep worked wonders and his kicking and defence was world class. The Blaina boy with the 'pop star looks' was so fiercely competitive, he didn't care much for playing for the Barbarians as they didn't want to win enough. When his Welsh Youth team lost 36-0 in an international he was ashamed. After realising there wasn't much press coverage of the game, he told people it was a 6-3 defeat only! He was critical to Newport's win over the All Blacks and even captained the British Lions.

Watkins was furious to be dropped for the 1966 Wallabies game. Making it worse, three of the Big Five claimed to have voted for him in the selection meeting. After 21 caps he went north for a then record fee of £13,000. Watkins was a huge success and is still fondly remembered in Salford as one of the greatest league players. Sadly, back in Wales, many petty-minded people shunned him for going north. But his place among the greats in both codes of rugby is assured.

1958–68 NOTABLE EVENTS IN WELSH HISTORY

• 1958: The Welsh football team make their only ever World Cup appearance and get knocked out by Brazil in the quarters. A teenager called Pelé scores his first goal for his country in the 1-0 win.

• 1959: The Flag of Wales (Y Ddraig Goch) is officially recognised as the Welsh national flag.

• 1960: Forty-five miners die in an accident in Six Bells Colliery in Abertillery.

• 1961: The village of Capel Celyn is destroyed intentionally to build a reservoir to serve the city of Liverpool.

• 1963: Welsh actor (and rugby nut) Richard Burton stars in Hollywood epic Cleopatra with his (twice!) wife, Elizabeth Taylor.

• 1965: The Welsh Office, a department of the UK Government, is established.

• 1966: 116 children and 28 adults are killed in the Aberfan disaster when a colliery waste tip collapses onto a school.

• 1967: The Welsh Language Act is passed, allowing the use of the language in official documents and legal proceedings.

1969–79: THE SECOND GOLDEN ERA

	PLAYED	WON	DRAWN	LOST
FIVE NATIONS	43	33	3	7
TOURISTS/TOURS	10	3	1	6
TOTAL	53	36	4	13

Championships

1969 (Triple Crown), 1971 (Grand Slam), 1975, 1976 (Grand Slam),

1978 (Grand Slam), 1979 (Triple Crown)

Shared Championships

1970, 1973

Other honours

1977 Triple Crown (France won Championship)

'The most important thing I have is the determination to get to the top, but even more important I have the determination to stay at the top.'

J.P.R. WILLIAMS

THE WINTERS OF MUCH CONTENT

For many, the 1970s – with its sideburns and sidestepping threequarters – IS Welsh rugby. That Wales would produce one of the most gifted generations of players ever to play the sport at the same time colour television became the norm was a lucky coincidence of history that has served the sideburned generation well. Not only did Wales thrive on the field, but off it too. The WRU led a global revolution in rugby with coaching innovations, national coaches and squad sessions. This filtered down through all levels of the game in Wales and produced a vibrant club scene at first-class and grassroots level.

Away from rugby, British and Welsh life underwent major changes in the 1970s, especially in the latter half of the decade. The early seventies saw a huge increase in car ownership, as vehicles and petrol became cheaper. In 1971, 91% of families had a TV and soon 64% of people had a washing machine. But there were black clouds approaching. An oil crisis in 1973 saw the cost of oil erupt and it sent shockwaves through the global economy as firms began to make thousands redundant. Many who kept their jobs found their income didn't keep pace with a huge rise in living costs. As energy costs were so expensive and industrial action from miners impacted fuel levels, the government of Edward Heath implemented the 'three-day week'. Non-essential businesses were only allowed three consecutive days of electricity. Even television was stopped after 10.30 p.m. to save energy.

There were constant battles between trade unions and the government over strikes from all sorts of industries and professionals such as miners, gravediggers, nurses and bin collectors. In the Winter of Discontent (1978–79), rubbish bins went uncollected, the dead weren't buried and some hospitals could only admit emergency patients. By the end of the 1970s, there would only be 54 coal mines in Wales (there were still 137 in 1959). Welsh nationalism was on the rise and Wales even had an (unsuccessful) referendum on having a Welsh devolved parliament. Some rugby fans began booing 'God Save the Queen' at internationals. Wales still sang this before games, with the Welsh anthem rarely played at away games at all.

The decade would end with the election of the UK's first female prime minister, Margaret Thatcher. It was an election result that would define the decade to come in Wales in more ways than one.

J.P.R. Williams – An icon of the 1970s in Wales.

TRAINING FOR A TRIPLE

Wales produced some thrilling rugby to win the 1969 Championship and Triple Crown, heralding the Second Golden Era. Bizarrely, France lost every game apart from a draw in Paris with Wales, denying the Dragons a slam. Wales's exciting attacking style was helped by new laws which prevented teams kicking to touch directly from outside their own 22 – opening up possibilities for full-backs who were no longer satisfied with their traditional defensive role.

Wales began full squad training sessions in 1969, led by Clive Rowlands. This was so controversial at the time that the IRFB debated whether it was against the amateur nature of the sport. The WRU asked clubs to restrict national squad members to one game a week during the season as clubs often played weekday games as well as Saturday matches.

This season some of the all-time greats for Wales made their debuts or cemented their places in the team. In the 17-3 win over Scotland, two players from London Welsh – J.P.R. Williams at full-back and Mervyn Davies at number eight – won their first caps. Players like Cardiff's Gerald Davies (winger/centre), Barry John (fly-half) and Gareth Edwards (scrum-half), were causing havoc with the support of centre John Dawes, flankers Dai 'The Shadow' Morris and John Taylor, as well as several other greats we'll soon be talking about.

MAURICE'S GRAND SLAM

1969 – Wales 30 England 9 (Cardiff Arms Park)

Cardiff winger Maurice Richards scored four tries in this demolition of England, equalling Willie Llewellyn's feat from 1899. The other Welsh try that day came from Barry John, who glided over like a 'ghost' and left multiple defenders clutching at thin air as he crafted one of his most famous scores. It was John's only Welsh try in Cardiff. He later said: 'I promise you, as much as the try itself I recall the happy faces, full of jubilation, and the wobbly yellow construction hats of the site-workers, "on duty" in that corner of Cardiff Arms Park. And it was a lovely feeling.'

Gareth Edwards is considered by many the greatest player of all time.

CAMEO CAP

In the 1969 8-8 draw with France in Paris, Phil Bennett became the first Welsh player to win a cap as a replacement. He came on for an injured Gerald Davies four minutes from time and never laid a hand on the ball. Replacements were a new concept and could only be used when a player was injured. Some traditionalists did not like the fact that caps were given for such 'cameos'.

THE SUICIDE TOUR OF '69

Sixty-four years and six games after first hosting the All Blacks, the Silver Ferns got to repay the favour when Wales went on their first tour to New Zealand, Australia and Fiji. The tour of Oceania involved three Tests, three domestic games in New Zealand and an uncapped match with Fiji. Fiji were still not deemed worthy of full Test status as a Welsh XV beat them by 33-11 in front of fans sitting in palm trees. The schedule was deemed suicidal and results proved the naysayers right. The key results were:

New Zealand 19 Wales 0 (Lancaster Park, Christchurch)
Once again, the All Blacks humbled Wales by 19 points to 0 as they had in 1924. Wales's hooker Jeff Young tugged on the jersey of Colin Meads and was rewarded with a broken jaw! Wales were totally overmatched in this series by one of the greatest Test packs of all time. New Zealand didn't need the assistance, but a home referee for this series didn't help matters.

New Zealand 33 Wales 12 (Eden Park, Auckland)
In the second Test referee Pat Murphy jumped in the air when All Black Fergie McCormick dropped a goal. McCormick bagged a then Test record of 24 points and afterwards the local media blasted the Welsh efforts.

Australia 16 Wales 19 (Sydney Cricket Ground)
The great Gerald Davies was fully converted to a wing on this tour, moving out from the centre, and was the key man in this game for Wales, scoring one and creating another for John Taylor. To date, this is the only Welsh victory over the Wallabies on their home soil.

A DIVISIVE START TO THE DECADE

When the Springboks came to play Wales in Cardiff as part of their 1969–70 tour of Britain and Ireland, it caused huge splits in Welsh rugby and wider society. In South Africa at the time there was a system of institutionalised racial segregation known as apartheid. This system saw black people oppressed while white people ran and controlled politics, culture, economics and all aspects of life. Non-white people could not play for the South African rugby side, for example, and visiting teams were usually encouraged (or ordered) to leave non-white players at home.

Throughout the tour the Springboks were greeted by protests and direct action. Before the Boks played Swansea, the clashes between protesters, police and fans were so violent the match was stopped at one point and became known as the 'Battle of Swansea'. A key organiser of the opposition to the tour was Peter

Hain, who would later become Welsh Secretary in government. He had a letter bomb sent to his house and, bizarrely, someone tried to frame him for a bank robbery by using a lookalike!

Some Welsh players took a personal stand too. John Taylor, who had seen apartheid first-hand with the Lions in 1968, honourably refused to be considered for selection for the Welsh game and even attended protests. Sadly, many in the game didn't want to think about the politics and just wanted to see the famous South Africans play.

1970 – Wales 6 South Africa 6 (Cardiff Arms Park)

Wales may have had their best result yet against the Boks, but this was another chance missed. South Africa had drawn with Ireland and lost to Scotland and England. In Wales, they lost to Newport and Gwent. Once again, the sides met in an embarrassing mudbath in Cardiff. Beaten up up front, it took a desperate late score from Gareth Edwards to salvage a draw for the home side, but the scrum-half was unable to add the conversion to steal it. To ward off protesters, the stadium had a huge police presence and the pitch was surrounded by barbed wire.

TEACHING THE WORLD TO PLAY

The make-up of the Welsh team continued to change with more teachers and educated professionals being represented and, as the economy changed, fewer manual workers such as miners and steelworkers. Part of the reason for the incredible success of London Welsh in the 1970s (who had a record seven players picked for one Lions tour) was the fact that many players studied in south-east England for their teaching qualifications. This allowed the exile club to pick from a deliciously creamy pot of talent.

1970 – SHARING THE GLORY WITH FRANCE

Wales had to share the Championship in 1970 with France after blowing their match in Dublin. The 1970s would see France and Wales as the top European teams.

THE CHICO COMEBACK

1970 – England 13 Wales 17 (Twickenham)

Wales were losing 13-6 with 20 minutes left when captain Gareth Edwards departed injured. To everyone watching, the injury sealed Wales's fate. In his place came Ray 'Chico' Hopkins for his first cap. Hopkins soon created a try for J.P.R. Williams (the third for a full-back for Wales), scored one himself and turned the game around. Despite his 20 minutes of glory, Hopkins never played for Wales again. He won one cap (as a replacement for Edwards again) for the 1971 Lions.

Wales scored four tries in total, the most they had scored at HQ. In the first half, the referee also had to be replaced after a collision left him with a broken bone in his leg and a dislocated shoulder.

EXTENDED TOILET BREAK

When Edwards left the field against England, a Welsh selector ran down from the stands to get Hopkins ready. On the way back to his seat, the official visited the toilet. He locked himself in and missed the famous comeback. He had to wait until the team returned to the dressing rooms to get out.

1970 – Ireland 14 Wales 0 (Lansdowne Road)

Wales were expected to claim another Triple Crown in Dublin but instead were taken to the cleaners in one of the biggest shocks in tournament history. It cost Edwards his role as captain and Wales the Grand Slam. Some even wanted Edwards dropped.

TRYING TIMES

From the 1971–72 season, tries were upgraded to four points, something that suited a Welsh team packed with finishers like J.P.R. Williams, Gerald Davies, John Dawes, Barry John, Gareth Edwards, John Bevan and Mervyn Davies.

THE SIXTH SLAM

Wales swept all before them in 1971 with a first Grand Slam since 1952. As a result, 13 Welsh players were selected (with another later sent out) for the 1971 Lions tour that beat New Zealand. Wales started the season easily dismissing England in Cardiff by 22-6 (J.P.R. played with a broken cheekbone for most of the game) and in their third match knocked Ireland off 23-9. The Scottish and French matches were the highlights. The Dragons' 9-5 win in Paris was their first success there for 14 years. Wales used just 16 players all Championship. It probably should have been 15, but centre Arthur Lewis pulled out of the Scottish game after he injured himself running to work!

1971 – Scotland 18 Wales 19 (Murrayfield, Edinburgh)

The lead changed hands six times in this all-time classic. Despite tries by flanker John Taylor, Gareth Edwards and Barry John, Wales trailed 18-14 with seconds remaining (Scotland had missed a sitter of a conversion to seal the game). After a clever line-out win from Llanelli's Delme Thomas (who had won three consecutive line-outs, including two Scottish ones) in the Scottish 22, J.P.R. Williams took the ball at speed in the line and fed Gerald Davies who used all his pace and swerve to score in the far right-hand corner. Left-footed Taylor then scored what was dubbed 'the greatest conversion since that of St Paul' to win it.

AN INCOMPLETE YEAR

Wales won all three of their Championship games in 1972,

including a 12-3 win at Twickenham. Due to rising political tension and terrorist action concerning Northern Ireland (it was a period of significant violence as Unionists and Irish Republicans waged bloody campaigns to fight for or against British rule), Scotland and Wales did not travel to Dublin. Although the Irish Republican Army claimed Wales were in no danger, death threats were sent to the WRU and leading clubs. It mattered little in the grand scale of things, but Wales were unable to complete a likely Grand Slam.

Gareth Edwards scored a try so heavenly, people joked a church should be built on the sacred spot where he touched down.

THE MIRACLE TRY

In 1972 Gareth Edwards scored one of the greatest solo tries of all time. Taking the ball from a maul-turned-ruck on his own ten-metre line, he burst down the blind side, knocked off defender Rodger Arneil and was suddenly in space. He charged to the Scottish ten-metre line, chipped over full-back Arthur Brown then, closely pursued by several defenders, used his left foot to kick ahead again inside the 22. As the ball ended up in the thick, browny-orange mud that encircled the pitch, he lunged for it just before the Scots arrived. Caked completely in dirt and with lungs burning, his walk back for the restart is one of rugby's most iconic images. It was so magnificent a feat, comedian Spike Mulligan proclaimed a church should have been built where Edwards scored!

THE SECOND GOLDEN ERA AND THE ALL BLACKS

Even during the Second Golden Era, Wales were unable to defeat New Zealand in multiple attempts. In addition to the two 1969 humiliations at what is considered the start of the Golden Era, Wales would lose at home in 1972 and 1978. Furthermore, an often forgotten uncapped match between full-strength teams took place in 1974. In terms of comparing the three Golden Eras, only the first one saw a Welsh side defeat the All Blacks.

1972 – Wales 16 New Zealand 19 (Cardiff Arms Park)

Joe Karam of New Zealand booted five penalties to dash Welsh hopes. There was also a try from infamous Kiwi prop

Keith Murdoch. After the game, Murdoch got in a fight in the nearby Angel Hotel. He was sent home in disgrace, but never arrived in New Zealand. He disappeared into the Australian wilderness. In almost 50 years before his death, he was only tracked down four times by journalists! The new friends he had made never even knew of his past.

A GAME IN DECLINE

In 1972, rugby writer J.B.G. Thomas wrote of the decline of interest in the game of rugby. He claimed this was down to the 'rival attractions of modern living; a more affluent society; the emancipation of women (amusing but true) and the challenge of other individual sports . . .'

IT'S GOOD TO SHARE

Following on from the no-result of 1972, there was another kind of no-result in 1973 – all five sides shared the Championship. With each team winning their home games and points difference not counting back then, it was officially a quintuple tie!

NEW LANDS AND NEW FOES

Wales travelled to Canada for the first time in 1973 where a Welsh XV, baking in their heavy cotton jerseys, started slowly before overcoming Canada 58-20. Back in Cardiff in October, a Welsh XV took Japan apart 62-14. Still not deemed worthy of Test status by rugby authorities, both teams would eventually come back to defeat the Dragons one day. Interestingly, the Japanese coach had been training as a kamikaze pilot before the Second World War ended.

A RARE WIN OVER TOURISTS

Wales beat the 1973 Wallabies 24-0. Tries came from Dai 'The Shadow' Morris, Gerald Davies and hooker Bobby Windsor of Pontypool on his debut. Phil Bennett, who had taken over from the now retired Barry John, kicked four penalties. Wales would beat Australia by an even bigger margin in 1975, with J.J. Williams scoring three tries in a 28-3 win.

TIMES ARE A CHANGIN'

In 1974, the regular fixtures started to rotate in the Five Nations, so it was no longer the traditional sequence of Wales playing England, Scotland and then Ireland. The idea was a Welsh one, and also included 'doubling up' games, so two games were played on the same weekend. One of the reasons there had been long opposition to the change of fixtures was that the RFU and SRU didn't want to move their traditional golf outing around the Calcutta Cup.

1974 – England 16 Wales 12 (Twickenham)

England's 1974 win was the Red Rose's only victory in the fixture between 1964 and 1979. The result was largely overshadowed by anger at the RFU's failure to play the Welsh national anthem. The Welsh players had expected to sing it and were baffled when the referee signalled the game was to begin. A fierce row broke out afterwards and the RFU secretary said: 'My committee is firmly of the opinion that when countries of the four Home Unions play at Twickenham we play "The Queen" only. We are all part of the United Kingdom and the national anthem . . . is "The Queen".'

GOING GREEN

Wales played a Tongan XV in Cardiff, in October 1974, winning 26-7. Tonga were a serious force. In 1973 they had won away in Australia. This match was notable as Wales wore green jerseys for the first time to avoid a colour clash. The next time they would do so, and the first time for a capped match, was against the same opponents in the 1987 World Cup. The Tongans were so cold in Cardiff that after the game they jumped in the stadium's famous old baths while still wearing their kit.

AN UNCAPPED MATCH AGAINST THE ALL BLACKS!
1974 – Wales XV 3 New Zealand 12 (Cardiff Arms Park)

It wasn't just matches with the likes of Tonga and Japan that were denied Test status. Wales and New Zealand picked their strongest teams and yet no caps were awarded for this Wednesday afternoon match. Why? Well, the All Blacks had been in Ireland to celebrate the IRFU's centenary. It was felt that if this match was capped, it would steal their thunder! Once again, Wales fell well short of the Kiwis.

The Pontypool front row were nicknamed the Viet-Gwent.

CHAMPIONS AGAIN

1975 – France 10 Wales 25 (Parc des Princes, Paris)

Wales, now coached by John Dawes and led by Mervyn Davies, won the 1975 Championship in style, despite losing narrowly in Edinburgh. The match in Paris was special as the famous Pontypool front row played together as a unit for the first time. Graham Price, Bobby Windsor and Charlie Faulkner were so feared and respected they had songs written about them. The legendary Price, making his debut, scored a magnificent try at the death, superbly gathering a ball after being part of an 80-metre kick and chase. It showed incredible fitness for a prop of any era, let alone the 1970s.

DISASTER AVERTED

A world record 104,000 fans packed into Murrayfield to see Scotland beat Wales 12-10 in 1975. The safe capacity of the ground was 70,000 and, with thousands more locked outside, things really could have gone terribly wrong. As a result, future matches were made all-ticket affairs.

1975 – Wales 32 Ireland 4 (Cardiff Arms Park)

Wales put in one of their finest performances of the era as they devastated Ireland and gave Irish legends like Willie John McBride a terrible end to their Test careers. Phil Bennett restored his reputation after the Murrayfield loss and Charlie Faulkner scored a famous try with the help of fellow front-rower Bobby Windsor. Other scores came from greats such as Gareth Edwards, J.J. Williams and Gerald Davies. It was a stylish way to claim the title.

WALES IN THE LAND OF THE RISING SUN

Wales continued their good relations with non-Test nations by touring Japan in 1975. The tour would have a long-term impact. A young Japanese man named Koji Tokumasu was so impressed by the flowing rugby of Wales he vowed to visit the country and learn more. He arrived in Wales with little money and nowhere to stay. He eventually got a job translating and another cleaning and, after staying two years, not the couple of weeks he planned, he took what he had learned and applied it back home. Eventually, as part of the Japanese Rugby Union, he helped drive the bid that took the World Cup to Japan in 2019.

On the field, Wales won the two uncapped matches by 56-12 and 82-4. The first match was played during the hottest Japanese September in 70 years and the Welsh players sucked on salt tablets to avoid cramps.

THE SEVENTH SLAM

Grand Slam number seven is arguably one of the finest in Wales's collection of a dozen. The Home Unions were bullied, battered and bewildered by a ruthless Welsh pack and poetic Welsh backs. The final match was an epic struggle between two sides going for the same prize and it took one of the finest tackles ever seen (and now completely illegal) to help Wales tame the French cockerel. Wales used just 16 players all tournament.

1976 GRAND SLAM

MATCH ONE: England 9 Wales 21 (Twickenham)

Perhaps the most dominant win Wales have ever recorded in London. The visitors were inspired by Gareth Edwards and a blood-soaked J.P.R. Williams, who grabbed two tries in his masterpiece performance. Williams overtook Billy Bancroft's cap record at full-back in this game. Captain Mervyn Davies, however, was not impressed by his team.

MATCH TWO: Wales 28 Scotland 6 (Cardiff Arms Park)

Another referee injury, but this time the official hobbled on for most of the game, refusing to come off. Phil Bennett became the all-time leading Welsh scorer as his 13 points took him to 92.

Phil Bennett and his magic sidestep.

Two Scottish fans visiting Cardiff decided to climb up on the roof of the Arms Park the night before the big match. It was all fun and games until the hatch they had come up through closed behind them. With just some scotch to keep them warm on a bitterly cold night, they were forced to wait it out until they were seen just before kick-off the next day.

MATCH THREE: Ireland 9 Wales 34 (Lansdowne Road)

Wales ignored supposed IRA death threats to inflict the third highest score Ireland had ever conceded. Eighteen of the points came in just six minutes! Phil Bennett had perhaps his sweetest moment in the jersey and bagged 19 points, equalling the record of Jack Bancroft and Keith Jarrett.

MATCH FOUR: Wales 19 France 13 (Cardiff Arms Park)

Mervyn Davies gave a heroic captain's performance, playing much of the game in extreme pain due to internal bleeding in his calf. It was his 38th consecutive Welsh appearance and he was then the most capped Welsh forward ever. Gareth Edwards also became the most capped Welsh international, overtaking the great Ken Jones. Late in the game, J.P.R. Williams made a huge shoulder-charge tackle to stop France's Jean-Francois Gourdon scoring in the corner. Illegal now, it was praised to the heavens. Mervyn Davies had led Wales to seven wins in his eight Championship games, as well as two titles. Wales's 102 points in 1976 was a Championship record.

A CRUEL FAREWELL

Just weeks after Grand Slam glory, Mervyn Davies collapsed while playing for Swansea in the Welsh Cup. He had suffered a brain haemorrhage. He recovered, but was never allowed to play again.

PUMA TEARS

In October 1976, a Welsh XV needed a last-minute penalty for a high tackle on J.P.R. Williams to beat Argentina in an uncapped match in Cardiff. It saved Wales's bacon as Phil Bennett kicked a 40-yarder to win it 20-19. The Pumas were in tears after. They would have been the only visiting team bar the All Blacks to win in the Arms Park since 1968.

TRIPLE CROWN–WINNING LOSERS

In 1977, Wales became the first team to win a Triple Crown but not win the Championship. A 16-9 defeat in Paris meant France made a clean sweep.

MARCH OF SHAME

In the 1977 Wales v Ireland match in Cardiff, Wales's second row Geoff Wheel and Ireland's number eight Willie Duggan became the first players to be sent off in Championship history. Punching was the reason, but there were no red cards back then. Players were simply ordered off. Duggan claims the referee asked if he would 'mind leaving the field'. The Irishman said he didn't mind as he was exhausted!

ANOTHER SLAM, BUT THE LAST FOR A GOOD WHILE

Before the 1978–79 season, some thought the pressure of Triple Crown competition would make some big Welsh names retire. And while some of the best players of all time were shortly to hang up their boots, it was not to be until after Wales had made a record eighth clean sweep and a first ever triple Triple Crown.

THE 1978 GRAND SLAM DECIDER
Wales 16 France 7 (Cardiff Arms Park)

Once again, the two mighty European teams of the 1970s clashed for Grand Slam glory. Phil Bennett was magnificent and became the first Welsh fly-half since Raymond Ralph in 1931 to score two tries in a game. Bennett was only able to play thanks to special supports in his boot, protecting an injured foot. Gareth Edwards dropped a goal in his last game for Wales after an amazing 53 consecutive caps. Bennett and Gerald Davies also played their final Championship games. Allan Martin in the second row had the game of his life. Prop Charlie Faulkner was 37 years old (he had hidden his age for much of his career). Some consider this the finest Welsh team of all time.

Wales: *J.P.R. Williams (Bridgend); J.J. Williams, Ray Gravell (Llanelli), Steve Fenwick (Bridgend), Gareth Evans (Newport);*

Phil Bennett (Llanelli, capt), Gareth Edwards (Cardiff); Tony Faulkner, Bobby Windsor, Graham Price (Pontypool), Allan Martin (Aberavon), Geoff Wheel (Swansea), Jeff Squire (Newport), Derek Quinnell (Llanelli), Terry Cobner (Pontypool).

J.P.R. IN THE PACK

Wales undertook a miserable tour of Australia in the summer of 1978, having been invited to help build up the depleted coffers of the Australian Rugby Union. Wales lost four of nine games and both very violent Tests. Injuries were so bad that by the end of the tour J.P.R. was selected as a flanker. Wales lost the internationals 18-8 and 19-17. Graham Price had his jaw broken in the second Test after a cheap hit from Steve Finnane. Wales almost refused to play the first Test after being told who the referee was (he had been openly biased in an earlier tour match). Tour matches down under at this point still tended to have home officials. On the plus side, future greats like Gareth Davies (fly-half) and Terry Holmes (scrum-half) made their debuts.

A GREAT THESPIAN PERFORMS
1978 – Wales 12 New Zealand 13 (Cardiff Arms Park)
Andy Haden burnt his name into Welsh folklore when he decided to employ a move that the All Blacks had planned for an emergency. With Wales looking like they were about to claim their first win over the All Blacks since 1953, Haden and teammate Frank Oliver dived out of a line-out, pretending

they had been shoved. Laughably pathetic from grown men, it worked. The referee Roger Quittenton later claimed he was penalising another offence, but most think he was conned. With injury time starting, Brian McKechnie slotted the kick and the Kiwis won 13 to 12. To his eternal shame, Haden, who actively supported playing in apartheid era South Africa, always boasted of his efforts and would repeat the dive in later games for a laugh.

For this All Black, the grass of Cardiff was a stage.

A DRAGON IN CZECHOSLOVAKIA?

In the Czech Republic there exists a short fictional film (by director Lun Sevnik and co-starring local French heartthrob Fabien Dagoury) detailing the preparations of a small Czech town, Nyrsko, who dared to take on mighty Wales in the 1970s. The 'documentary' looks at how the locals built goalposts from trees they chopped down themselves and trained by the light of car headlights as the Dragons came to communist Czechoslovakia to take on little old Nyrsko! Amazingly, in real life, Nyrsko didn't even found a rugby team until 2016.

FOUR TRIPLES ON THE TROT

The Golden Era of the 1970s ended with a fourth consecutive Triple Crown, a feat only ever matched by England in the 1990s. Despite an epic performance from Terry Holmes in Paris, Wales fell 14-13, missing out on a Grand Slam. Nonetheless, the title went to Wales. The great team of the 1970s was slowly breaking apart through injury and retirement and this was to be the last burst of glory until a shared title in 1988 and an outright one in 1994.

1979 – MATCH FOUR: Wales 27 England 3 (Cardiff Arms Park)

England captain Bill Beaumont had said his side would win this. If Wales had scored 27 fewer points, Bill would have been correct. This was the biggest English battering in this fixture since 1905. Mike Roberts, 33, came into the second row and out of semi-retirement for his first cap in four years and took Beaumont to the cleaners while also nicking a try.

A SIGN OF THINGS TO COME

Wales closed the decade of glory off with a one-point win in an uncapped match over an excellent Romanian team in Cardiff. While many were surprised, in hindsight it was a sign that the world order was shifting. As for the Romanians, they would have a huge impact on Wales in the coming decade.

1969–79: THE STAR PLAYERS

GARETH EDWARDS

Club: Cardiff
Position: Scrum-half
Caps: 53 (1967–78)
(British Lions, 10 caps, 3 points)
Points: 88 (20 tries, 2 conversions, 1 penalty, 3 drop goals)

Born to a miner father in the small village of Gwaun-cae-Gurwen, Gareth Edwards is considered by many as the greatest rugby player ever. A natural athlete, as a youth he was driven to his limits physically by Bill Samuel, his P.E. master. Edwards made his Welsh debut at 19 in Paris and was captaining the team by age 20.

His 20 tries were a Welsh record at the time (shared with Gerald Davies) and he won an astonishing 53 consecutive caps. When he first trained with Barry John he said: 'You've got to concentrate all the time, because I can get passes out of certain situations that other scrum-halves wouldn't dream about.' Whether for Wales, Cardiff, the British Lions or the Barbarians, his determination, raw talent and competitiveness took him to the limits of what players could do in the sport. He was knighted in 2015.

J.P.R. WILLIAMS

Clubs: Bridgend, London Welsh
Position: Full-back
Caps: 55 (1969–81)
(British Lions, 8 caps, 3 points)
Points: 36 (6 tries, 2 conversions, 3 penalties)

Sideburns, blood, bandages and headbands. John Williams is one of the great icons of rugby and up there among the finest full-backs to grace the game. Williams won Junior Wimbledon in 1966 but knew rugby was his true calling. He took advantage of the 1968 law changes which ended the direct kick to touch outside a team's own 22, allowing full-backs to become more attacking. A superb attacker, his six tries were remarkable for a player in his position at the time and he helped redefine what people expected from the position. Five of his tries came against England, a team he never lost to in ten clashes. Fierce, brave, a devastating defender and not shy of throwing a punch, he was a rock for Wales.

BARRY JOHN

Clubs: Llanelli, Cardiff
Position: Outside-half
Caps: 25 (1966–72)
(British Lions, 5 caps, 30 points)
Points: 90 (5 tries, 6 conversions,
13 penalties, 8 drop goals)

So good, even the Kiwis called him 'The King' after his feats with the 1971 Lions. He retired at 27, sick of the monster that was fame (the final straw had been a woman curtseying before him at a public event). In his short career he became a true legend of the sport. He could drift through defenders like a ghost, throw dummies that opponents knew were coming but would still hopelessly buy, and tear full-backs apart with his tactical kicking.

Laid-back and confident of his ability, when he first trained with Gareth Edwards, he cut the session short by saying, 'You chuck it, Gar, and I'll catch it.'

PHIL BENNETT

Club: Llanelli
Position: Outside-half
Caps: 29 (1969–78)
(British Lions, 8 caps, 44 points)
Points: 166 (4 tries, 18 conversions,
36 penalties, 2 drop goals)

Another of the many great Welsh fly-halves, Bennett won

two of his first five caps as a replacement and drifted between wing, centre, fly-half or full-back. After Barry John retired, he took possession of the sacred number ten jersey until he hung his own boots up. With a lethal and explosive sidestep, pace, masterful kicking skills and a strategic brain, Bennett had it all. He led Wales eight times and only lost once to France, earning Wales two Triple Crowns and a Grand Slam. He finished as Wales's top scorer to that point in history.

A fiercely proud Welshman, he once gave a team talk ahead of the England game that went: 'Look what these ******** have done to Wales. They've taken our coal, our water, our steel. They buy our homes and live in them for a fortnight every year. What have they given us? Absolutely nothing. We've been exploited . . . controlled and punished by the English – and that's who you are playing this afternoon!'

MERVYN DAVIES

Clubs: London Welsh, Swansea
Position: Number eight
Caps: 38 (1969–76)
(British Lions, 8 caps)
Points: 7 (2 tries)

'Merv the Swerve' is always in the mix when discussions arise about the best player ever to play number eight and many regard him as the best ever Welsh captain. As skipper he took Wales to two Championship titles including a Grand Slam. In 38 caps he only saw defeat eight times. A non-stop worker, superb in rucks and mauls, Davies was most proud of his tackling. He once said that 'one good tackle gives me more pleasure than ten tries'. He claimed to have made at least 40 try-saving tackles for Wales. He was also an incredibly successful British Lion in 1971 and 1974. Davies's 'Mexican moustache' was his attempt to look more aggressive. His career was cruelly cut short by a brain haemorrhage.

GRAHAM PRICE

Club: Pontypool
Position: Prop
Caps: 41 (1975–83)
(British Lions, 12 caps, 4 points)
Points: 8 (2 tries)

Price was part of the legendary Pontypool front row that played together for Wales 19 times. Aided by the infamous Pontypool fitness regime of coach Ray Prosser, Price was a tough man with a seemingly inexhaustible engine. His reward for an epic try in Paris, which saw him cover almost 80 metres chasing a series of hacked-on balls, was extra fitness training from Prosser, who decided the French props couldn't have been very good if he was still able to run so much.

After his broken jaw against Australia, Price kept his weight up with a liquid diet that included over six pints of milk a day. It is generally agreed he is the greatest tight-head prop Wales (and possibly the Lions) ever had.

GERALD DAVIES

Clubs: London Welsh, Cardiff,
Cambridge University
Position: Wing, centre
Caps: 46 (1966–78)
(British Lions, 5 caps, 9 points)
Points: 72 (20 tries)

Despite being among the elite wingers in the history of rugby, Davies was originally a centre and considered his selection on the wing a demotion. He made the most of his apparent downgrade and scored a then joint record 20 tries for Wales. His combination of speed, swerve, agility and deadly finishing made him the stuff of nightmares for opponents.

A Lion in 1968 and 1971, he declined the South African tour of 1975 due to his views on apartheid. After rugby he went on to become one of the most eloquent writers on the sport and in 2019 became president of the WRU.

1969–79 NOTABLE EVENTS IN WELSH HISTORY

• 1969: Two members of the paramilitary Welsh nationalist group Mudiad Amddiffyn Cymru (Movement for the Defence of Wales) attempt to plant a bomb outside government offices in Abergele but blow themselves up.

• 1972: The first ever hypermarket in Wales opens for shoppers in Caerphilly.

• 1974: Welsh soap opera *Pobol Y Cwm* appears on television for the first time.

• 1978: The BBC release *Grand Slam*, a cult comedy about Welsh fans travelling to Paris to watch Wales play.

• 1979: Welsh voters reject the establishment of a Welsh Assembly by a ratio of four to one.

1980–94: BLEAK TIMES

	PLAYED	WON	DRAWN	LOST
FIVE NATIONS	60	24	2	34
NON-CHAMPIONSHIP TESTS	30	16	0	14
WORLD CUP (INCL. QUALIFIERS)	13	10	0	3
TOTAL	103	50	2	51

Championships

1994

Shared Championships

1988 (Triple Crown)

World Cups

Third Place (1987), Pool Stage (1991)

'My only dangerous opponent was the referee
– he put his finger in my eye.'

ROMANIA'S MIRCEA PARASCHIV AFTER
THRASHING WALES 24-6 IN 1983

SCARLET HORROR SHOW

After the Second Golden Era, Welsh rugby declined. Then got worse. Then got horrid. Then got unspeakably embarrassing. Countries that Welsh fans at the end of the 1970s didn't even know existed, let alone played rugby, would come into Cardiff Arms Park and triumph. Old rivals like New Zealand would go from respecting Wales as a serious rival, to feeling pity, even contempt, for what they had become.

The 1980s were not much fun off the pitch either. The recession of the 1970s trundled on. The economic hardship caused an even bigger split in society and many Welsh communities, devastated by the further decline of traditional industries, felt alienated and angry at 'faraway' Westminster. Margaret Thatcher was prime minister through the whole decade and her policies and actions split the Welsh as much as the rest of the UK. Her opposition to trade unions (the 'enemy within') played a huge role in the bitter battle between the establishment and striking miners in 1984–85.

Thatcher also took Britain into the Falklands War in 1982, defending two territories in the South Atlantic from Argentina. The rights and wrongs of this were fiercely debated and many Welsh soldiers died or suffered serious injuries fighting it. Also that year, the Welsh language channel S4C began broadcasting after years of political struggle and protests when it seemed the concept would be abandoned by the UK government.

In 1992, with Thatcher gone, it seemed Wales would supply the next prime minister, with polls predicting Labour's Neil Kinnock would win. Like his compatriots on the rugby field, Kinnock ended up losing.

THE GRIM DECLINE AND
FALL OF THE WELSH EMPIRE

1980 – England 9 Wales 8 (Twickenham)

It's a massive oversimplification, but many point to the England game of 1980 as the end of the golden days and the departing point for a descent into sporting hell. After a violent, but big win against France in Cardiff, Wales came to Twickenham with lots of media fuss about the dark arts, especially concerning players like flanker Paul Ringer. After both teams had been warned by the referee for fighting, Ringer hit England's John Horton high and late in the 14th minute and was sent off. Wales outscored England two tries to none, missed five penalties and led 8-6 with minutes left. But a last-gasp penalty from Dusty Hare put England on their way to Grand Slam glory, their first since 1957.

THE RINGER EFFECT

The fallout from the loss to England was huge. Due to concern about the game's brutal image, the Welsh forwards were told to behave themselves and that foul play had to be eliminated. To this day, many argue this chopped off the legs that had built the success of the 1970s. But while there is no doubt the pack had part of their weaponry taken from them, this was only one small reason why Wales would go off the rails. Quite simply, the rugby world was moving on and the fantastic innovations Wales had brought to rugby, both on the coaching front and on the field, were no longer enough. Just as at the end of the

First Golden Era, too many blazers, players and fans refused to let go of past glories.

A HUNDRED YEARS

On 26 July 1980, the WRU marked the start of its 100th anniversary season with a Centenary Gala Opening. Taking place at the Arms Park, everyone from the Welsh national side to the Welsh schools team were there. Military bands marched, male voice choirs sang and guardsmen lifted the fancy new WRU flag with a new grand coat of arms. The Red Devils parachute team even hopped in from the sky carrying notes from the presidents of the other Five Nations teams.

A message of congratulations from the Queen in London, placed in a specially made rugby ball, had been dispatched ten days earlier and was carried by a relay of runners all the way to Cardiff. However, when it was opened it was damaged by all the British rain it had seen. Off the field, an overly optimistic WRU had also produced far too much centenary merchandise and struggled to sell it! On and off the grass, the centenary season was a flop.

AN UNHAPPY BIRTHDAY
1980 – Wales 3 New Zealand 23 (Cardiff Arms Park)

New Zealand arrived to help kick off the centenary celebrations and spoilt the mood for everyone. The four tries they scored were the most Wales had conceded at home since 1960. Wales only managed a penalty goal. Happy birthday! Following on, Wales scored just two tries in the Championship as they scraped home wins against England and Ireland and lost both away games.

The All Blacks ruined Wales's big birthday bash.

BY THE BOOK

Under the amateur regulations of the times, retired players such as Barry John, Phil Bennett, Mervyn Davies, Gareth Edwards and J.P.R. Williams were lost to the game and could not coach as they had taken payment for writing books about their life in rugby.

OLYMPUS HAS FALLEN

Wales started the 1981–82 season by beating Australia and

France at home. It would be the last win against France until 1994, and for the best part of four decades the Dragons would rarely scorch the Wallabies again.

1982 – Wales 18 Scotland 34 (Cardiff Arms Park)

Where to begin? After 27 consecutive undefeated home games in the Five Nations stretching back to 1968, Wales were shocked by the Scots. The visitors had not won in Cardiff for two decades and their 34 points were the most Wales had ever conceded at home.

HOME FROM HOME

After the 23-9 win over Ireland in 1983, Wales would not win a home fixture against them until 2005. In that period, however, Wales would win seven times against the Irish in Dublin and once in New Zealand!

DEFEAT BEHIND THE IRON CURTAIN

1983 – Romania 24 Wales 6 (23 August Stadium, Bucharest, Romania)

After a reasonable Five Nations, Wales travelled to communist Romania. Pontypool's Eddie Butler at number eight led a side with six debutants as caps were given by Wales against a team from a country outside the IRFB for the first time.

The giant Romanian forwards brushed the Welsh pack aside on four occasions through line-out drives to score. Wales were never in the game. Afterwards, many of the Welsh players gave their opposite numbers their kit and items like chewing gum and toiletries that were difficult to obtain in communist Europe.

MARK BROWN MAKES HISTORY

Wales's horror show in Bucharest saw Pontypool flanker Mark Brown make his debut. Brown, who went on to win six caps, became the first black player to represent Wales. Shamefully, it could not be said that there hadn't been black talent in the Welsh game. But great players like Billy Boston and Clive Sullivan were lost to rugby league and were never given a fair chance in union.

TAKING CHANGE FROM THE CHANGING ROOM

During the 1984 win over Ireland, a thief climbed into the Welsh dressing room at Lansdowne Road via a ventilation shaft and stole £800! Wales were luckier on the field and won 18-9 with a try from centre Rob Ackerman.

CONTINUING CALAMITIES

In 1984 Wales won in Dublin and London, but lost both home Championship games for the first time since 1963. France won in Cardiff for the first time since 1968 and Scotland won two on the bounce in Cardiff for the first time ever. The year was rounded off with a 28-9 record home loss to Australia, the most Wales had ever conceded at this point to a touring team.

THE SENSITIVE BIG FIVE

1985 – Wales 24 England 15

The Big Five were never known for their people skills. After Wales lost in Paris, they selected the team to face England in the final Championship match with A.N. Other at fly-half, saying they wanted more time to consider whom to play there. Gareth Davies, who had played in the last three games, retired on principle. When they eventually asked Davies to play, he refused. Another Davies, Jonathan Davies, took his place and the incredible talent line of the Welsh number ten shirt continued. Davies scored a try (after comical fumbling from English full-back Chris Martin) and dropped a goal. The great line-out forward Robert Norster had a stormer and another key forward of the era, Phil Davies, made his debut at number eight.

THE LONG BOOT

When Wales's full-back Paul Thorburn opted to kick at goal from way inside his own half against Scotland at Cardiff in 1986, most assumed it was just a way to get the ball deep down field. His wind-assisted kick from 64.2 metres was a success and is still the longest score at Test level. Even more impressive it was done with no kicking tee.

"The posts are down there somewhere."

A PUNCHY TOUR OF PARADISE

As preparation for the inaugural World Cup in 1987, Wales undertook an historic tour of Fiji, Tonga and Western Samoa. While Wales won all three Tests and three non-Tests, it was a brutal trip. Wales defeated Fiji 22-15 in Suva, with Richard Moriarty (captain) and Paul Moriarty becoming the first brothers to play in the pack for Wales since 1937. The tour ended with a 32-14 win in the burning heat (32° Celsius) in Apia against Samoa. But it was the Tongan game that would go down in infamy. A game so violent, some believe the tape was destroyed so the IRFB could not punish the teams for what happened (a live broadcast was not possible).

1986 – Tonga 7 Wales 15 (Nuku'alofa, Tonga)

This match, played in front of the King of Tonga wearing ski googles, almost never happened. Moments before the teams were due to run out, a window was broken by accident in the Welsh dressing room. The police arrived and, with batons waving around, wanted to arrest several players. Ex-international Derek Quinnell restrained several police and eventually the president of the WRU was able to calm things.

After the anthems, the Welsh team had to go up in the stand to greet the king. The game soon descended into a series of mass brawls. Tongan prop Tevita Bloomfield is supposed to have knocked down or knocked out at least four players. He chased centre Bleddyn Bowen (a policeman) into the crowd and the crowd threw Bowen back onto the pitch! Things got so nasty that after winger Adrian Hadley was knocked out, scrum-half Robert Jones asked captain Moriarty to actually take the team off to stop someone getting killed. Glen Webbe, meanwhile, became the second black player to be capped for Wales when he replaced Hadley.

REVENGE IS A DISH BEST SERVED IN WELSH

After the Tongan fight, the hosts wanted someone from Wales to speak in Welsh during the post-match function. Jonathan Davies got up and said that this was the worst place he had ever been, the food was awful and that Tonga were the dirtiest team he'd ever seen. The locals, not understanding, cheered and applauded.

WINTER OF MEDIOCRITY

Wales's 1987 Five Nations was a grim one. The sole victory was in the 'Battle of Cardiff' against England (19-12), a game so violent that the RFU banned four English players afterwards. One of the only bright spots in the Championship was the debut of Ieuan Evans of Llanelli on the wing. He would go on to become one of the most beloved of players. As preparation for the first ever World Cup, it was dismal. This was also Wales's longest period without a title since the 19th century.

WOMEN IN SCARLET

Wales Women 4 England Women 22 (Pontypool Park, Pontypool)

On 5 April 1987, the first Welsh international match for a women's team took place in Pontypool. Led by Liza Burgess, it was a historical moment for women's sport in Wales. In 2018, Burgess, who went on to win 87 Welsh caps, was inducted into the World Rugby Hall of Fame.

1987 WORLD CUP (NEW ZEALAND & AUSTRALIA)

It seems incredible now, but the IRFB was for a long time opposed to the idea of the World Cup. Then again, if you've been paying attention to their efforts to seemingly hinder the growth of the game so far, perhaps it isn't that incredible.

The Home Unions (especially Ireland and Scotland) were the most against it, fearing it would lead to professionalism. The French, to their credit, supported the concept if the likes of Romania and Italy could be involved. And so, in 1987, New Zealand and Australia hosted the first ever World Cup and rugby would never be the same again.

Captain: Richard Moriarty
Coach: Tony Gray

POOL GAMES

Wales 13 Ireland 6 (Athletic Park, Wellington)

Just over a month after Ireland again won in Cardiff, Wales had their revenge. Tough-as-teak centre John Devereux led the way, Jonathan Davies dropped two goals and goal-kicking machine Paul Thorburn added a penalty. The mercurial midfielder Mark Ring grabbed the first ever Welsh World Cup try. Years later Ring was in a pub quiz when the tiebreaker question for his team to win was 'Who scored Wales's first World Cup try?' He answered incorrectly!

Wales 29 Tonga 16 (Showgrounds, Palmerston North)
Wales, wearing green for the first time in a capped international, were flat, but did enough. Winger Glen Webbe scored a hattrick of tries, but suffered a horrendous and tournament-ending concussion after a dangerous tackle from Tali Ete'aki. His third try was a stunner, but he had no memory of it.

Wales 40 Canada 9 (Rugby Park, Invercargill)
Ieuan Evans scored four tries in a game, putting him alongside Maurice Richards (1969, v England), Reggie Gibbs (1908, v France) and Willie Llewellyn (1899, v England).

QUARTER-FINAL
Wales 16 England 3 (Ballymore, Brisbane)
This encounter was considered the worst of the World Cup. Wales didn't care. Those that stayed awake saw tries from John Devereux, Gareth Roberts and Robert Jones put Wales through with ease. After it, most of the squad went drinking for two days.

SEMI-FINAL
Wales 6 New Zealand 49 (Ballymore)
For many, this was the day the rivalry between the two nations ended. This was a global humiliation. The All Blacks would cruise to the title and Wales were like the buzzing of flies to them for all the resistance offered. Making it worse, after being knocked out cold by Kiwi captain Wayne Shelford in clear view of everyone, Wales's second-row Huw Richards was sent off for a punch on All Black Gary Whetton. It summed up the contest.

It was lights out for Wales in possibly the most horrific loss in Welsh rugby history to that point.

THIRD PLACE PLAY-OFF

Wales 22 Australia 21 (Rotorua International Stadium, Rotorua)

Wales won a thriller with a dramatic last gasp score by Adrian Hadley. Paul Thorburn hit the sweetest of conversions from the far-left touchline to seal a famous victory and claim third place (to date Wales's best result). In truth, it covered up the problems in Welsh rugby. Australia had been down to 14 men for most of the game after a sending-off. Wales had beaten a dismal England and been so badly annihilated by the All Blacks it should have set alarm bells ringing. Manager Clive Rowlands, after the All Blacks massacre, had been asked what Welsh rugby would do after such a loss. His response summed up the lack of Welsh ambition: 'Go back to beating England every year.'

FALSE DAWN: PART I

Led by Bleddyn Bowen (South Wales Police), Wales followed their World Cup odyssey with the first Triple Crown since 1979 and a shared Championship. It was a flicker of hope before a blazing fire of self-destruction.

1988 TRIPLE CROWN

MATCH ONE: England 3 Wales 11 (Twickenham)
Wales travelled to HQ with four outside-halves in the backline, including Anthony Clement of Swansea picked at full-back on his first full cap (he had never played the position previously). Wales's Adrian Hadley finished two exceptional tries as a good pack performance was backed up by the slick passing of Robert Jones, the jinking and stepping of Jonathan Davies and the deadly running of Bleddyn Bowen.

MATCH TWO: Wales 25 Scotland 20 (Cardiff Arms Park)
In one of the all-time classics, Wales rallied from 20-10 down to put themselves on for the Triple Crown. Jonathan Davies's

solo grubber try from a scrum and Ieuan Evans's sidestepping of five defenders have burned themselves into the eyeballs of thrilled Welsh fans they have been shown so many times on television. It briefly felt like the 1970s.

MATCH THREE: Ireland 9 Wales 12 (Lansdowne Road)

After a nerve-wracking late win in Dublin (with Paul Thorburn hitting a winner deep in injury time), Wales fell in the rain 10-9 to France to miss out on a Grand Slam, but the future seemed bright. The light, however, was from an oncoming express train.

WELSH LAMBS SLAUGHTERED IN NEW ZEALAND

Wales followed up their Five Nations heroics with a disaster in the Land of the Long White Cloud. They won just two of eight games. The Tests were lost by an unfathomable 52-3 and 54-9 (it was still the four-point try era)! New Zealand scored ten tries in the first game and eight in the second. Wales got one in total (although it was the score of the series as Jonathan Davies ran 60 metres to finish a try Mark Ring launched on his own line). As Wales stood under the posts for yet another conversion during a game against North Auckland, one home fan took out a bugle and played 'The Last Post', the music played to commemorate soldiers who have fallen in battle. Just months after taking Wales to the Triple Crown, coach Tony Gray was fired.

The 'Last Post' was played by a fan to the Welsh team in 1988.

EASTERN WARRIORS SACK THE ARMS PARK

Romania showed their win in 1983 on home soil was no fluke, by coming to Cardiff in 1988 and repeating their heroics with a 15-9 win. It was a nightmare second game for new coach John Ryan as the huge Romanian pack throttled the toothless Dragons and fly-half Gelu Ignat kicked the home side off the park. Two of the visiting side, including captain Florică

Murariu, died within the year during the 1989 revolution that ended communism in the country.

By 1988, Romania were two wins from two against Wales.

YEARS OF FAMINE

Wales's loss to Romania caused panic and anger in Welsh rugby. Jonathan Davies, who was captain for the loss, took an unfair amount of abuse and decided to turn professional. In the coming years he would be followed by an astonishing array of talent, including John Devereux, David Young,

Scott Quinnell, Allan Bateman, Scott Gibbs, Paul Moriarty, Rowland Phillips and Mark Jones.

Wales narrowly avoided their first ever Five Nations whitewash with a surprise win over England in the rain of Cardiff in 1989. But in 1990, not even a change of coach (Ron Waldron came in after a 34-6 thrashing at Twickenham) could stop Wales losing all four games.

WALES LOSE TO A SMALL PART OF WALES

A Welsh XV, warming up for the fateful visit of the 1989 All Blacks (Wales lost 34-9) played a game against Bridgend. The club side not only had several players missing through injury, but had their own stars, such as Mike Hall, Glen Webbe and Mike Griffiths, lining up against them. Wales led 17-6 at the interval and, laughably, conceded 18 points to lose 24-17. In many ways the result summed up the whole shambolic era.

AN ILL-FITTING CAP

In 1990 the WRU were accused of devaluing the jersey by awarding caps against the Barbarians, a club team. Bizarrely, Wales went on to do the same on three other occasions. However, on the other six times they've played the Barbarians no caps were given. Making things worse in 1990, Wales lost 31-24.

A YEAR OF SHAME

The 1991 Five Nations saw Wales lose 25-6 in Cardiff to

England – the first home loss to them since 1963. The only highlights of the game for fans were the debuts of centre Scott Gibbs and fly-half Neil Jenkins. Both were just 19. Wales conceded their worst ever total in the Five Nations (114) while again failing to win a game, managing only a draw with Ireland. But, it gets worse . . .

THE NIGHTMARE OF OZ

Wales's 1991 Australian tour managed to make the 1988 tour of New Zealand seem a fun jolly. Wales won only half of their six games, but their losses to New South Wales (71-8) and Australia (63-6) were a new low. Both were the worst two results by Wales (capped and uncapped) since 1881. But it got worse. The Welsh players drunkenly fought among themselves at the post-match dinner and centre Mike Hall got his hand cut open by glass. The WRU had to officially apologise to the ARU. After the New South Wales defeat, one paper wrote that the home side had 'buried the mutilated carcass of Welsh rugby'. With the World Cup months away, coach Ron Waldron stepped down and was replaced by Alan Davies.

The 1991 *Welsh Rugby Annual* marked the nightmare season by putting a black border around its cover to mark the death of international rugby in Wales.

1991 WORLD CUP (UK AND FRANCE)

The one good thing about the 1991 World Cup for Welsh fans

was the nightmare was over in the space of a week, even if the shame would linger forever.

Captain: Ieuan Evans
Coach: Alan Davies

THE POOL GAMES

Wales 13 Western Samoa 16 (Cardiff Arms Park)

Samoa, not invited to the 1987 World Cup, beat, battered and bruised Wales with tackling the likes of which Cardiff had never seen. Three Welsh players left injured (all broken by Samoa's Apollo Perelini) as the Arms Park was rocked to its core. The result meant Wales needed to beat both Argentina and Australia.

Western Samoa stormed the Arms Park and shocked world rugby.

Wales 16 Argentina 7 (Cardiff Arms Park)

The only thing to praise about this midweek win was it ended a run of eight home games without a win! The great Mike Rayer made his first start at full-back with a strong defensive game.

Wales 3 Australia 38 (Cardiff Arms Park)

Wales continued to set unwanted records as they suffered their worst ever home defeat and let in six tries. Australia, who went on to lift the World Cup, won 28 line-outs to two! The day was summed up when with 12 minutes remaining, and Wales losing 28-3, winger Arthur Emyr tried a drop goal. The only thing it did was damage a few blades of grass. Wales crashed out in their own backyard and would need to qualify for the next World Cup.

A WIN . . . AT HOME!

Wales began to improve under Alan Davies as coach and in 1992 won away to Ireland and at home to Scotland. The latter win was the Dragons' first win at home in the Five Nations for three years. A 24-0 loss to England (who won a second consecutive Grand Slam) and the fact that Wales only scored two tries all tournament reminded people the dark days were not over.

FALSE DAWN: PART II
1993 – Wales 10 England 9 (Cardiff Arms Park)

Wales shocked the title favourites with a first win over England since 1989. Flanker Emyr Lewis kicked ahead harmlessly in his own half just before half-time with Wales trailing 9-3. England winger Rory Underwood, who had gifted Wales a win in 1989 on the same ground, casually jogged after it like he was out for a Sunday stroll. Captain Ieuan Evans pounced, kicked ahead and scored a famous try to offer Wales hope that a corner had been turned. It was followed by a 20-0 stuffing by Scotland and losses to Ireland and France.

WINGING IT

After Wales were utterly taken apart up front against Scotland in their 20-point beating, the Welsh selectors spent nearly eight hours picking the team to face Ireland. The result? One change. The position? Left wing! Wayne Proctor was dropped for Nigel Walker, the former Olympic hurdler and fastest man in Welsh rugby.

CANADIAN PUTS BOOT INTO LAND OF HIS FATHER

1993 – Wales 24 Canada 26 (Cardiff Arms Park)

Wales continued crafting new rugby disasters with a new level of cluelessness and tactical ineptitude. At one point, fly-half Adrian Davies looked up to the coaches in the stands in despair and confusion about game tactics. For reasons unknown, at the death and with Wales leading by one try, Anthony Clement put an up-and-under up from his own 22 instead of clearing. Canada's Al Charron scored from the subsequent possession and Gareth Rees, son of a Welshman, kicked a famous winner. All Wales's points had come from eight Neil Jenkins penalties.

FALSE DAWN: PART III

Wales won the 1994 Championship outright, thanks to points difference, which was now used to separate teams and prevent the regular outcome of shared titles. It was the first full title since 1979 and it seemed the occasional green shoots shown under coach Alan Davies were starting to take root. Sadly, a slow start at Twickenham cost Wales a Grand Slam as they lost 15-8 in the final game. Captain Ieuan Evans collected the Five Nations trophy (introduced in 1993) with a slightly embarrassed look.

1994 CHAMPIONSHIP WIN

MATCH ONE: Wales 29 Scotland 6 (Cardiff Arms Park)

In the lashing rain of Cardiff, replacement wing Mike Rayer slid in for two famous tries (such a feat was rare for replacements in that era) to help Wales to their biggest Championship win in 15 years. Hooker Garin Jenkins was reported to the police by a Scottish fan for throwing a punch!

MATCH TWO: Ireland 15 Wales 17 (Lansdowne Road)

MATCH THREE: Wales 24 France 15 (Cardiff Arms Park)

Wales finally beat France after 12 years. Scott Quinnell, son of Derek, scored one of the great Welsh forward tries, running nearly half the pitch and bouncing off or fooling multiple defenders. Wales wore green socks, not red, as in previous games referees had been confused about foul play as France also had red socks. It paid off as with no TMO back then,

Quinnell's try was almost disallowed for him stepping into touch, until the officials realised it was a red sock of France that had gone out. The game was sealed with another half-pitch run for a try, this time by speedster Nigel Walker.

MATCH FOUR: England 15 Wales 8 (Twickenham)

*Nigel Walker could seem a
blur on the field with his speed.*

WILD MAN OF THE WOODS

Llanelli flanker Mark Perego won nine caps for Wales. He was a fanatical fitness freak and would run in ice-cold rivers, half naked, carrying an axe with which to chop wood. It was said he would sometimes go for a run AFTER games, even internationals!

THIRTEEN-GAME YEAR

Wales played an astonishing 13 games in 1994. In the early days of rugby it could take a player four or five years to earn so many caps. Here's some of 1994's highlights (and lowlights – this is the 1990s after all!).

Portugal 11 Wales 102 (Lisbon University)
Wales broke the 100-point mark for the only time in this bizarre World Cup qualifier. The local TV station, unsure of how to show rugby, spent more time showing replays of conversions rather than tries.

Spain 0 Wales 54 (Madrid University)
Another World Cup qualifier against a nation most people at the time didn't even realise played rugby.

Western Samoa 34 Wales 9 (Chanel College, Apia)
In blistering heat, Wales again fell to Samoa in their biggest defeat since 1991 against Australia in Cardiff.

Romania 9 Wales 16 (Stadionul Dinamo, Bucharest)

Wales finally beat Romania in a capped match in what was a World Cup seeding match. It was darn close though and needed Ieuan Evans's 21st try for Wales, taking him past Gareth Edwards and Gerald Davies in the all-time list.

Wales 12 South Africa 20 (Cardiff Arms Park)

The Springboks returned to international rugby after the end of apartheid in South Africa. It had been 24 years since the two sides had met, but the result was business as usual.

1980–94: THE STAR PLAYERS

TERRY HOLMES

Club: Cardiff
Position: Scrum-half
Caps: 25 (1978–85)
(British Lions, 1 cap)
Points: 36 (9 tries)

Terry Holmes, aged just 21, had the unenviable job of taking over from Gareth Edwards at Cardiff and Wales. Nonetheless, he soon made his own mark as one of the greats. One of the most powerful scrum-halves to have played the game, Holmes scored nine tries for Wales and 123 for Cardiff. Captain of his country five times, he left for rugby league in 1985.

ROBERT NORSTER

Club: Cardiff
Position: Second row
Caps: 34 (1982–89)
(British Lions, 3 caps)
Points: 8 (2 tries)

In the pre-lifting era, Robert Norster was considered one of the world's best jumpers. His total of 34 caps was, at the time, a joint Welsh record for a lock shared with Allan Martin. He was twice a British Lion and until he lost his place in the second Lions Test against Australia in 1989 he was never dropped at the top level. No other player won more caps for Wales in the 1980s and he was key to much of the (little) success Wales had. He almost missed out on his first try for Wales as he started celebrating before placing the ball down and an Irish player tackled him. After retirement he was team manager for Wales from 1991 until 1995.

JONATHAN DAVIES

Clubs: Neath, Llanelli, Cardiff
Position: Outside-half
Caps: 32 (1985–97)
Points: 81 (5 tries, 2 conversions, 13 drop goals)

Many argue that Jonathan Davies is as great as anyone who

ever played number ten for Wales. He had a lethal sidestep, incredible acceleration, a huge boot and supreme confidence. Despite the fact he usually played behind a poor or average Welsh pack, he still produced many moments of sheer magic. A determined tackler and able to look after himself physically, in 1988 he won man of the match in Wales's record 54-9 loss to New Zealand. Sadly, his best years were lost to rugby league, when he signed with Widnes for a record fee. A huge success in both the UK and Australia, Davies returned to win five more caps after rugby went pro in 1995.

ROBERT JONES

Club: Swansea
Position: Scrum-half
Caps: 54 (1986–95)
(British Lions, 3 caps)
Points: 19 (4 tries)

Robert Jones was famous for a golden pass that gave his half-back partners vital extra moments on the ball. Never a great try-scoring threat, Jones was a master tactician, street-smart and a superb box kicker. In 1989 his kicking in Cardiff in the rain drove the fancied English to ruin. A tough cookie, he was famous for being in the thick of the violent rearguard action that helped the 1989 Lions beat Australia. He equalled Gareth Edwards's scrum-half cap total of 53 and won one cap as a replacement wing.

IEUAN EVANS

Clubs: Llanelli, Bath
Position: Wing
Caps: 72 (1987–98)
(British Lions, 7 caps, 4 points)
Points: 157 (33 tries)

In the dark, dark age of Welsh rugby in the 1980s and 1990s, there were very few bright sparks for fans to fix their eyes on. Ieuan Evans wasn't just a bright flicker of light, but a vast burning bonfire of brilliance. Playing behind some of the worst packs of forwards to ever wear the scarlet of Wales and often having either no ball or bad ball, he still shone out as one of the great wingers of the modern era. Unlike his celebrated peers such as England's Rory Underwood and Australia's David Campese, Evans could defend too.

The complete footballer, he had speed, a lethal sidestep, a clever footballing brain and, as his famous try against England in 1993 showed, he had a decent boot on him in a foot race. The Pontarddulais wing's attacking verve earned him the nickname 'Merlin the Magician' from legendary TV commentator Bill McLaren. He scored a then record 33 tries for Wales, smashing the previous record of 20 held by Gareth Edwards and Gerald Davies. He scored more tries at the Arms Park than any other Welsh player, but only won on 13 of his 32 games there. He captained Wales 28 times, also a record for the time (broken in 2012 by Ryan Jones).

Ieuan was also a three-time British Lions tourist and scored the winning try in the deciding Test against Australia in 1989. Amazingly, Ieuan did all this despite a series of major injuries, including dislocating his right shoulder five times and horrifically dislocating his ankle (the author was very close to this and can assure you, it was grim).

1980–94 NOTABLE EVENTS IN WELSH HISTORY

• 1980: Gwynfor Evans (Plaid Cymru leader) declares he will go on hunger strike if the government does not keep its promise to create a Welsh-language television channel.

• 1981: According to the UK census, only 18.9% of the Welsh population are Welsh speakers, the lowest ever total.

• 1982: Thirty-two Welsh Guards are killed when the ship *Sir Galahad* is sunk in the Falklands War.

• 1983: Welshman Neil Kinnock becomes leader of the Labour Party.

• 1984: Welsh band The Alarm release their debut album; they would go on to be one of the most successful Welsh bands in America during the 1980s.

• 1984–85: The UK miners' strike shakes the social, cultural and economic fabric of Wales.

• 1986: The last pit in the Rhondda – Maerdy Colliery – closes.

• 1988: The *New Welsh Review* literary magazine is founded and the Hay-on-Wye literature festival begins.

• 1991: The Welsh football team shock the sporting world with a 1-0 win over Germany in Cardiff during Euro qualifiers.

• 1992: Welsh actor Anthony Hopkins wins the Best Actor Oscar for *The Silence of the Lambs*.

• 1993: The Welsh language is given parity with English in the Welsh public sector.

• 1994: It becomes legal for shops to open on a Sunday for the first time.

1995–2004: THE DAWN OF PROFESSIONALISM

	PLAYED	WON	DRAWN	LOST
FIVE/SIX NATIONS	45	14	1	30
NON-CHAMPIONSHIP TESTS	50	29	0	21
WORLD CUP	12	6	0	6
WORLD CUP WARM-UP GAMES*	6	4	0	2
TOTAL	113	53	1	59

*Listed separately due to their experimental nature and mass substitutions. Full caps were awarded, however, and they are considered full internationals.

Championships

None

Shared Championships

None

World Cups

Pool Stage (1995), Quarter-finals (1999, 2003)

'We are bigger, better, faster and stronger . . .'
GEOFF EVANS, WALES'S 1995 WORLD CUP MANAGER,
COMPARES WALES TO THE ALL BLACKS

SLOWLY MOVING OUT OF THE DARK AGES

It is said that when the historic decision was made in 1995 to turn rugby professional, one old IRFB committee member repeatedly banged his head on the wall while moaning in despair. People took it that seriously.

By the time of the 1995 World Cup, rugby could no longer justify increasing time demands on players or reaping in huge ticket and television deals and not paying players. Professionalism in Wales initially brought lots of money, but not a great deal of professionalism. Amateur committees and officials were suddenly arranging massive player contract deals with no idea what they were doing. At one point, despite appalling results, Wales were supposedly the highest paid team in the world. Meanwhile, many players were happy to be big fish in a small pond: taking the money and fame in Wales, but failing to meet the growing standards the rest of the rugby world was applying. Finally though, led primarily by foreign coaches, things began to get better and happier times arrived.

The late 1990s in Wales saw significant political change as the nation voted for the establishment of the National Assembly for Wales, after rejecting the idea in the 1970s. While the referendum result was extremely close, some commentators argued the result reflected a growing sense of national confidence and a desire for a more inclusive style of politics with greater local autonomy. Culturally, this period coincided with 'Cool Cymru', a movement fuelled by the success of Welsh musicians, film-makers, fashion designers, athletes and artists. The UK Britpop scene was exploding around the world, and Welsh bands like the Manic Street Preachers, Stereophonics,

Catatonia and Super Furry Animals gave Wales its own distinct rock scene. Coupled with the redevelopment of areas like Cardiff Bay and the building of the Millennium Stadium (which was one of the most hi-tech stadiums in the world when it opened), Wales was undergoing a cultural renaissance and putting on a proud face to the world.

THE SHAM-LIKE LAST DAYS OF SHAMATEURISM

The final amateur Championship of 1995 was a dark one. Wales suffered their second ever Five Nations whitewash and scored just one try (Robert Jones's first ever in the tournament on his 51st cap). Coach Alan Davies was forced to resign and, learning nothing from 1991, Wales went into a World Cup with a brand-new coach. This time Wales went for an Australian in Alec Evans, who had successfully rebuilt the Cardiff team of the era.

1995 WORLD CUP (SOUTH AFRICA)

The 1995 World Cup was so dramatic they made into a Hollywood movie. South Africa was making its debut, the great Jonah Lomu blasted his way into rugby folklore and Nelson Mandela, the former revolutionary turned president, wore a Springbok shirt as he handed the trophy to the host nation. The symbolism of a man who was imprisoned for 27 years by the authorities wearing the jersey associated with the regime that locked him up played a major part in uniting the home nation.

Wales and Ireland's 1995 World Cup match was a horror show.

Wales's contribution was less spectacular. It was ghastly. In an effort to turn things around quickly, new coach Alec Evans stacked the team with Cardiff players (eight played against Japan) and took the captaincy from Ieuan Evans and gave it to his Cardiff skipper Mike Hall. As in 1990 and 1991, tribal and club splits within the squad only further derailed Welsh efforts.

Captain: Mike Hall
Coach: Alec Evans

POOL GAMES

Wales 57 Japan 10 (Free State Stadium, Bloemfontein)
Winger Gareth Thomas scored three tries on his debut as Wales, wearing green, recorded their solitary win in the tournament.

Wales 9 New Zealand 34 (Ellis Park, Johannesburg)

Welsh manager Geoff Evans absurdly boasted pre-game that Wales were bigger and better than the All Blacks. About the only small victory Wales had was that Jonah Lomu was switched to the opposite wing from Ieuan Evans. Lomu didn't score, but he didn't need to.

Wales 23 Ireland 24 (Ellis Park)

An abomination of a contest between two awful teams. Neither side deserved to win. Wales were ordered by the coaches to play as little rugby as possible and to hope for mistakes from Ireland. It was hard to have any sympathy in defeat. Wales, again, were out in the pool stages.

THE PROFESSIONALS

1995 – South Africa 40 Wales 11 (Ellis Park)

This game against the new world champions, just 70 days after the World Cup, was the first time the Dragons took to the field as professionals. The experience for Cardiff second row Derwyn Jones was a short one. At 2.08m (6ft 10in), he was at that point by far the tallest Welsh player in history (until Luke Charteris arrived in 2004). With lifting not allowed in the line-out then, he was a more than useful target. After some shirt pulling as Wales's Mark Bennett scored in the fifth minute, Springbok Kobus Wiese hit Jones hard from behind and knocked him out cold. Game over. Wiese was not sent off, but Wales's hooker Garin Jenkins was red-carded later for a punch.

PROFESSIONALS BY NAME (NOT BY NATURE)

Wales, now coached by Kevin Bowring and led by hooker Jonathan Humphreys, lost the opening three games of the 1996 Championship, putting them on a record streak of eight losses in the Five Nations. The only win came against France in the final match. Amazingly, it cost France the title.

Wales followed this grim Championship with another nightmare tour of Australia. The upside was that there were no punch-ups between the squad in the after-match functions. The downside was just two wins from eight and Test losses of 56-26 and 42-3. Wales also conceded 69 in a non-Test match.

PRODIGAL SONS RETURN

Once rugby union turned pro, to the delight of despairing Welsh fans, it allowed exiled league players to return. Against Italy in 1996, Scott Gibbs returned to the team. The next game would see the comeback of the man most missed by the nation in the barren winters that had followed the 1988 Triple Crown: Jonathan Davies.

1996 – Wales 19 Australia 28 (Cardiff Arms Park)

So far had Wales fallen, a 28-19 loss, in which the Dragons had led with 20 minutes to go, was almost seen as a moral victory. Jonathan Davies with his first cap for eight years couldn't quite steer Wales over the line. Gareth Thomas scored the longest try by a Welshman at Cardiff when he returned an interception over 90 metres.

UNBLEACHED WALES

In 1997 against the USA in Cardiff, Wales wore their first non-green change kit. The main colour was 'ecru' (which comes from French for raw or unbleached) with dark blue and red hoops. It was the start of a continuing fashion for change shirts that were designed to boost income.

FAREWELL TO ARMS

1997 – Wales 13 England 34 (Cardiff Arms Park)

Wales said goodbye to the grand old Cardiff Arms Park after 113 years by taking a beating from their biggest enemy. The stadium was to be demolished for the creation of the Millennium Stadium for the 1999 World Cup, which Wales were to host. It was a sad way to end it all. Jonathan Davies played his final game for Wales and Rob Howley grabbed the last international try at the ground.

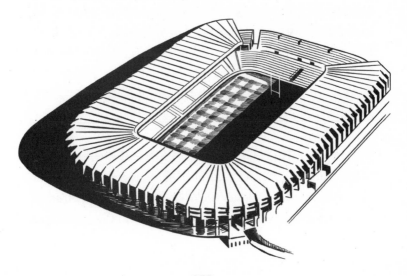

BLONDES HAVE ALL THE PENALTIES

For the 1997 tour to North America, Gareth Thomas, Leigh Davies, Arwel Thomas and Nathan Thomas had dyed their hair peroxide blonde. They were told to change it when, in the narrow win over Canada (28-25), they kept getting pinged for offside. The Welsh analysts believed they stuck out so much they caught the ref's attention and appeared offside when they weren't.

WANDERING WALES

With Cardiff Arms Park gone, Wales had to find new homes during their wait for a new stadium. Against Romania in 1997 they played in North Wales for the first time, winning 70-21 at the Racecourse Ground in Wrexham. It was the first home game away from Cardiff since 1954.

Next up, the Dragons returned to Swansea to beat Tonga 46-12. Swansea, being Swansea, it rained heavily. A mere 6,589 fans attended. Italy came to Stradey in 1998, the first Welsh game there since 1893 and the days of Arthur Gould! It was Ieuan Evans's last cap. For the big games London's Wembley Stadium was home for two seasons and Wales started their tenancy with another thrashing by the All Blacks (42-7).

TRAGIC END TO PROMISING CAREER

In December 1997, 25-year-old Welsh captain and world-class open side Gwyn Jones broke his neck playing for Cardiff. Initially it appeared he may be paralysed from the neck down.

Thankfully, Jones was able to learn to walk again and went on to build a successful medical and broadcasting career.

FROM DISGRACE TO HOPE
1998 – England 60 Wales 26 (Twickenham)
Allan Bateman scored two of Wales's four tries, one of which remains one of the greatest tries ever scored at Twickenham as he rounded off a move started near the Welsh line by a magnificent Gareth Thomas break. The problem was, England scored eight as the Dragons conceded the most points in Five Nations history. After the game, Neil Jenkins, whom Bowring had insisted on playing at full-back, said he would never play number 15 again. Speedy Nigel Walker suffered a career-ending injury after four minutes and captain Rob Howley declared it the worst week of his career.

1998 – Wales 0 France 51 (Wembley Stadium)
After recovering from the Twickenham massacre with wins against Scotland and Ireland, Wales outdid themselves with a shattering loss to Grand Slammers France. It was the biggest losing margin the tournament had ever seen. France's fly-half Thomas Castaignède toyed with Wales like a kitten does an injured mouse. It was the first time Wales had failed to score against France and every Welsh back-rower collected a yellow card. Wales wore black socks on a black day. Coach Kevin Bowring was soon gone.

1998 – A year of shame.

1998 – South Africa 96 Wales 13 (Loftus Versfeld, Pretoria)
If Bok hooker Naka Drotske had held a simple pass, Wales
would have conceded an unimaginable century of points. This
was the lowest point in the history of the national team and
was the conclusion to a six-match tour of Africa, in which
Wales lost five. Wales, missing several top players (some of
whom were accused of dodging the tour), were led by caretaker
coach Dennis John. The world champions jogged in 15 tries
and coach Nick Mallett blasted the quality of the visitors.

THE ORACLE OF WALES

After the Pretoria massacre, coach Dennis John was widely mocked for saying Wales would beat the Springboks within a year. It was an incredible prediction. And, incredibly, it was correct.

THE REDEEMER ARRIVES

In desperation, the WRU controversially turned to a non-Welshman to lead Wales. New Zealander Graham Henry was sensationally appointed as the highest paid coach in world rugby. His impact was immediate. Wales's next game after the 96-13 loss to the Boks was a rematch at Wembley. The 'home' side stormed into a 14-0 lead and led 20-17 with a few minutes left on the clock. Frustratingly, a streaker interrupted proceedings, Wales lost their concentration (that's what Henry said!) and the Boks stole a dramatic 28-20 win.

The game was a turning point. Henry demonstrated the potential of the players was huge, if only tribalism, petty politics and the toxic drinking culture could be cleaned up.

CULTURE SHOCK

Wales's flicker of hope against the Boks was followed by losses to Scotland and Ireland. Graham Henry admitted later he underestimated the impact of fans on the Five Nations and the cultural importance to players. He was utterly baffled to see thousands of Welsh fans invading Edinburgh on the eve of his first Championship match and asked fellow managers what was happening! He could scarcely believe 20,000-plus fans, most without tickets, would travel to an away game.

1999 – France 33 Wales 34 (Stade de France, Paris)

After two losses, with the two hardest games to come, Wales looked set for a whitewash as they travelled to a city they had not won in since 1975. France, hoping to stay on track for a third Grand Slam, had little to fear from a side they had beaten 51-0 the year before. What followed was one of the most spectacular Welsh displays of all time. Neil Jenkins kicked 19 points as Wales ran riot with a mixture of power up front and artistry with ball in hand. Tries from flanker Colin Charvis, winger Dafydd James and second row Craig Quinnell shook the world. Tears and beer flowed.

1999 – Wales 32 England 31 (Wembley)

England's coach Clive Woodward was asking officials where the team needed to head to claim the Six Nations trophy when, two minutes into injury time, Scott Gibbs blazed his way to immortality by beating one third of the English team to score. Jenkins kicked the extras to round off one of the most magnificent kicking displays in tournament history (scoring 22 on the day). It was perhaps Jenkins's finest game and included a sublime pass for Shane Howarth to score in the corner. The last-minute win cost England the title, the Grand Slam and the Triple Crown. Scotland won the last ever Five Nations instead before Italy joined the Championship in 2000.

"Guide us, O though great Redeemer."

HYPE AND EXPECTATIONS

Wales followed up their extraordinary results against France and England by becoming the first British side to win a series in Argentina, winning both internationals. Wales even rallied from 23-0 down in the first game, a then world record. What followed in the next match was to put Welsh fans and media into a state of hysteria, especially with a home World Cup just around the corner.

1999 – Wales 29 South Africa 19 (Millennium Stadium, Cardiff)

Less than a year after losing 96-13, as Dennis John predicted, Wales beat the Springboks after 93 years of trying. In a half-built stadium (Wales almost had to wear hard hats when they came out to warm up) with 27,000 privileged fans, Wales made history. Centre Mark Taylor scored the first try at the ground, Gareth Thomas scored another and Neil Jenkins, in the form of his life, kicked 19 points. With Wales beating Canada, France and the USA (uncapped) ahead of the World Cup, expectations were sky high.

1999 WORLD CUP (WALES)

With the paint still fresh on the Millennium Stadium, Wales hosted the World Cup with a nation feverishly dreaming of glory. Although Wales were the official hosts, the Home Unions and France held some games too (which is why those nations voted for Wales to host it). With Wales having suffered so many years of rugby humiliation and pain, it was perhaps inevitable that fans got so carried away going into the tournament. As it always eventually does, reality made an entrance and an under-firing Wales exited at the quarters. At least it was better than the pool stage exits of 1991 and 1995.

Captain: Rob Howley
Coach: Graham Henry

POOL GAMES

(all games at the Millennium Stadium)

Wales 23 Argentina 18

Following singing from Shirley Bassey, Bryn Terfel and Max

Boyce, a nervy Wales did just enough to beat the Pumas. Management felt the opening ceremony activities that took place as Wales warmed up overwhelmed the players emotionally. Scott Quinnell and brother Craig were in tears during the warm-up and Scott Gibbs, seeing them, turned back around to the dressing room before he too got started sobbing.

Wales 64 Japan 15
Wales 31 Samoa 38
Once again, the Samoans spoiled a home World Cup party for Wales. Wales conceded five tries and scored only three (two from scrum penalty tries). Scott Quinnell said he had never been so battered and bruised in his career. It also ruined Wales's chance of equalling their own record of 11 consecutive wins from 1907 to 1910. Luckily for the home side, they still made the quarter-finals. It was Samoa's third consecutive win over Wales and they led the series 3-2. One positive was Neil Jenkins became the all-time record Test scorer, beating Michael Lynagh's tally of 911.

QUARTER-FINAL

Wales 9 Australia 24
The eventual tournament winners shut Wales down completely on a rain-soaked day. While two Australian tries should have been disallowed, the Wallabies were by far the best side in the tournament and the defeat effectively ended what had been another false dawn in Welsh rugby. Consistent with Welsh rugby history, a high was to be followed by a series of crashing lows.

*Neil Jenkins kicked his way to the top of
the world during the 1999 World Cup.*

NEW MILLENNIUM, SAME SCRIPT

Wales's 2000 Six Nations campaign brought wins against
Ireland, Scotland and Italy, but regression to 1998 level
humiliations to France (losing 36-3) and England (46-
12). Similarly, 2001 brought fresh, if familiar, horrors, with
England winning 44-15 in Cardiff. The shame didn't stop
several players going on the beer! The Henry era was becoming
equal parts hope and horror.

2001 – France 35 Wales 43 (Stade de France)

Once again the poetry of Paris inspired Wales, who threw the form book out of the window and ran riot with four tries, Rob Howley scoring the most spectacular. Taking the ball on the edge of his own 22 after a number eight pick-up from Quinnell, he went 75 metres and turned French full-back Jean-Luc Sadourny inside out on his way to the line. Neil Jenkins scored an astonishing 28 points, getting a 'full house' with a try, four conversions, three penalties and two drop goals. The total meant he surpassed 1,000 points for Wales.

LIONS KILL OFF A DRAGON AND MAKE A KIWI

Coach Graham Henry made the fatal mistake of agreeing to coach the Lions team to Australia while still Welsh coach. The losing tour damaged his relationship with several Welsh players who smarted at his preference to pick others over them after he had been telling them they were the best when he was Welsh coach. In addition, Wales continued to suffer nasty losses, the worst of them being a dreadful 36-6 loss in Cardiff to Ireland and a stuffing at home to Argentina 30-16. The latter saw Graham Henry go along with the WRU's demand he pick Iestyn Harris at fly-half to boost ticket interest. Harris was a convert from rugby league and was thrust into the shirt after just 200 minutes of rugby union. It badly backfired. Henry began facing criticism from within for his large pay packet and for the lack of fitness of star players like Scott Quinnell.

The final straw was a scarcely believable 54-10 loss in Dublin in 2002. Henry resigned and would soon become the All Blacks' coach. His replacement was Steve Hansen, another Kiwi who had earlier joined Henry's Welsh management.

GRANNYGATE

Another nail in the coffin of Henry's reign was the Grannygate scandal. With Wales's small playing pool, Henry wished to search the world for more talent with Welsh family connections. Two of the key players he uncovered were former All Black and full-back Shane Howarth, who qualified via a Cardiff-born grandfather, and Brett Sinkinson, who also claimed to have a Welsh grandfather. Howarth had won 19 caps and Sinkinson 14 before it was found that neither player could actually really prove their Welsh ancestry. It was a global scandal and ended Howarth's Welsh career (although it seems in his case his family had really believed his grandfather was Welsh). Sinkinson eventually qualified on residency.

FIERY ONE-CAP WONDER

Lock James Griffiths of Swansea came on as a replacement to make his debut for Wales in a 50-6 win over Samoa in 2000. Twenty-one seconds after entering the field he was leaving it with a yellow card for a shoulder charge. He never won another cap.

FOUNDATIONS AND FAILURE

Steve Hansen's era bitterly divided players and public. The new coach maintained that the culture, skill level and fitness were so far off where they needed to be that the entire national set-up would have to be rebuilt, no matter what the results on the pitch. Several key players such as Martyn Williams and

Gareth Thomas backed the Kiwi's methods, but an early defeat to England (50-10 in 2002) did him no favours.

THE IRAQ DICTATOR AND THE WELSH CAPTAIN

In 2003 Wales lost to Italy for the first time, falling 30-22 in Rome. Near the end of the national catastrophe, television cameras caught Wales's Colin Charvis, who had been subbed, grinning. There was outrage. A national newspaper poll had him placed as the second most hated man in Wales after terrorist Osama bin Laden. Even Iraqi dictator Saddam Hussein picked up fewer votes.

TEN OUT OF TEN

Approaching the 2003 World Cup, Wales suffered their worst run of results in history. Wales lost consecutive games to New Zealand (43-17), Italy (30-22), England (26-9), Scotland (30-22), Ireland (25-24), France (33-5), Australia (30-10), New Zealand (55-3), Ireland (35-12) and England (43-9). The tenth loss of that series was to a second-string England in a World Cup warm-up. Only a win against a weakened Romania and a summer Scotland team ended the rut and saved Hansen being fired right before the World Cup.

CIVIL WAR AND COSTLY COMPROMISE

Against the backdrop of international humiliation, Wales domestically were doing what they do best: fighting among themselves. The club game in Wales was suffering financially with not enough money to go around and too much of what there was being spent on players and teams that were too far off the level needed. After years of debate and bitterness, five 'regional' teams (or stand-alones in the case of Cardiff and Llanelli) were created. The teams to play in top-flight cross-border competitions were the Llanelli Scarlets, Neath-Swansea Ospreys, Celtic Warriors, Cardiff Blues and Gwent Dragons. The Celtic Warriors had barely got out of the starting gate when the money ran out and they folded. The concept continues to divide the rugby community.

2003 WORLD CUP (AUSTRALIA)

With Wales coming in off a series of poor results, expectations for this tournament were less than low. The spark that followed was as mesmerising as it was mysterious. To this day, debate rages about how much it was the product of wise coaching and to what extent a fluke of circumstances.

Captain: Colin Charvis
Coach: Steve Hansen

POOL GAMES

Wales 41 Canada 10 (Telstra Dome, Melbourne)

Wales, wearing white, won with a waltz. Bizarrely, squad captain Charvis did not represent a club at this point as he was without a contract and seeking a team. Former Welsh captain Paul Thorburn blasted Steve Hansen as 'pig-headed' as the criticism continued.

Wales 27 Tonga 20 (Canberra Stadium, Canberra)
Substitute flanker Martyn Williams only played 20 minutes, but hit a drop goal and grabbed a try in a poor team display.

Wales 27 Italy 15 (Canberra Stadium)
Twelve points from Iestyn Harris and tries from Dafydd Jones, Mark Jones and Sonny Parker booked Wales's place in the quarters. Italy were ludicrously playing their fourth game in 14 days.

Wales 37 New Zealand 53 (Telstra Stadium, Sydney)
With Wales qualified for the quarters and having not beaten the All Blacks since 1953, Hansen changed ten players for this match – effectively admitting defeat. The Kiwis scored a try in the second minute and all seemed set for the usual massacre as New Zealand burst into a 28-10 lead. Yet when Shane Williams, who wasn't first choice or much of a favourite of Hansen, scored in the 45th minute, Wales led 34 to 28! It was one of the all-time classic World Cup games, and the other Welsh tries came from Colin Charvis, Sonny Parker and Mark Taylor. The killer blow came with 11 minutes left when at 38-37, Justin Marshall threw a magnificent forward pass to put Doug

Shane Williams, stepping into Welsh rugby history.

271

Howlett over and Wales had the stuffing knocked out of them. Unlike they would in the 2007 World Cup, the All Blacks made no fuss about the forward pass. Wales may have lost, but the fans were happy to see some of the best rugby in years.

QUARTER-FINAL
Wales 17 England 28 (Suncorp Stadium, Brisbane)
Wales outscored eventual cup winners England by three to one on the try front and gave Goliath a huge scare. However, poor kicking, a lack of confidence in winning positions and a fantastic substitute appearance from Mike Catt broke Welsh hearts. Wales again played some spectacular stuff and Stephen Jones scored one of the greatest Welsh tries after rounding off a stunning counter-attack that was started deep in the Welsh half by twinkle-toed Shane Williams. Wales were out, but there was hope again.

BACK TO EARTH
Steve Hansen in his final Championship could only lead Wales to wins against Scotland and Italy, as Wales were soundly beaten by the other nations. Mike Ruddock was named as the new Welsh coach ahead of a bizarre (and largely unsuccessful) tour to Argentina and South Africa.

2004 – Wales 25 New Zealand 26 (Millennium Stadium)
For the first time since the 1970s, Wales took New Zealand to the wire. But in a mix-up with less than four minutes left and Wales getting a penalty in the Kiwis' 22, Gareth Thomas asked Gavin Henson to go for goal. However, the coaches, knowing time was almost up, had tried to get instructions on to the

field to go for a try. Thomas thought the stadium clock (as it had been in a recent game) was correct and that more time remained. He was mistaken and his team missed their chance at immortality.

Wales 98 Japan 0 (Millennium Stadium)
Wales scored 14 tries and Gavin Henson converted every one! Colin Charvis became the first Welsh forward to score four tries in a game.

1995–2004: THE STAR PLAYERS

ROB HOWLEY
Clubs: Bridgend, Cardiff, Wasps
Position: Scrum-half
Caps: 59 (1996–2002)
(British & Irish Lions, 2 caps)
Points: 50 (10 tries)

Rob Howley sits among the pantheon of legendary Welsh scrum-halves. At times, along with Scott Quinnell, he was considered one of Wales's only true danger men and despite the extra attention from defenders, still created havoc and produced spectacular solo tries. Incredibly fit and blessed with rapid speed, Howley was captain during Wales's ten-match winning streak in 1999. He went on to be Welsh attack coach (and often caretaker coach) under Warren Gatland.

GARETH THOMAS

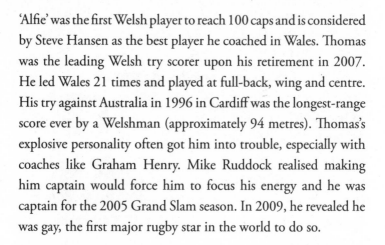

Clubs: Bridgend, Cardiff,
Toulouse, Celtic Warriors
Position: Wing, full-back, centre
Caps: 100 (1995–2007)
(British & Irish Lions, 3 caps, 5 points)
Points: 200 (40 tries)

'Alfie' was the first Welsh player to reach 100 caps and is considered by Steve Hansen as the best player he coached in Wales. Thomas was the leading Welsh try scorer upon his retirement in 2007. He led Wales 21 times and played at full-back, wing and centre. His try against Australia in 1996 in Cardiff was the longest-range score ever by a Welshman (approximately 94 metres). Thomas's explosive personality often got him into trouble, especially with coaches like Graham Henry. Mike Ruddock realised making him captain would force him to focus his energy and he was captain for the 2005 Grand Slam season. In 2009, he revealed he was gay, the first major rugby star in the world to do so.

NEIL JENKINS

Clubs: Pontypridd, Cardiff
Position: Fly-half, full-back, centre
Caps: 87 (1991–2002)
(British & Irish Lions, 4 caps, 41 points)
Points: 1,049 (11 tries, 130 conversions, 10 drop goals)
For a man who won so many caps and smashed record books,

Wales's 'Ginger Monster' was massively underappreciated for most of his career. Lacking the jinking flair Welsh fans expect from their outside-halves, Jenkins was repeatedly dropped, shuffled to centre and full-back, and generally maligned and misunderstood, despite his kicking often being the only thing to keep Wales competitive.

Graham Henry, considered one of the greatest coaches of all time, saw how critical he was and built his Welsh team around him. Jenkins responded with his best run in a Welsh shirt. He made his debut aged 19 for Wales and was unfortunate to mainly play his career behind a mediocre, even toothless, pack. In 1997 he kicked the Lions to glory in South Africa. On retirement he was the highest scorer in Test history and had also scored 5,557 club points.

COLIN CHARVIS

Clubs: Swansea, Tarbes, Newcastle, Newport Gwent Dragons
Position: Back row
Caps: 94 (1996–2007)
(British & Irish Lions, 2 caps)
Points: 110 (22 tries)

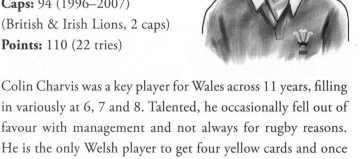

Colin Charvis was a key player for Wales across 11 years, filling in variously at 6, 7 and 8. Talented, he occasionally fell out of favour with management and not always for rugby reasons. He is the only Welsh player to get four yellow cards and once got two in consecutive games against the Pumas. Charvis also collected tries. His 22 tries are a record for a Welsh forward at Test level. He once nabbed four in a game against Japan (a record for an international forward). He became the first Welsh player to be capped playing from France when he was playing with Tarbes.

SCOTT GIBBS

Clubs: Swansea, Neath
Position: Centre
Caps: 53 (1991–2001)
(British & Irish Lions, 5 caps, 5 points)
Points: 50 (10 tries)

Scott Gibbs made his debut aged just 19. Nicknamed 'Car Crash' for the force with which he would tackle attackers or smash defenders, Gibbs was an intensely physical and competitive player. He had no interest in the fame and attractions around rugby, often disappearing after matches rather than going drinking. In the amateur days he was so far ahead of his fellow national players physically, that coach Ron Waldron once made him strip off and stand on a chair to show them what they should look like. Gibbs's most famous moments came in his bone-shattering 'Player of the Series' performances for the 1997 Lions in South Africa and his dazzling winning try against England in 1999. He would have won more caps but spent two seasons in rugby league.

1995–2004 NOTABLE EVENTS IN WELSH HISTORY

- 1996: An oil tanker runs aground on the south-west coast of Wales, causing one of the worst oil spills the world has seen.

- 1997: Wales narrowly votes for devolution.

- 1999: The National Assembly for Wales holds its first session.

- 2001: The FA Cup Final is held in Cardiff due to the redevelopment of Wembley.

- 2004: The Wales Millennium Centre opens in Cardiff.

2005–21: A THIRD GOLDEN ERA?

	PLAYED	WON	DRAWN	LOST
SIX NATIONS	85	54	2	29
NON-CHAMPIONSHIP TESTS	84	35	3	46
WORLD CUP	23	14	0	9
WORLD CUP WARM-UP GAMES*	14	6	0	8
AUTUMN NATIONS CUP	4	2	0	2
TOTAL	210	111	5	94

*Listed separately due to their experimental nature and mass substitutions. Full caps were awarded, however, and they are considered full internationals.

Championships

2005 (Grand Slam), 2008 (Grand Slam),

2012 (Grand Slam), 2013, 2019 (Grand Slam), 2021 (Triple Crown)

World Cups

Pool stage (2007), Quarter-finals (2015), Semi-finals (2011, 2019)

'Welsh supporters are like a shower which is either too hot or too cold. You either have to get the players down from the clouds or pick them up from the floor. There is no perspective.'

GRAHAM HENRY

THE REVIVAL

After 27 years of famine, Wales were finally able to taste Grand Slam glory again. In typical Welsh style, success was followed swiftly by collapse, and then success again. Under another Kiwi, Warren Gatland, Wales would claim another three Grand Slams (equalling the achievements of the First and Second Golden Eras) as well as reach two World Cup semi-finals. For many, this was another Golden Era.

As a nation, Wales underwent significant political change in the 2010s. In 2011, 21 of the 22 Welsh counties voted 'Yes' in a referendum to increase direct law-making powers for the Welsh Assembly. This enhanced Wales's ability to make decisions in areas such as health and education. More political change followed in 2016, when 52.5% of voters in Wales voted to leave the European Union, helping to take the UK 'out' of Europe. The Brexit vote bitterly divided the country and surprised many as Wales was one of the biggest beneficiaries of EU funding.

A YEAR FOR ROMANTICS

Fresh from the near miss against New Zealand, Mike Ruddock's Wales entered the Six Nations with fans hoping for something to cheer. Despite the bookies having Wales at 40/1 to do it, the Dragons ended 27 years of pain to claim a ninth Grand Slam.

2005 GRAND SLAM

MATCH ONE: Wales 11 England 9 (Millennium Stadium)

Wales's last victories against England had been in 1999, 1993 and 1989. Only captain Gareth Thomas had tasted success against the reigning world champions. Shane Williams squeezed in the left corner after a beautiful pass from number eight Michael Owen for the key try. But the day belonged to Gavin Henson. A virtuoso display included two humiliating tackles on poor 18-year-old debutant Mathew Tait and the winning penalty, kicked in his silver boots from 43.9 metres out with four minutes left on the clock. It was his first kick of the game and, legend has it, as he ran over to collect the ball for his kick he told his captain, 'Tell the boys to start celebrating!'

After the English win, the precious match jerseys of Stephen Jones and Tom Shanklin went missing. A public appeal was made by Gareth Thomas to return the shirts and, perhaps feeling guilty, the crook returned the shirts in the post!

MATCH TWO: Italy 8 Wales 38 (Stadio Flaminio, Rome)

MATCH THREE: France 18 Wales 24 (Stade de France)

France led 15-6 at the interval, but should have been ahead by more. Only committed defence by the visitors, especially Gareth Thomas (who departed at half-time with a broken thumb), kept Wales in it. Just five minutes after the second half started, Wales had two tries through Martyn Williams, both the result of some fantastic open running rugby. Suddenly, Wales sensed glory. A dramatic end saw them cling on for dear life on their own line for several minutes as the final seconds ticked away. The Slam was on.

MATCH FOUR: Scotland 22 Wales 46 (Murrayfield)

Skippered by Michael Owen, fluid, fast and beautiful Wales stormed into a 38-3 lead by the break, before easing off in the second 40 minutes. With so much misery since 1980, young Welsh fans thought they were living in some alternate reality.

Ronan O'Gara's bizarre offside claims were ignored and Gethin Jenkins helped Wales towards fortune and glory.

MATCH FIVE: Wales 32 Ireland 20 (Millennium Stadium)

On a glorious spring day in Cardiff, tens of thousands of fans streamed into Cardiff just to watch the match on a giant screen OUTSIDE the ground! Some reports claimed over 250,000 people came into the city for the game. Prop Gethin Jenkins scored one of the all-time classic tries, charging down a kick from Irish fly-half Ronan O'Gara 40 metres out, then following up by showing his football skills and falling on his own hack ahead to score. Wales never looked back. To tears and cheers, full-back Kevin Morgan finished off a superb break from Tom Shanklin to put the seal on one of the most iconic games in Welsh history.

FORTUNE AND GLORY

The players of the eight Welsh teams who had won the Grand Slam before 2005 didn't earn a penny, and most struggled to get even basic expenses out of the tight-fisted WRU. Those who played all five games in this Grand Slam, Wales's first of the professional era, earned £30,000.

HITTING THE SELF-DESTRUCT BUTTON

The autumn that followed the glorious Grand Slam was largely glum. A New Zealand team led by the previous two Welsh coaches, Graham Henry and Steve Hansen, put Wales to the sword 41-3. Next Wales struggled to an 11-10 win over Fiji and then fell to the Springboks 33-16. The only positive was when a black-clad Wales pipped Australia 24-22. It was the first win against Australia since 1987. The results led some critics to claim the Grand Slam had been built on foundations of sand.

Rumours began to circulate of player discontent, coaches being undermined and conflict behind the scenes. Wales opened the 2006 Championship with a humiliating 47-13 thrashing in London and just 48 hours after beating a 14-man Scotland, Mike Ruddock was gone. Not even a year after the wonders of the

Grand Slam and Wales were again a shambles. Under Australian caretaker coach Scott Johnson, Wales were smashed in Dublin, limped to a draw with Italy and lost to France.

A TELEVISION NASTY

The rumours, accusations and drama around Ruddock's departure were so great that captain Gareth Thomas appeared on TV to shout his side of the story. In an excruciating bit of television, Thomas battled with the far calmer former captain Eddie Butler. The appearance did little to quell rumours of player power and after returning home the stressed Thomas suffered a mini stroke. Butler claims that for doing his job he was fired from the *Scrum V* show by former Welsh wing Nigel Walker.

REVIVAL OF THE SPIRIT OF THE '90s

Wales appointed Gareth Jenkins as coach after the 2006 Six Nations. A former Llanelli and Wales B flanker, he had coached some fantastic Llanelli sides over the years, but probably came to the Welsh job too late. Sandwiched between the 2005 and 2008 Grand Slams, Wales were more like the embarrassment of a side that had disgraced the 1990s than the force they should have been.

HISSY FIT

In 2005, to mark the centenary of Tests between the sides, Wales had the All Blacks repeat the format of that first ever game when the haka was performed before the Welsh anthem. The WRU had even consulted a Maori chief about this request, who agreed the haka was performed to invite a response and was therefore a suitable request. But when asked again for the 2006 match, the NZRFU said they would do their haka in private in the changing room. Which they did, kind of. They still allowed the TV cameras in. Captain Richie McCaw said that the haka 'is about spiritual preparations and we do it for ourselves'. Some considered this a bit rich seeing as the NZRFU use it to sell German sporting goods and jewellery in commercials.

THE FALL CONTINUES

After giving debuts to the likes of Alun Wyn Jones, James Hook and Ian Evans in a two-match losing series in Argentina, Jenkins's Wales returned to Cardiff in November for a draw with Australia, a dull win over the Pacific Islands (combo of Fiji, Tonga and Samoa) and a thrashing of Canada. But in the real test against New Zealand, Wales were again taken apart 45-10. The Dragons then went on to lose to everyone in the 2007 Six Nations apart from England on the final day in Cardiff. Player power again raised its head with claims that senior players were dictating training or quarrelling whenever they were asked to do tough contact sessions.

A DIFFERENT KIND OF NIGHTMARE IN OZ

Wales lost a two-match series in Australia in the summer of 2007. Wales led the first Test by 17-0, and were even winning with less than a minute left. The side looked so unsure of themselves in holding the lead, they panicked. Scrum-half Gareth Cooper needlessly kicked away solid possession in good field position to allow the Wallabies one last chance at winning the game. They took it and won 29-23 with a long-range try. The following week Wales threw in the towel and lost 31-0. Players as well as management were accused of drinking heavily on the tour as Wales confirmed their reputation as poor tourists.

AN INTERVIEW AS BAD AS THE RESULT
2007 – England 65 Wales 5 (Twickenham)
England picked a huge pack for this World Cup warm-up. Everyone knew they planned to take on Wales up front. Everyone, that is, apart from Gareth Jenkins who said after, 'We didn't expect the game plan England initiated.' Despite conceding nine tries, Jenkins (with a straight face) said, 'Defensively we targeted areas that we actually achieved – we said we had to make 90% tackle completions and we did.'

YOUNGEST TEST 50
Classy scrum-half Dwayne Peel reached 50 caps for Wales aged just 25 and within six years. Gareth Edwards's 53 consecutive caps had taken him 11 years.

2007 WORLD CUP (FRANCE)
If you want to start a debate in a Welsh rugby club that will

go on all night, ask people to decide which Welsh World Cup was the worst: 1991, 1995 or 2007. Once again, Wales were involved in one of the tournament's most exciting and dramatic tussles. Once again, Wales lost. Completing a South Seas hat-trick that started with Samoa in 1991 and 1999, Wales suffered a brainless loss to an inspired Fijian team.

With a player pool not vastly different to the one available for the 2005 and 2008 Grand Slams, Wales were dreadful. Having home advantage for the key pool match with Australia (a thank you for voting for France to host the World Cup) counted for nothing. Even during a World Cup, many Welsh players could not stay off the beer. The squad and management duly paid for it with yet another exit before the knockout stages.

Captain: Gareth Thomas
Coach: Gareth Jenkins

POOL GAMES
Wales 42 Canada 17 (Stade de la Beaujoire, Nantes)
Wales 20 Australia 32 (Millennium Stadium)
For the third time, Wales lost at home in a World Cup to Australia. Tactically poor, the scoreline flattered Wales.

Wales 72 Japan 18 (Millennium Stadium)
Wales 34 Fiji 38 (Stade de la Beaujoire)
Part of Wales's preparation for this game included a day drinking at a racecourse. Like Apollo Creed in *Rocky II*, Wales idiotically got involved in a style of fight they could not win. Despite the 1st XV being apparently unable to defend

Another World Cup humiliation.

remotely well in training against the rest of their own squad, the Dragons played a loose game that allowed Fiji to play to their deadly strengths. Two of Wales's five tries came when their opponents were down a man. Fiji fully deserved this famous win and Shane Williams's showboating dive for his try (his team were 15 points down at the time) looked even sillier after the game. Once again Wales were involved in a classic match for all the wrong reasons. Gareth Thomas won his 100th and final cap and scored his 40th try. Gareth Jenkins was sacked the next morning in a car park.

I MUST BREAK YOU

Wales turned again to the Land of the Long White Cloud when looking to put the national team back together and chose Warren Gatland. His coaching pedigree included Ireland, Connacht and Wasps. As his defence coach, he appointed ex-league legend Shaun Edwards. The two were to reshape the mentality and standards of the national side and take Wales from a punching bag to feared punchers. After taking over, Gatland told the press: 'I'm going to tell the players that now there's time to train I'm going to try and break a couple of them.'

RETURN OF THE DRAGON

After ending a wait of 27 years for a Grand Slam in 2005, Wales grabbed another three years later, with essentially the same bunch of players that had been humiliated at the World Cup a few months before. It was to begin what is arguably another Golden Era. However, much like the second one, it was to bring relatively little success against the might of the All Blacks, Wallabies and Springboks.

IF YOU HAVEN'T BUST YOUR LEG AND YOU AREN'T KNOCKED OUT, GET IN THE DEFENSIVE LINE!

Shaun Edwards's advice to injured players was blunt.

2008 – GRAND SLAM

MATCH ONE: England 19 Wales 26 (Twickenham)

There was bemusement and amusement when Gatland announced 13 Ospreys in a Welsh team trying to win at Twickenham for the first time since 1988. Only Mark Jones (Scarlets) and Martyn Williams (Cardiff) broke up the Ospreys' dominance. The figure surpassed the 1948 Welsh team that had ten Cardiff players at the same venue.

With just over 20 minutes remaining, England led 19-6. Inspired by captain Ryan Jones and the boot of James Hook, Wales edged back to 19-12. Then the visitors hit the home side with a one-two sucker punch. Hook deftly tied up three defenders to put Lee Byrne in at the corner. Just a few minutes later scrum-half Mike Phillips charged down a kick and, after a clever pick-up from Gethin Jenkins and quick passing from Martyn Williams (brought out of his post-World Cup retirement), Phillips finished off in the corner. Wales had broken their latest Twickenham hoodoo.

THERE'S NO PLACE LIKE . . .
THE AWAY DRESSING ROOM

One of the first things Gatland did as coach was swap Wales's dressing room at the Millennium Stadium with the smaller 'away' one. Some thought this was because the home dressing room was considered unlucky by rugby and football teams who had a poor record using it. At one point, a doctor of feng shui was called in to try and bring some luck! But Gatland simply thought the home dressing room was impractical as he couldn't see all the players at once.

MATCH TWO: Wales 30 Scotland 15 (Millennium Stadium)
Jamie Roberts made his debut on the wing as Wales comfortably beat Scotland. Shane Williams, in the form of his life, grabbed two tries and Hook another. As a sign of how ruthless Gatland was, Hook's 31 points in two games was not enough to see him retain his place and he was on the bench for the next game.

MATCH THREE: Wales 47 Italy 8 (Millennium Stadium)
A Welsh line-out mix-up gave Italy a soft try. It was the second of the Championship that Edwards's defence had given up and, astonishingly, was the last one too.

MATCH FOUR: Ireland 12 Wales 16 (Croke Park, Dublin)
Shane Williams scored a beauty, dancing over in minimal space as a superb defensive effort kept the Irish frustrated. It was Wales's first appearance at the sacred Croke Park ground while Lansdowne Road was being rebuilt to increase capacity by a few thousand.

MATCH FIVE: Wales 29 France 12 (Millennium Stadium)
Shane Williams made the most of his almost supernatural reaction skills to punish the French for a loose ball and hacked his way over cleverly to score his 41st try and become the all-time leading try scorer for his country. Martyn Williams signed off the Grand Slam in style with a late try. Wales had risen from the ashes and Gatland now had to live up to the excessive optimism he had created in Welsh fans.

SOUTHERN STRUGGLES

When the All Blacks rocked up to Cardiff for the 2008 autumn games, Wales had lost three games to South Africa (two away, one home). These results, and the All Blacks one about to come, were to be a continuing theme of Gatland's Wales team. Wales regularly beat the likes of Ireland, England and Scotland, yet for a long time all these sides picked up far better results than Wales against the big three from the southern hemisphere.

WALES OFFEND KIWIS BY LOOKING AT THEM

2008 – Wales 9 New Zealand 29 (Millennium Stadium)

Another haka, another controversy. After the All Blacks performed their challenge, Wales stood their ground staring intensely back, waiting for New Zealand to leave their place and prepare for kick-off. Wales would not budge first. It led to an intense 83-second stand-off, with the crowd's roar adding a thrilling soundtrack. Bizarrely, after the game, All Black Ma'a Nonu said: 'What the Welsh did wound us up . . . The Haka is a war dance. If you're going to stand there like that then in the past people would have charged, but it's a rugby match and you can't do that. People back home will have been hurt . . . standing in the way like they did is asking for a fight.' Irony, it seems, is a concept lost on Nonu. Wales led 9-6 at the break, but faded as their old foe eventually came up convincing winners.

2008 – Wales 21 Australia 18 (Millennium Stadium)

This was to be Wales's last win over Australia for 14 games

(until 2018) and their final win over a big three southern hemisphere team until victory over the Boks in 2014. Jamie Roberts played on for 15 minutes with a fractured skull after crashing into and injuring Stirling Mortlock.

2009 – Wales Women 16 England Women 15 (Taff's Well)
After 22 years of trying, including some painfully one-sided results, Wales Women defeated England. It couldn't have been any more dramatic, taking an injury-time penalty kick from full-back Non Evans to finally end the Dragons' curse against the Red Roses.

WORLD CHAMPIONS

Wales shocked the rugby world by winning the 2009 Rugby World Cup Sevens in Dubai. Impressively, it came just a few years after the WRU had disbanded the sevens squad. To this day, it is the only major tournament Wales have ever won in the shortened game.

THE GOLF BUGGY INCIDENT

After a dramatic 2010 comeback win over Scotland (Wales won 31-24 after trailing 24-14 in the 77th minute), Welsh number eight Andy Powell made world headlines by stealing a golf buggy in the early hours of the next morning while drunk and driving it down the motorway to get some cigarettes! He was arrested and the Welsh management clamped down hard on what players could do afterwards when celebrating home wins. Jamie Roberts later said he believed the incident helped make the team more professional and played a part in later success.

YOUNG GUN

When Tom Prydie (Ospreys) made his debut against Italy in 2010, he became the youngest player ever to play for Wales. He was aged just 18 years and 25 days. The previous holder of that record was Norman Biggs back in 1888.

BACK TO MEDIOCRITY

In the run-up to the 2011 World Cup, Wales went through a rocky period. The 2010 summer Tests saw defeat at home to South Africa and two losses (one very big) in New Zealand. Next came a terrible autumn series in which Wales lost to Australia (25-16), South Africa (29-25) and New Zealand (37-25). There was also a poor 16-16 draw with Fiji. When England beat Wales 26-19 in Cardiff to begin the 2011 Six Nations, Wales had lost seven and drawn one from their last eight. One positive had been an outstanding debut from 18-year-old wing George North, who scored twice against South Africa – the youngest ever to score two tries in his first Test and the first player to do so on debut against the Boks.

2011 WORLD CUP (NEW ZEALAND)

But for three kickers having an off day on the same day, Wales should have made their first final. 2011 will always conjure up nightmares for Welsh fans due to the collective emotional trauma of captain Sam Warburton's semi-final red card. Gatland's Wales sneaked into the tournament under the radar with no one expecting much and ended up having to regret missing a chance to beat a nervous Kiwi side in the final (who managed to scrape home in controversial circumstances to win their first title since 1987). Warburton, who made his debut for Wales in 2009, became the youngest ever World Cup captain in this tournament. He was just 22 years old.

Captain: Sam Warburton
Coach: Warren Gatland

POOL GAMES

Wales 16 South Africa 17 (Westpac Stadium, Wellington)

When Wales conceded a try to Frans Steyn in just the third minute, the rugby-watching world thought: 'Here we go again.' Led by a stunning 20-tackle performance by Sam Warburton (whom the Boks praised as a 'pain'), Wales took it to the wire. The Welshmen led 16-10 after 65 minutes, but the Boks pulled back a try to sneak a win. Suddenly, Wales looked a real handful.

Wales 17 Samoa 10 (Waikato Stadium, Hamilton)

At the third attempt, Wales beat Samoa in a World Cup. They were somewhat fortunate to meet a Samoa team with an unforgiving fixture schedule, but a Shane Williams try and the boots of James Hook and Rhys Priestland took them through. Priestland at fly-half was an unexpected star of the tournament for Wales, only getting his chance at the number ten shirt due to a late warm-up injury to Stephen Jones in a World Cup preparation match.

Wales 81 Namibia 7 (Yarrow Stadium, New Plymouth)
Wales 66 Fiji 0 (Waikato Stadium)
Wales somewhat avenged their 2007 World Cup loss.

QUARTER-FINAL
Wales 22 Ireland 10 (Westpac Stadium)
A supremely confident Ireland were blown away as Shane Williams scored from the kick-off. Mike Phillips and centre Jonathan Davies scored the other tries. The Welsh defence was a thing of beauty, with flanker Dan Lydiate at the forefront of a chop-tackle blitz that cut down the fancied Irish carriers before they could get going. Ahead of the game, Liam Toland wrote in the *Irish Times* that 'Ireland will win . . . In Priestland, Wales have a grey man. He is neither one thing nor the other and he will cost Wales the match tomorrow . . . muscle has a memory and so too this Irish team. Warburton does not know what he's facing . . .'

SEMI-FINAL
Wales 8 France 9 (Eden Park, Auckland)
Any Welsh fan who watched this match will take it to their grave. Twenty minutes in and skipper Sam Warburton was red-carded for a tip tackle. Technically correct the decision

may have been, but it shocked the world as far worse tackles had occurred in the tournament and not even been yellows. It was the start of a new drive by the IRB to make the tackle area safer and such decisions were much rarer in 2011. Despite the shock card (the commentators initially missed it and even Wales's centre Jonathan Davies didn't realise for several minutes), Wales still should have won. Kicks, some relatively simple, were missed by James Hook, Stephen Jones and Leigh Halfpenny. Wales had enough ball and chances, even though lacking a man, but fell agonisingly short.

The tipping point in Wales's World Cup.

THIRD PLACE PLAY-OFF
Wales 18 Australia 21 (Eden Park)

A PACKED HOUSE . . . 12,000 MILES AWAY
Wales's semi-final brought 61,345 fans to the Millennium Stadium at 9 a.m. on a Saturday to watch the game on a giant screen.

TWO YEARS OF CHAMPIONSHIP GLORY
Wales built on their World Cup run by sweeping all before them in the 2012 Six Nations, claiming their second Gatland Grand Slam. It was to be followed by a Championship win the following year too under caretaker coach Rob Howley (Gatland was on sabbatical with the Lions). The success only further underlined what a tragic waste 2006 and 2007 had been. It wasn't all glory though, because in between Six Nations success came a sorry lot of summer and autumn rugby.

2012 GRAND SLAM
MATCH ONE: Ireland 21 Wales 23 (Aviva Stadium, Dublin)
The chaos around tip tackle officiating continued, with Wales the main beneficiaries this time in their first game in Ireland's new stadium. Jonathan Davies grabbed two tries, but the visitors trailed 16-15 when second-row Bradley Davies was

only yellow-carded for upending and dropping a player OFF the ball in the 64th minute. Ireland soon added a try. At 75 minutes Wales were back at full strength and George North powered over with three minutes to go but the conversion was wide and they trailed by one. Then it was Ireland's turn to get a yellow for a tip tackle, this time Stephen Ferris on Ian Evans (who later embarrassingly admitted to milking it). Leigh Halfpenny kicked the winner with 13 seconds left.

MATCH TWO: Wales 27 Scotland 13 (Millennium Stadium)
MATCH THREE: England 12 Wales 19 (Twickenham)

Wales claimed their first Triple Crown at HQ thanks to a late try from replacement centre Scott Williams. He stripped English giant Courtney Lawes on halfway, kicked ahead, gathered five metres from the English line and scored. In the final play of the game, England almost went over in the corner, but a reckless (legal) tackle from Leigh Halfpenny and an excellent wrap tackle from Jonathan Davies held David Strettle up. After a tense TMO review, Wales could celebrate. Halfpenny suffered a head injury for his trouble. Wales celebrated by nipping to the Twickenham car park to get into a van which had been converted into a mobile cryotherapy chamber!

MATCH FOUR: Wales 24 Italy 3 (Millennium Stadium)
MATCH FIVE: Wales 16 France 9 (Millennium Stadium)

A superb finish from Alex Cuthbert helped Wales to glory. Dan Lydiate (The Silent Assassin) had one of his most celebrated defensive performances, notching 20 tackles, many of them bone-shudderingly painful. It was Sam Warburton's 13th game as captain, but his first in Cardiff in a Six Nations game.

THE ICEMEN COMETH!

A major factor in the success Wales enjoyed under Gatland was their fitness. Wales frequently won Championship games late, with their superior fitness seeing them through. A key part of their fitness regime were terrifying trips to Poland. In a remote camp in the woods, Wales would do up to five incredibly physical fitness sessions daily (everything from swimming to weights to sprints) and recover by frequently stepping into cryotherapy chambers. Players would spend several minutes in them at temperatures between −70 and −130°C! All sweat had to be wiped off before entering or players would suffer burns!

A SORROWFUL SUMMER AND A GLOOMY AUTUMN

Sandwiched between 2012 and 2013 Six Nations glory was a run of poor results against non-European teams. Wales lost three Tests in Australia in the summer of 2012,

Sam Warburton.

despite leading two of the games with seconds remaining. The autumn again saw Wales lose in injury time to Australia and also brought losses to New Zealand (33-10), Argentina (26-12) and their old enemies Samoa (26-19).

CHAMPIONS AGAIN AFTER
FINAL DAY DRAMA IN 2013

Wales 30 England 3 (Millennium Stadium)

Wales began their 2013 with a 2012 hangover, trailing Ireland 23-3 at the break in Cardiff. Wales rallied but fell 30-22, their eighth consecutive loss. Amazingly, the men in scarlet went on to win in Paris (16-9), in Rome (26-9) and Edinburgh (28-18). On the final day of the Championship, England came to Cardiff confident of a Grand Slam. They left with their tail between their legs as Wales racked up their biggest winning margin ever over their old foes. Alex Cuthbert scored two tries, one of them after superb threequarter-like skills from flanker Justin Tipuric. Halfpenny and Biggar kicked the other points. Not only had England had the Grand Slam snatched away from them, Wales were champions on points difference.

A RARE SOUTHERN WIN

In November 2014 Wales picked up a rare win over a big southern hemisphere team. A daft Liam Williams foul had cost Wales a famous win in the second Test of the summer tour to South Africa (31-30). Wales followed up their usual autumn losses to Australia (33-28) and New Zealand (34-16), before kicking their way to a 12-6 win over the Springboks. Sam Warburton later told journalist Ross Harries that there was a mental block when it came to games against the big three, saying: 'There are 23 guys in a squad, and perhaps 15 of them genuinely think they're going to win. That means there are eight that don't. They'd be happy to get within seven points.'

2015 WORLD CUP (ENGLAND)

Wales went into the World Cup just across the border after losing the 2015 Six Nations on points difference, an opening-day loss to England at home costing them a Grand Slam. They entered the 2015 World Cup as part of the 'Pool of Death', with England and Australia as group rivals. Before the tournament began Gatland lost key players Leigh Halfpenny and scrum-half Rhys Webb to injury in a controversial extra final warm-up against Italy. Worse was to come as Wales appeared cursed and injuries came like snowflakes in a snowstorm. Nonetheless, Wales were to record one of their most famous wins ever and narrowly miss out on another semi-final.

Captain: Sam Warburton
Coach: Warren Gatland

POOL GAMES

Wales 54 Uruguay 9 (Millennium Stadium)
Wales 28 England 25 (Twickenham)
An injury-ravaged Wales helped knock England out of their own tournament with a stunning late rally in London. Already

without several players such as Jonathan Davies, Leigh Halfpenny, Cory Allen, Eli Walker and Rhys Webb, Wales lost Scott Williams, Hallam Amos and Liam Williams during the game too. In the 71st minute, scrum-half Lloyd Williams, a replacement winger, made the most famous Welsh cross kick since 1953 and scrum-half Gareth Davies picked up the ball with his fingertips to score. Biggar soon after rounded off one of the great Welsh kicking displays to add a penalty (giving him a flawless total of eight kicks from eight) and put Wales in the lead. The ravaged Dragons, who had trailed by ten in the second half, hung on. When Australia also beat England in their game, the hosts emulated the 1991 Welsh team in exiting at the pool stage.

ANOTHER VICTORY LIKE THIS AND WE'LL BE RUINED!

Wales 23 Fiji 13 (Millennium Stadium)
Wales 6 Australia 15 (Twickenham)
Once again Wales lost to the Wallabies in a World Cup. Even having two extra men due to two Aussie yellow cards at the same time couldn't get Wales over the line. Australia went on to lose to New Zealand in the final.

QUARTER FINAL
Wales 19 South Africa 23 (Twickenham)
Wales again lost narrowly to the Boks in a World Cup as their poor record against the big southern boys continued. Warburton's men, falling apart at the seams through injury, led until the 75th minute, when Fourie du Preez broke Welsh hearts with a try from a sublime Duane Vermeulen pass.

THE DRAGON FINALLY FINDS ITS CLAWS FOR A SPRINGBOK
Wales had to wait 12 games and 93 years for victory over South Africa. But after the famous 1999 result, Wales went a further 16 matches without success against them. After the 2014 win, Wales then went on a splendid streak of five victories from six matches (tragically the only loss was the 2015 World Cup defeat). All of Wales's wins came in Cardiff, except for one rather bizarre game played in Washington on the way to a two-match series against Argentina!

MADE IT, MAM! TOP OF THE WORLD!

In Warren Gatland's final season, Wales won their third Grand Slam of his reign. The title run was at the core of a 14-match winning streak that broke the 11-game record hanging over from the First Golden Era. The run even (very briefly) put Wales atop the World Rugby rankings for the first time. With bogey teams Australia and South Africa among the scalps claimed in the sequence, Welsh fans dared to start dreaming of something special in the upcoming 2019 World Cup.

Top of the world for 14 glorious days!

MATCH ONE: France 19 Wales 24 (Stade de France)

Wales trailed 16-0 in Paris, but as they had won seven from eight against the French since the 2011 semi-final loss, they never lost hope. In the 46th minute, the Dragons finally got on the scoreboard with a try from Tomos Williams and two from George North. It gave Wales another dramatic comeback win.

MATCH TWO: Italy 15 Wales 26 (Stadio Olimpico, Rome)
MATCH THREE: Wales 21 England 13 (Principality Stadium)

Gatland's Wales ended a run of four successive losses to Eddie Jones's England in a smart, disciplined and physical win. England led 10-3 at the break, but Wales wore England down and tries from second row Cory Hill and winger Josh Adams sealed the deal.

MATCH FOUR: Scotland 11 Wales 18 (Murrayfield)
MATCH FIVE: Wales 25 Ireland 7 (Principality Stadium)

A smart chip over the Irish defence from classy outside-half Gareth Anscombe in the first 70 seconds fell sweetly into the hands of Hadleigh Parkes who promptly fell over the line to give Wales control. Anscombe kicked six penalties and a conversion to shut down any hopes the visitors had of stopping the Welsh title charge. In a sign of how far Wales had come since the bleak years of the 1980s and 1990s, some fans were upset that Ireland were able to score in the final play of the match.

2019 WORLD CUP (JAPAN)

Wales, World Cups and heartache go together like crisps and bread or cookies and cream, and 2019 was in some ways the worst of all. Wales had never had a better chance to win it. After finally beating Australia in the tournament for the first time since 1987, Wales lost narrowly at the death to their new World Cup nemesis South Africa in the semi-final. The following week, the Springboks demolished England by 32-12. With Wales having beaten England in the Six Nations earlier in the year, the final result only made the semi-final loss worse to take.

Off the field, Wales had huge support from Japanese fans. Fifteen thousand locals greeted Wales at one training session and had even learnt to sing the Welsh national anthem. The games, facilities and domestic interest helped make the event one of the greatest in rugby history.

Captain: Alun Wyn Jones
Coach: Warren Gatland

POOL GAMES

Wales 43 Georgia 14 (City of Toyota Stadium, Toyota)
Wales 29 Australia 25 (Tokyo Stadium, Chōfu)
Wales finally beat a major southern hemisphere nation in a meaningful World Cup match, allowing them to ultimately win the pool. The men in red led 26-8 after 46 minutes thanks to a haul that included two drop goals from Dan Biggar and Rhys Patchell and tries from Gareth Davies and Hadleigh

Parkes. Australia though pulled back to 26-25, but Wales held on and opened up a very winnable path to the final.

Wales 29 Fiji 17 (Ōita Stadium, Ōita)
Wales 35 Uruguay 13 (Kumamoto Stadium, Kumamoto)

QUARTER-FINAL
Wales 20 France 19 (Ōita Stadium)

Another knockout game with France, another red card and another one-point result. Unlike 2011, this time the red card was for France. Wales's Gallic rivals had stormed into a 12-0 lead in just eight minutes. An opportunist try from back-rower Aaron Wainwright got Wales back in touch. Then, an unprovoked moment of madness saw French second-row Sébastien Vahaamahina throw an elbow to the face of Wainwright and get sent off. Wales were poor, grabbed a controversial try and the French, ultimately, blew it. Gatland admitted the better team lost. After the infamous Sam Warburton match eight years before, nobody in Wales was complaining.

Aaron Wainwright runs for glory.

SEMI-FINAL

Wales 16 South Africa 19 (International Stadium Yokohama, Yokohama)

Wales again fell cruelly short and Gatland and Edwards's reign finished with another grievous loss in the dying minutes to South Africa. As in 2015, the Dragons' shallow playing pool cost them dearly as injuries and fatigue hampered the cause. Wales gave their all in a titanic struggle between two brutal teams, but ultimately their physical style and defensive approach took its toll. After a Josh Adams try tied things up at 16-16 with 15 minutes to go, Welsh fans felt like magic was about to happen. However, a 76th-minute penalty from deadly Handre Pollard ended the dream.

THIRD PLACE PLAY-OFF

Wales 17 New Zealand 40 (Tokyo Stadium)

A GRIM SOUTHERN RECORD

The main downer on what some call a Third Golden Era was the failure to win major southern hemisphere clashes. Here is the summary of 2008–19 results against SANZAR nations.

	PLAYED	WON	LOST	WIN RATE
AUSTRALIA	16	3	13	18.75%
SOUTH AFRICA	16	5	11	31.25%
NEW ZEALAND	12	0	12	0%
TOTAL	44	8	36	18.2%

ONE KIWI FOR ANOTHER AS
2020 TURNS INTO A NIGHTMARE

Gatland's departure saw Wales turn to a fourth New Zealand coach. Wayne Pivac, who had enjoyed success with the Scarlets, took up the hot seat. After a crushing 42-0 win over Italy in the 2020 Six Nations, the hot seat started to melt with losses to Ireland, France and England. Unfortunately, the 2020 Championship was almost beaten by an opponent no one had ever had to face before. The conclusion to the tournament was delayed as the coronavirus pandemic brought a halt to the competition and meant (perhaps thankfully) Wales's summer tour to New Zealand and Japan was cancelled, as well as the planned autumn matches.

When the Six Nations resumed in October, coronavirus restrictions and the Principality Stadium's unavailability (it was at one point being used as an emergency hospital) saw Wales based at Llanelli. For safety reasons, no spectators were admitted to Parc y Scarlets as an uninspired Wales submitted to a poor Scottish side. It was Scotland's first win in Wales in 18 years. The result saw Wales plummet to ninth in the world rankings.

Wales then took part in the Autumn Nations Cup with the Six Nations teams as well as Georgia and Fiji. The event, ultimately won by England, was designed to fill the void left by the cancellation of the autumn matches and bring in vital money from television broadcasters as the coronavirus devasted the finances of rugby organisations. Wales continued their spectacular drop from the heights of 2019, with grim losses to England and Ireland and shaky wins over Georgia and Italy. So low had Wales fallen, Pivac, after Wales lost 24-13 to England, took comfort in the fact that the English had kicked penalties against Wales, rather than kick to the corner to try and score tries. He claimed it showed 'respect'. After how high Wales had risen in 2019, fans felt it was an odd thing to take pride in.

THE RED CHAMPIONSHIP

2021 ranks amongst the strangest years in the long history of Welsh rugby. After the disasters of 2020, many pundits predicted Wales would be tussling for fifth place in the Six Nations with lowly Italy. Instead, led by Alun Wyn Jones, they won the Six Nations and came just seconds short of another Grand Slam. The journey to that title was a peculiar one with covid restrictions preventing fans attending matches and a lot of talk about the colour red.

2021 CHAMPIONSHIP WIN

MATCH ONE: Wales 21 Ireland 16 (Principality Stadium)
Wales, often slow Championship starters, were looking good in the opening 15 minutes when Ireland's Peter O'Mahony was red carded for a dangerous clear out on Welsh prop Tomas Francis (Ospreys). It was the Irish player's second such sending off of the season. Yet the dismissal seemed to galvanise the visitors as Wales began looking uncomfortable and by the break, they trailed 13-6. Tries from George North and teenage sensation Louis Rees-Zammit (Gloucester), who had been capped aged 19 in the autumn of 2019, eventually helped get Wales ahead.

In the dying moments though, Ireland almost snatched it. With seconds remaining, in space and with options around him, scrum-half Gareth Davies pointlessly kicked a short distance ahead to give Ireland a vital free possession which allowed them to keep the game alive. The Irish got into a strong attacking position and forced a penalty. Ireland opted to kick to the corner and, based on the game's momentum, had a very good shot at a try from the subsequent line-out. Wales were spared though. In going for the corner, Ireland's Billy Burns overegged his kick and the ball went dead.

MATCH TWO: Scotland 24 Wales 25 (Murrayfield)

Another match, another red card. This was the first time Wales had seen their opponent's have a player dismissed in consecutive Test matches. With Scotland leading 17-15, Scottish prop Zander Fagerson was given his marching orders for driving his shoulder into prop Wyn Jones's (Scarlets) head in a ruck in the 54th minute.

But before that, Wales looked dreadful and after just 25 minutes trailed 17-3 before scores from Liam Williams and Louis Rees-Zammit helped put Wales back in the mix. The red card galvanised Scotland though and after 65 minutes they led 24-20. Then came a moment of magic from Rees-Zammit. A sublime chip and chase, after taking the ball on the half-way line, ended up with him scoring on the right wing. It was hard to know what was more remarkable, his pace, or the fact he actually appeared to be jogging when he was in fact running far faster than anyone else on the field could hope to. Wales held on and were suddenly on for the Triple Crown.

MATCH THREE: Wales 40 England 24 (Principality Stadium)
Another win, another controversy. Wales claimed their 22nd Triple Crown by racking up their highest ever score against England. Josh Adams bagged a try after claiming a clever cross kick from Dan Biggar after it looked like Wales would kick a penalty at the posts. However, the referee had told England captain Owen Farrell to talk to his team about their discipline and the visitors claimed they didn't have time to reset. Later in the first half, everyone, including the player concerned (Louis Rees-Zammit), thought there had been a knock on prior to a try from Liam Williams. However, the try was given. Wales were both making and riding their luck.

At 62 minutes the score was 24-24 after scrum-half Kieran Hardy (Scarlets) had claimed Wales's third try. Substitute fly-half Callum Sheedy helped build a Welsh lead with several penalties before another substitute, second row Cory Hill, rounded things off with a bonus point try.

MATCH FOUR: Italy 7 Wales 48 (Stadio Olimpico)
Hooker Ken Owens claimed two tries in Rome. Others came from Taulupe Faletau, George North, Callum Sheedy and Louis Rees-Zammit.

MATCH FIVE: France 32 Wales 30 (Stade de France)
Wales lost in the most heart-breaking fashion imaginable after having a Grand Slam in their hands before throwing it away in injury time. Unbelievably, France's Paul Willemse got a red card in the 68th minute for contact around the eye of Wyn Jones. This was the third red card for a Welsh opponent in just five games. The Dragons led by 30-20 at the time and it seemed one of the most

A year of unexpected glory and a smattering of red.

unlikely clean sweeps ever was all but in the bag. But then came one of the most extraordinary climaxes in Championship history. Under huge pressure, the visitors conceded two yellow cards with Faletau (72 minutes) and Liam Williams (74 minutes) sent to the bin. France took advantage of the fact they now had an extra man and scored a try in the 77th minute to make it 30-27 to Wales.

With 98 seconds left, Wales were given a knock-on advantage just inside the French half. Instead of taking a scrum (many teams would have intentionally dropped a ball or made sure they had no advantage), Wales tried to run down the clock with ball in hand and were penalised for sealing off at a ruck. From the subsequent line-out, taken seconds before the clock went into the red, France put together 11 phases to go over in the corner and smash the Grand Slam dream.

Wales had a nervous wait to see if France could score enough against Scotland the following week to claim the title themselves, but they fell short. Wales were again Championship winners. It was their 28th outright title.

A RED SUMMER

Wales played three Tests in Cardiff in the summer, shorn of ten players who were with the British and Irish Lions in South Africa. After dismantling Canada 68-12, Argentina arrived for a two-match series. The games were meant to take place in Argentina, but covid travel restrictions forced a change. Wales were unable to take advantage of another red card in their favour in the first Test and had to settle for a 20-20 draw, before losing the second game 33-11.

A RED AUTUMN

Wales played four autumn games and saw two of their opponents pick up red cards. It meant Wales had benefited from six sending offs in one calendar year. To give context as to how remarkable that was, it is worth noting that the first six dismissals of a Welsh opponent had taken place between 1888 and 2006 (it was not possible to be sent from the field before 1888). The increase was clearly a reflection of the differences in officiating in the modern era and the concerns about head injuries. In total there have been 16 sending offs against Wales in the entire history of international rugby. In contrast, Wales have had eight players dismissed.

The autumn campaign kicked off with a near farcical clash with New Zealand. The game was played outside the official international window as the WRU needed the cash injection. It meant several first-choice players based outside of Wales could not be selected. With injuries ravaging the squad, over 20 players were unavailable for Wayne Pivac and the All Blacks strolled home 54-16. A narrow loss to world champions South Africa followed (23-18), followed by red card assisted wins over Fiji (38-23) and Australia (29-28).

2020 and 2021 typified the swings of fortune and glory that run throughout the national team's history. Romance and despair are in a constant dance, which is what makes the journey of following them so fascinating and rewarding. Here's to the next 140 plus years of Welsh fortune, sorrow and joy.

2005–21: THE STAR PLAYERS

GETHIN JENKINS

Clubs: Cardiff, Celtic Warriors,
Pontypridd, Toulon
Position: Prop
Caps: 129 (2002–16)
(British & Irish Lions, 5 caps)
Points: 20 (4 tries)

One of the fittest men ever to play for Wales, Gethin Jenkins performed like a hybrid prop/flanker with an incredible ability to seemingly cover every inch of the field in open play. Skilful as well as strong, his footballing abilities were never better highlighted than through his solo tries against Ireland in 2005 or Namibia in 2011.

In 2015 he broke the then world record for caps for a forward, overtaking the 119 appearances by England's Jason Leonard. He was a cornerstone of the 2005, 2008 and 2012 Grand Slams. In 2020, he joined Wayne Pivac's coaching team.

LEIGH HALFPENNY

Clubs: Scarlets, Cardiff, Toulon
Position: Full-back, wing
Caps: 96 (2008 to present)
(British & Irish Lions, 4 caps, 49 points)
Points: 778 (15 tries, 74 conversions,
185 penalties)

No braver tackler has ever pulled on the red shirt. His lack of regard for his own health in defence has provided Wales with several famous wins (England in 2012 in particular) while coming at the cost of great personal injury.

Most famous with the general public perhaps for his laser-like kicking, some of his most important contributions to Wales are often missed by the casual fan. His expert defensive positioning and ability to read the game is a thorn in the side of opposing players, who know that whenever he is on the field, their kicking options are severely limited.

ALUN WYN JONES

Clubs: Ospreys, Swansea
Position: Second-row, flanker
Caps: 149 (2006 to present)
(British & Irish Lions, 12 caps)
Points: 45 (9 tries)

In terms of his stamina, longevity, inspirational role and sheer force of will, Alun Wyn Jones is arguably the most important player Wales has ever had. Even after 150 plus Test matches, he still sprints between training drills 'like a teenager'. Fanatically competitive on and off the field, Jones is as admired outside of Wales as he is in it.

Jones made his debut in 2006, but was still at the top of his game when he captained Wales to the 2019 Grand Slam, winning player of the tournament in the process. In 2021 he led Wales to an unexpected Six Nations title and was at the helm for the Lions in South Africa. The most capped international player in the history of rugby, his retirement will leave one of the biggest holes in any Welsh side ever. Before his injury in the autumn series of 2021, Jones had played in 19.8% of all Welsh tests since 1881. He has led Wales 48 times, more than any other player.

SAM WARBURTON

Clubs: Cardiff
Position: Flanker
Caps: 74 (2009–17)
(British & Irish Lions, 5 caps)
Points: 25 (5 tries)

Sam Warburton led his nation 49 times, the most in Welsh history. He also twice led the British & Irish Lions. The youngest ever World Cup captain, Warburton built a fierce reputation as a tough, abrasive back-row forward with an incredible ability to time and steal a turnover or slow down ball, despite brutal targeting from opponents. Like Halfpenny, Warburton's fearless approach to the game took a brutal toll on his body and cost him many more caps and ultimately ended his career early. After an international he would have to crawl up his stairs at home for days as he was too battered to walk up them.

The ultimate professional, Warburton was at the forefront of a younger generation who rejected the excessive drinking culture that had contributed to so much underachievement by otherwise talented teams.

TAULUPE FALETAU

Clubs: Dragons, Bath
Position: Number eight
Caps: 86 (2011 to present)
(British & Irish Lions, 4 caps,
5 points)
Points: 40 (8 tries)

Taulupe Faletau has been a core figure of Wales's success since 2011. A wonderfully gifted footballer, his ability to make yards from the back of a retreating scrum or from bad ball is uncanny. Even more exciting, it isn't brute force which usually gets his side out of trouble, but some of the best footwork in the modern game. He became the 131st Welsh captain when he took on the role against Italy in the 2018 Six Nations. The back-row combination he formed with Dan Lydiate and Sam Warburton is one of the most iconic in Welsh history.

GAVIN HENSON

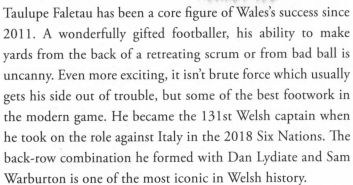

Clubs: Swansea, Ospreys, Saracens,
Toulon, Cardiff
Position: Centre, fly-half, full-back
Caps: 33 (2001–11)
(British & Irish Lions, 1 cap)
Points: 130 (3 tries, 29 conversions,
18 penalties, 1 drop goal)

Gavin Henson split public opinion like no Welsh player since the days of Arthur Gould. But his obsession with his hair, dislike of his own wrists, his celebrity girlfriends and poor drinking capacity distracted from his extraordinary rugby abilities. Martyn Williams called him undoubtedly the most naturally talented player he ever played with. He was quick, powerful, smart, had a fantastic boot and at times almost inter-dimensional passing skills. If anyone doubts Henson's importance to Wales, they need look no further than the key role he played in the 2008 Grand Slam under Gatland. He won 11 of the 12 games he started in the Six Nations and was the first player to represent Wales U19, Wales U21, Wales A and Wales in one calendar year. Injury and fallouts with coaches meant he never graced a World Cup.

ADAM JONES

Clubs: Ospreys, Cardiff
Position: Prop
Caps: 95 (2003–14)
(British & Irish Lions, 5 caps)
Points: 10 (2 tries)

A three times Grand Slammer, Adam Jones (nicknamed 'Bomb') is one of the best tight heads to grace the Welsh shirt. Bizarrely treated by Steve Hansen, who would often substitute him after just 30 minutes, Jones soon became one of the rocks of the Welsh pack during a 95-cap career. His ability to scrummage low and awkwardly shift his weight caused opponents no end of trouble and gave Wales the foundations to dominate in the tight. One of modern rugby's great characters, his Welsh career had a sad end when he responded less than diplomatically to being axed from the squad for the 2015 Six Nations. When injuries gave Wales a headache at tight head, Gatland said he would not beg Jones to return. He was never capped again.

2005–20 NOTABLE EVENTS IN WELSH HISTORY

• 2006: The new Senedd building opens in Cardiff.

• 2007: Merthyr Tydfil is named the unhealthiest place to live in the UK. Eight of the top ten places on the list are in Wales.

• 2008: Tower Colliery, the last working deep coal mine in Wales, closes.

• 2009: For the first time ever, the England cricket team play an Ashes Test match in Cardiff.

• 2010: Barry-born Julia Gillard becomes the first female prime minister of Australia.

• 2011: Although only 35% of voters turn out, the majority of those who vote in the Welsh devolution referendum want increased law-making powers.

• 2012: The National Assembly for Wales (Official Languages) Act 2012 is the first Act passed in Wales to become law in over 600 years.

• 2013: The sky over the Brecon Beacons National Park is named as an International Dark Sky Place, with the aim of protecting it from light pollution.

• 2014: Wales hosts the NATO Summit. It has never been held outside London before when in the UK.

• 2016: 52.5% of voters in Wales in the referendum to leave the European Union vote to leave.

• 2018: Cardiff's Geraint Thomas becomes the first Welshman ever to win the Tour de France.

• 2020: After a lengthy and passionate campaign, The National Assembly for Wales becomes Senedd Cymru.

SHIRTS AND STADIUMS:
WHERE THEY PLAYED AND WHAT THEY WORE

PLAYING KITS

England and Wales have each other's numbers

The 1922 Championship saw Wales and England agree to number their teams for the first time. However, the system was not standardised for a long time. This meant great outside-halves, such as Cliff Morgan in the 1950s, often wore a six, not a ten, as the numbers could start with the full-back being number one. At one point Wales left out the number 13 to avoid bad luck. And from the 1930s to the 1950s, Wales often wore letters instead of numbers.

Numbering players was distasteful to the Scots. During the 1920s, Scotland asked visiting teams not to number players, and Wales meekly agreed. When King George V attended a Calcutta Cup match and asked why the players were not numbered, he was told by the SRU president that 'this is a rugby match, not a cattle sale'. The 1905 match between Wales and New Zealand was the first time both teams in a Welsh game wore numbers.

In 1991, Wales copyrighted a version of their three feathers crest and signed a deal with kit manufacturer Cotton Traders to produce official shirts. The era of the constantly changing kit and expensive replica gear had begun.

EARNING YOUR SHIRT

At the start of the 20th century, jerseys were not given for each match. WRU policy was: 'All players must return old jerseys before obtaining new ones.'

*For images of all the shirts Wales have worn, see the colour section in the middle of this book.

STADIUMS

'Twickenham with those Rolls-Royces and bottles of champagne. Lansdowne Road and its terraces, Murrayfield and the Scottish gloom, even Parc des Princes. They all have their charms and quirks. But if you are an All Black and you're looking for rugby and especially a Test, then Cardiff Arms Park is the place.' – **Graham Mourie, New Zealand (1976–82)**

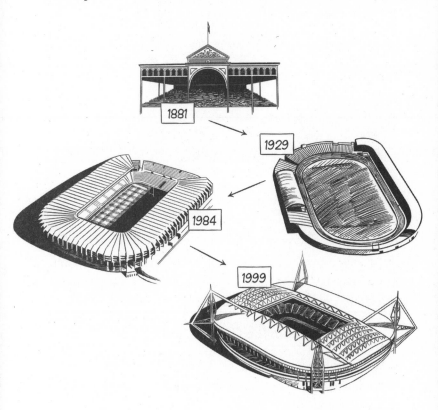

CARDIFF ARMS PARK TO PRINCIPALITY STADIUM

Cardiff Arms Park was generally regarded as the cathedral of rugby by players and fans across the world. Here's a short timeline of the history of the sacred land and the stadiums that later stood upon it.

• **17th century:** Sir Thomas Morgan builds a stately home that was to become known as the Red House. This became in the 18th century a coaching inn called the Cardiff Arms Hotel.

• **1803:** The Cardiff Arms Hotel (and the swampy meadow behind it) become the property of the famous Bute family.

• **1848:** Cardiff Cricket Club plays on the ground.

• **1867:** The Bute Estate charges a 'peppercorn rent' of one shilling each year for use of the grounds and the area narrowly avoids becoming a cattle market.

• **1874:** The first rugby game is held at the site.

• **1876:** The newly formed Cardiff RFC practises at the Arms Park.

• **1878:** The Cardiff Arms Hotel is demolished.

• **1881:** The first stand for cricket is built for £50. Charging for attending sporting games is a new and very unpopular thing and providing covered and 'comfortable' stands helps justify the fees. The stand was built 'for the convenience of the spectators and the ladies in particular.'

• **1884:** The first Welsh game held at the Arms Park sees Wales beat Ireland.

• **1885:** The first grandstand is pulled down and a new one erected at a cost of £362. Boards are put down to stop spectators sinking in the mud.

- **1890s to 1910:** Soccer is played at the Arms Park.
- **1904:** A new pavilion is built. Previously, club teams changed in the Grand Hotel in Westgate Street and international teams in the Angel Hotel. After the game, players would mingle with supporters on their way back to the changing rooms.
- **1911–12:** The grandstand and temporary tiers are demolished and replaced by a new structure that increases seating capacity to 3,000 and standing room to 40,000.
- **1922:** The 4th Marquess of Bute sells the land to the Cardiff Arms Park company for £30,000. Cardiff Athletic Club gets the ground on a 99-year lease.
- **1930s:** The WRU consider building a new ground at Sloper Road or Bridgend (they even buy land there).
- **1933–34:** A new double-decker stand opened at the Arms Park increases capacity overall to 56,000 and '. . . provision is made on the ground floor of the stand for the service of refreshments, two counters, each 76 feet long, running the full length of the stand, so that spectators can get refreshments on the ground, as is done at Twickenham'.
- **1936:** The Marquess of Bute, annoyed by the new north stand built in 1934 ruining his view, allows flats to be built on Westgate Street to block out his view of the stadium.
- **1940s:** Players such as Bleddyn Williams complain of greyhound racing at the ground and the 'grubby puddles' left by dogs!
- **1941:** A German bomb destroys the North Stand and sections of the West Terrace and South Stand.
- **1953:** The WRU confirm all future Welsh home games will be held in Cardiff only.

- **1958:** The Empire Games are held at the stadium and a cinder athletic track is placed around the pitch.
- **1960s:** Bridgend is again considered for an alternative stadium.
- **1962:** It is decided to split the Arms Park into two rugby grounds. A new, smaller one for Cardiff RFC (today's Cardiff Arms Park) with the main ground for internationals. To fund the plans a debenture ticket scheme is launched and there are soon complaints that too many debentures are taken up by commercial interests and rich folk.

HOME SWEET HOME

There was a joke in the 1960s that the old stadium would not burn down due to all the fans weeing in the ancient, leaking urinals. In 1968 referee Air-Vice-Marshal G.C. 'Larry' Lamb took control of the Wales v Scotland match. When shown to his dressing room he thought it was a broom cupboard and the WRU were playing a joke. With gale-force wind and rain pouring in through a window, he indicated he may not wish to return to referee again in such poor conditions. The WRU were embarrassed enough to upgrade to far more impressive facilities.

- **1968:** The WRU take the freehold of the south ground (site of today's stadium) from Cardiff Athletic Club.
- **1970:** A new North Stand is built and Cardiff's ground is finished. At the opening game at the new stadium, 40,000 watch a John Dawes-led Welsh XV beat an RFU invitational

side 26-11. The ground is technically The National Stadium, but everyone calls it Cardiff Arms Park.

LIKE A BOWLING LAWN

In 1978 legendary All Black Graham Mourie was asked how New Zealand pitches compared to the new one at the Arms Park. He replied they had many like them, but they used them for 'tennis and bowls'.

• **1980:** The new double-tiered East Terrace opens at a cost of £900,000 ready for the WRU centenary season. The scoreboard is fancy for the time, being able to write out things like welcoming messages to visiting teams! Underneath is a dining room to entertain guests. During the 1980s there were an average of seven cats in the stadium at any one time to keep seagulls away. Pickpockets were a problem. Once, after a game, 14 wallets, empty of money, were found in the toilet cisterns.

• **1984:** The National Stadium is finally complete with a new South Stand. The capacity is now 65,000 (but safety regulations later changed this to 53,000). The rebuilding had taken 15 years and cost £9 million (four times what it was planned at). Writer David Parry-Jones wrote: '. . . it was to a reborn and perfectly formed Cardiff Arms Park which nevertheless enshrined within its new concrete ramparts the racial memory of a nation at play.'

• **1997:** The final Welsh game is played at Cardiff Arms Park (there had been 174 matches there). Wales lose to England.

The final game is Cardiff v Swansea in the Welsh Cup, fittingly won by the capital club.

• **1999:** The new Millennium Stadium is completed just in time for the 1999 World Cup. It cost £121 million. At the time of construction it was considered one of the finest stadiums in the world.

• **2016:** The stadium is renamed the Principality Stadium.

Mike Rayer slides in for one of his two iconic tries against Scotland in 1994.

• **2020:** Due to the coronavirus, the Principality Stadium is temporarily turned into an emergency hospital. Wales play their home games (without fans present) in Llanelli at Parc y Scarlets.

RESULTS AND RECORDS

All stats correct as of December 2021

CHAMPIONSHIPS (HOME NATIONS, FIVE NATIONS, SIX NATIONS)

OUTRIGHT TITLES (28)

1893, 1900, 1902, 1905, 1908, 1909, 1911, 1922, 1931, 1936, 1950, 1952, 1956, 1965, 1966, 1969, 1971, 1975, 1976, 1978, 1979, 1994, 2005, 2008, 2012, 2013, 2019, 2021

SHARED TITLES (12)

1888, 1906, 1920, 1932, 1939, 1947, 1954, 1955, 1964, 1970, 1973, 1988

GRAND SLAMS (12)

1908, 1909, 1911, 1950, 1952, 1971, 1976, 1978, 2005, 2008, 2012, 2019

TRIPLE CROWNS (22)

1893, 1900, 1902, 1905, 1908, 1909, 1911, 1950, 1952, 1965, 1969, 1971, 1976, 1977, 1978, 1979, 1988, 2005, 2008, 2012, 2019, 2021

BEST WORLD CUP POSITIONING

THIRD (1987)

FOURTH (2011, 2019)

WORLD RUGBY RANKING

HIGHEST: 1st (2019)

LOWEST: 10th (2007, 2013)

MOST CAPS (ALL TIME)

NAME	CAPS	DEBUT	FINAL GAME	WINS
ALUN WYN JONES	149	2006 (ARGENTINA)	-	74
GETHIN JENKINS	129	2002 (ROMANIA)	2016 (SOUTH AFRICA)	61
STEPHEN JONES	104	1998 (SOUTH AFRICA)	2011 (AUSTRALIA)	43
GEORGE NORTH	102	2010 (SOUTH AFRICA)	-	57
GARETH THOMAS	100	1995 (JAPAN)	2007 (FIJI)	51
MARTYN WILLIAMS	100	1996 (BARBARIANS)	2012 (BARBARIANS)	44
DAN BIGGAR	95	2008 (CANADA)	-	52
ADAM JONES	95	2003 (ENGLAND)	2014 (SOUTH AFRICA)	47
COLIN CHARVIS	94	1996 (AUSTRALIA)	2007 (SOUTH AFRICA)	42
MIKE PHILLIPS	94	2003 (ROMANIA)	2015 (IRELAND)	44
JAMIE ROBERTS	94	2008 (SCOTLAND)	2017 (NEW ZEALAND)	48

MOST CAPS (DEBUT BEFORE PROFESSIONALISM IN 1995)

NAME	CAPS	DEBUT	FINAL GAME	WINS
GARETH THOMAS	100	1995 (JAPAN)	2007 (FIJI)	51
GARETH LLEWELLYN	92	1989 (NEW ZEALAND)	2004 (NEW ZEALAND)	38
NEIL JENKINS	87	1991 (ENGLAND)	2002 (ROMANIA)	44
IEUAN EVANS	72	1987 (FRANCE)	1998 (ITALY)	30
GARIN JENKINS	58	1991 (FRANCE)	2000 (SOUTH AFRICA)	34
J.P.R. WILLIAMS	55	1969 (SCOTLAND)	1981 (SCOTLAND)	37
ROBERT JONES	54	1986 (ENGLAND)	1995 (IRELAND)	22
GARETH EDWARDS	53	1967 (FRANCE)	1978 (FRANCE)	35
SCOTT GIBBS	53	1991 (ENGLAND)	2001 (ITALY)	24
SCOTT QUINNELL	52	1993 (CANADA)	2002 (CANADA)	30

MOST POINTS

PLAYER	POINTS	CAPS	CAREER	POINTS PER GAME AVG.*
NEIL JENKINS	1,049	87	1991–2002	12.1
STEPHEN JONES	917	104	1998–2011	8.8
LEIGH HALFPENNY	778	96	2008–	8.1
DAN BIGGAR	532	95	2008–	5.6
JAMES HOOK	352	81	2006–15	4.3
PAUL THORBURN	304	37	1985–91	8.2
SHANE WILLIAMS	290	87	2000–11	3.3
GEORGE NORTH	215	102	2010–	2.1
ARWEL THOMAS	211	23	1996–2000	9.2
GARETH THOMAS	200	100	1995–2007	2.0

*Rounded to one decimal place.

MOST TRIES

NAMES	TRIES	CAPS	CAREER	TRIES PER GAME AVG.*
SHANE WILLIAMS	58	87	2000–11	0.7
GEORGE NORTH	43	102	2010–	0.4
GARETH THOMAS	40	100	1995–2007	0.4
IEUAN EVANS	33	72	1987–98	0.5
COLIN CHARVIS	22	94	1996–2007	0.2
GERALD DAVIES	20	46	1966–78	0.4
GARETH EDWARDS	20	53	1967–78	0.4
TOM SHANKLIN	20	70	2001–10	0.3
RHYS WILLIAMS	18	44	2000–05	0.4
REGGIE GIBBS	17	16	1906–11	1.1
JOHNNIE WILLIAMS	17	17	1906–11	1.0
KEN JONES	17	44	1947–57	0.4
ALEX CUTHBERT	17	48	2011-	0.4
LIAM WILLIAMS	17	74	2012-	0.2
JOSH ADAMS	17	35	2018-	0.5

*Rounded to one decimal place.

RESULTS BY DECADE

DECADE	PLAYED	WON	DRAWN	LOST	WIN %
1881–89	19	5	2	12	26.32
1890–99	27	11	1	15	40.74
1900–09	35	28	1	6	80.00
1910–19	22	15	0	7	68.18
1920–29	42	17	3	22	40.48
1930–39	34	18	3	13	52.94
1940–49	13	6	1	6	46.15
1950–59	43	29	2	12	67.44
1960–69	48	20	6	22	41.67
1970–79	46	32	3	11	69.57
1980–89	60	30	1	29	50.00
1990–99	98	48	1	49	48.98
2000–09	117	55	3	59	47.01
2010–19	129	71	2	56	55.04
2020–	22	10	1	11	45.45
TOTAL	**755**	**395**	**30**	**330**	**52.32%**

RESULTS BY TEST MATCH TYPE

TEST TYPE	GAMES	WON	DRAWN	LOST	WIN%
CHAMPIONSHIP (FOUR/FIVE/SIX NATIONS)*	486	260	26	200	53.50
NON-CHAMPIONSHIP/ NON-WORLD CUP	**197**	**93**	**4**	**100**	**47.21**
WORLD CUP WARM-UPS	20	10	0	10	50.00
WORLD CUP (INCLUDES QUALIFIERS)	**48**	**30**	**0**	**18**	**62.50**
AUTUMN NATIONS CUPS	4	2	0	2	50.00
TOTAL	**755**	**395**	**30**	**330**	**52.32**

* Includes the 1908 and 1909 French tests, not part of the Home Championship, but counted as part of the 1908 and 1909 Grand Slams.

RESULTS PER OPPONENT
(CAPPED GAMES ONLY)

OPPONENT	GAMES	WON	DRAWN	LOST	WIN%
ARGENTINA	20	13	1	6	65.00
AUSTRALIA*	44	13	1	30	29.55
BARBARIANS	4	2	0	2	50.00
CANADA	13	12	0	1	92.31
ENGLAND	137	60	12	65	43.80
FIJI	13	11	1	1	84.62
FRANCE	101	51	3	47	50.50
GEORGIA	3	3	0	0	100.00
IRELAND	132	70	7	55	53.03
ITALY	30	27	1	2	90.00
JAPAN	10	9	0	1	90.00
NAMIBIA	4	4	0	0	100.00
NEW ZEALAND	36	3	0	33	8.33
NZ ARMY TEAM	1	0	0	1	0.00
NZ MAORIS	1	1	0	0	100.00
PACIFIC ISLANDERS	1	1	0	0	100.00
PORTUGAL	1	1	0	0	100.00
ROMANIA	8	6	0	2	75.00
SAMOA	10	6	0	4	60.00
SCOTLAND	127	74	3	50	58.27
SOUTH AFRICA	37	6	1	30	16.22
SPAIN	1	1	0	0	100.00
TONGA	9	9	0	0	100.00
URUGUAY	2	2	0	0	100.00
USA	7	7	0	0	100.00
ZIMBABWE	3	3	0	0	100.00
TOTAL	755	395	30	330	52.32

*Includes 1927 match with NSW Waratahs, now classed as an Australian team.

SCORING TOTALS 1881-2021

TEAM	TRIES	PENALTY TRIES	CONVS	PENS	DROP GOALS	GOALS FROM MARK	POINTS
WALES	1636	24	1021	1286	130	3	13260
OPPONENTS	1429	11	876	1178	133	4	11577

RESULTS BY HEAD COACH

COACH	PERIOD	GAMES	WON	DRAWN	LOST	WIN %
DAVID NASH	1967–68	5	1	1	3	20.00
CLIVE ROWLANDS	1969–74	29	18	4	7	62.07
JOHN DAWES	1975–79	24	18	0	6	75.00
JOHN LLOYD	1980–82	14	6	0	8	42.86
JOHN BEVAN	1983–85	15	7	1	7	46.67
TONY GRAY	1986–88	24	15	0	9	62.50
JOHN RYAN	1988–90	9	2	0	7	22.22
RON WALDRON	1990–91	10	2	1	7	20.00
ALAN DAVIES	1991–95	35	18	0	17	51.43
ALEC EVANS*	1995	4	1	0	3	25.00
KEVIN BOWRING	1995–98	29	15	0	14	51.72
DENNIS JOHN*	1998	2	1	0	1	50.00
GRAHAM HENRY	1998–2002	34	20	1	13	58.82
LYNN HOWELLS*	2001	2	2	0	0	100.00
STEVE HANSEN	2002–04	31	11	0	20	35.48
MIKE RUDDOCK	2004–06	20	13	0	7	65.00
SCOTT JOHNSON*	2006	3	0	1	2	0.00
GARETH JENKINS	2006–07	20	6	1	13	30.00
NIGEL DAVIES*	2007	1	0	0	1	0.00
WARREN GATLAND	2008–19	125	70	2	53	56.00
ROBIN McBRYDE*	2009, 2013, 2017	6	5	0	1	83.33
ROB HOWLEY*	2012, 2013, 2016, 2017	20	10	0	10	50.00
WAYNE PIVAC	2020–	22	10	1	11	45.45
TOTAL	1967–2021	484	251	13	220	51.86

*Caretaker coach

TEAM RESULTS BEFORE HEAD COACH POSITION (1881–1967)

GAMES	WON	DRAWN	LOST	WIN %
271	144	17	110	53.14

RESULTS ACCORDING TO NATIONALITY OF REFEREE (NEUTRAL)

REFEREE'S UNION	GAMES	WON	DRAWN	LOST	WIN %
ARGENTINA	8	5	0	3	62.50
AUSTRALIA	44	22	0	22	50.00
CANADA	1	0	0	1	0.00
ENGLAND	208	113	6	89	54.33
FRANCE	87	42	3	41	49.43
IRELAND	161	88	9	64	55.66
ITALY	2	1	0	1	50.00
NEW ZEALAND	54	25	2	27	46.30
SCOTLAND	128	69	9	50	53.91
SOUTH AFRICA	50	26	0	24	52.00

Note: On three occasions in Welsh Tests, the starting referee has been injured and replaced by a referee of a different union. For these we have counted only the nationality of the starting referee.

RESULTS FOR GAMES WITH NON-NEUTRAL REFEREES

REFEREE'S UNION	GAMES	WON	DRAWN	LOST	WIN %
AUSTRALIA	3	1	0	2	33.33
ENGLAND	2	0	1	1	0.00
IRELAND	1	1	0	0	100.00
NEW ZEALAND	2	0	0	2	0.00
SOUTH AFRICA	1	0	0	1	0.00
WALES	2	0	0	2	0.00
TOTAL	**11**	**2**	**1**	**8**	**18.12**

Note: This table looks at games when a referee has been either from the WRU or the union of the opposing team. These mainly occurred in the early years of international rugby or in touring games during the amateur era.

MOST GAMES AS CAPTAIN

NAMES	GAMES	WINS	TEST CAREER
SAM WARBURTON	49	23	2009-2017
ALUN WYN JONES	48	26	2006-
RYAN JONES	33	18	2005-2014
IEUAN EVANS	28	13	1987-1998
COLIN CHARVIS	22	11	1996-2007
ROBERT HOWLEY	22	15	1996-2002

LEAGUE LOSSES

Wales lost 154 capped players to league before the game went professional. That works out at about 25% of capped players in the amateur era.

RESULTS: 1881–2021

Notes for Games 1 to 19

G – Goal (a converted try)

T – Try

DG – Drop goal

GFM – Goal from mark

Abbreviations/Glossary

Test = refers to non-tournament/non-World Cup match

Test (1) or (2) or (3) – reference to first, second or third match in a 'Test series'

HN = Home Nations (earlier version of the Six Nations)

5N = Five Nations (earlier version of the Six Nations)

6N = Six Nations

WC = World Cup

WCQ = World Cup qualifier

WCW = World Cup warm up

AUTC = Autumn Nations Cup

GAME	DATE	TYPE	H/A	CITY	CAPTAIN	OPPONENTS	RESULT	SCORE (FOR)	SCORE (OPP)	COACH
1	19/02/1881	TEST	AWAY	BLACKHEATH	JAMES BEVAN	ENGLAND	LOST	NIL	7G, 1DG, 6T	N/A
2	28/01/1882	TEST	AWAY	DUBLIN	CHARLES LEWIS	IRELAND	WON	2G, 2T	NIL	N/A
3	16/12/1882	HN	HOME	SWANSEA	CHARLES LEWIS	ENGLAND	LOST	NIL	2G, 4T	N/A
4	08/01/1883	HN	AWAY	EDINBURGH	CHARLES LEWIS	SCOTLAND	LOST	1G	3G	N/A
5	05/01/1884	HN	AWAY	LEEDS	CHARLES LEWIS	ENGLAND	LOST	1G	1G, 2T	N/A
6	12/01/1884	HN	HOME	NEWPORT	CHARLES LEWIS	SCOTLAND	LOST	NIL	1DG, 1T	N/A
7	12/04/1884	HN	HOME	CARDIFF	HENRY SIMPSON	IRELAND	WON	1DG, 2T	NIL	N/A
8	03/01/1885	HN	HOME	SWANSEA	CHARLES NEWMAN	ENGLAND	LOST	1G, 1T	1G, 4T	N/A
9	10/01/1885	HN	AWAY	GLASGOW	CHARLES NEWMAN	SCOTLAND	DRAW	NIL	NIL	N/A
10	02/01/1886	HN	AWAY	BLACKHEATH	CHARLES NEWMAN	ENGLAND	LOST	1G	1GFM, 2T	N/A
11	09/01/1886	HN	HOME	CARDIFF	FRANK HANCOCK	SCOTLAND	LOST	NIL	2G, 1T	N/A
12	08/01/1887	HN	HOME	LLANELLI	CHARLES NEWMAN	ENGLAND	DRAW	NIL	NIL	N/A
13	26/02/1887	HN	AWAY	EDINBURGH	ROBERT GOULD	SCOTLAND	LOST	NIL	4G, 8T	N/A
14	12/03/1887	HN	NEUTRAL	BIRKENHEAD	THOMAS CLAPP	IRELAND	WON	1DG, 1T	3T	N/A
15	04/02/1888	HN	HOME	NEWPORT	THOMAS CLAPP	SCOTLAND	WON	1T	NIL	N/A
16	03/03/1888	HN	AWAY	DUBLIN	THOMAS CLAPP	IRELAND	WON	NIL	1G, 1DG, 1T	N/A
17	22/12/1888	TEST	HOME	SWANSEA	FRANK HILL	NZ MAORIS	WON	1G, 2T	NIL	N/A
18	02/02/1889	HN	AWAY	EDINBURGH	FRANK HILL	SCOTLAND	LOST	NIL	2T	N/A
19	02/03/1889	HN	HOME	SWANSEA	ARTHUR GOULD	IRELAND	LOST	NIL	2T	N/A
20	01/02/1890	HN	HOME	CARDIFF	FRANK HILL	SCOTLAND	LOST	1	5	N/A
21	15/02/1890	HN	AWAY	DEWSBURY	ARTHUR GOULD	ENGLAND	WON	1	0	N/A
22	01/03/1890	HN	AWAY	DUBLIN	ARTHUR GOULD	IRELAND	DRAW	3	3	N/A
23	03/01/1891	HN	HOME	NEWPORT	WILLIAM BOWEN	ENGLAND	LOST	3	7	N/A
24	07/02/1891	HN	AWAY	EDINBURGH	WILLIAM THOMAS	SCOTLAND	LOST	0	15	N/A
25	07/03/1891	HN	HOME	LLANELLI	WILLIAM THOMAS	IRELAND	WON	6	4	N/A
26	02/01/1892	HN	AWAY	BLACKHEATH	ARTHUR GOULD	ENGLAND	LOST	0	17	N/A
27	06/02/1892	HN	HOME	SWANSEA	ARTHUR GOULD	SCOTLAND	LOST	2	7	N/A
28	05/03/1892	HN	AWAY	DUBLIN	ARTHUR GOULD	IRELAND	LOST	0	9	N/A
29	07/01/1893	HN	HOME	CARDIFF	ARTHUR GOULD	ENGLAND	WON	12	11	N/A
30	04/02/1893	HN	AWAY	EDINBURGH	ARTHUR GOULD	SCOTLAND	WON	9	0	N/A
31	11/03/1893	HN	HOME	LLANELLI	ARTHUR GOULD	IRELAND	WON	2	0	N/A
32	06/01/1894	HN	AWAY	BIRKENHEAD	ARTHUR GOULD	ENGLAND	LOST	3	24	N/A
33	03/02/1894	HN	HOME	NEWPORT	ARTHUR GOULD	SCOTLAND	WON	7	0	N/A
34	10/03/1894	HN	AWAY	BELFAST	FRANK HILL	IRELAND	LOST	0	3	N/A
35	05/01/1895	HN	HOME	SWANSEA	ARTHUR GOULD	ENGLAND	LOST	6	14	N/A
36	26/01/1895	HN	AWAY	EDINBURGH	ARTHUR GOULD	SCOTLAND	LOST	4	5	N/A
37	16/03/1895	HN	HOME	CARDIFF	ARTHUR GOULD	IRELAND	WON	5	3	N/A
38	04/01/1896	HN	AWAY	BLACKHEATH	ARTHUR GOULD	ENGLAND	LOST	0	25	N/A
39	25/01/1896	HN	HOME	CARDIFF	ARTHUR GOULD	SCOTLAND	WON	6	0	N/A
40	14/03/1896	HN	AWAY	DUBLIN	ARTHUR GOULD	IRELAND	LOST	4	8	N/A
41	09/01/1897	HN	HOME	NEWPORT	ARTHUR GOULD	ENGLAND	WON	11	0	N/A
42	19/03/1898	HN	AWAY	LIMERICK	WILLIAM BANCROFT	IRELAND	WON	11	3	N/A

GAME	DATE	TYPE	H/A	CITY	CAPTAIN	OPPONENTS	RESULT	SCORE (FOR)	SCORE (OPP)	COACH
43	02/04/1898	HN	AWAY	BLACKHEATH	WILLIAM BANCROFT	ENGLAND	LOST	7	14	N/A
44	07/01/1899	HN	HOME	SWANSEA	WILLIAM BANCROFT	ENGLAND	WON	26	3	N/A
45	04/03/1899	HN	AWAY	EDINBURGH	WILLIAM BANCROFT	SCOTLAND	LOST	10	21	N/A
46	18/03/1899	HN	HOME	CARDIFF	WILLIAM BANCROFT	IRELAND	LOST	0	3	N/A
47	06/01/1900	HN	AWAY	GLOUCESTER	WILLIAM BANCROFT	ENGLAND	WON	13	3	N/A
48	28/01/1900	HN	HOME	SWANSEA	WILLIAM BANCROFT	SCOTLAND	WON	12	3	N/A
49	17/03/1900	HN	AWAY	BELFAST	WILLIAM BANCROFT	IRELAND	WON	3	0	N/A
50	05/01/1901	HN	HOME	CARDIFF	WILLIAM BANCROFT	ENGLAND	WON	13	0	N/A
51	09/02/1901	HN	AWAY	EDINBURGH	WILLIAM BANCROFT	SCOTLAND	LOST	8	18	N/A
52	16/03/1901	HN	HOME	SWANSEA	WILLIAM BANCROFT	IRELAND	WON	10	9	N/A
53	11/01/1902	HN	AWAY	BLACKHEATH	GWYN NICHOLLS	ENGLAND	WON	9	8	N/A
54	01/02/1902	HN	HOME	CARDIFF	GWYN NICHOLLS	SCOTLAND	WON	14	5	N/A
55	08/03/1902	HN	AWAY	DUBLIN	GWYN NICHOLLS	IRELAND	WON	15	0	N/A
56	10/01/1903	HN	HOME	SWANSEA	TOM PEARSON	ENGLAND	WON	21	5	N/A
57	07/02/1903	HN	AWAY	EDINBURGH	LLEWELLYN LLOYD	SCOTLAND	LOST	0	6	N/A
58	14/03/1903	HN	HOME	CARDIFF	GWYN NICHOLLS	IRELAND	WON	18	0	N/A
59	09/01/1904	HN	AWAY	LEICESTER	GWYN NICHOLLS	ENGLAND	DRAW	14	14	N/A
60	06/02/1904	HN	HOME	SWANSEA	WILLIE LLEWELLYN	SCOTLAND	WON	21	3	N/A
61	12/03/1904	HN	AWAY	BELFAST	WILLIE LLEWELLYN	IRELAND	LOST	12	14	N/A
62	14/01/1905	HN	HOME	CARDIFF	WILLIE LLEWELLYN	ENGLAND	WON	25	0	N/A
63	04/02/1905	HN	AWAY	EDINBURGH	WILLIE LLEWELLYN	SCOTLAND	WON	6	3	N/A
64	11/03/1905	HN	HOME	SWANSEA	WILLIE LLEWELLYN	IRELAND	WON	10	3	N/A
65	16/12/1905	TEST	HOME	CARDIFF	GWYN NICHOLLS	NEW ZEALAND	WON	3	0	N/A
66	13/01/1906	HN	AWAY	LONDON	GWYN NICHOLLS	ENGLAND	WON	16	3	N/A
67	03/02/1906	HN	HOME	CARDIFF	GWYN NICHOLLS	SCOTLAND	WON	9	3	N/A
68	10/03/1906	HN	AWAY	BELFAST	GWYN NICHOLLS	IRELAND	LOST	6	11	N/A
69	01/12/1906	TEST	HOME	SWANSEA	GWYN NICHOLLS	SOUTH AFRICA	LOST	0	11	N/A
70	12/01/1907	HN	HOME	SWANSEA	RICHARD OWEN	ENGLAND	WON	22	0	N/A
71	02/02/1907	HN	AWAY	EDINBURGH	BILLY TREW	SCOTLAND	LOST	3	6	N/A
72	09/03/1907	HN	HOME	CARDIFF	RHYS GABE	IRELAND	WON	29	0	N/A
73	18/01/1908	HN	AWAY	BRISTOL	ARTHUR HARDING	ENGLAND	WON	28	18	N/A
74	01/02/1908	HN	HOME	SWANSEA	GEORGE TRAVERS	SCOTLAND	WON	6	5	N/A
75	02/03/1908	TEST	HOME	CARDIFF	EDWARD MORGAN	FRANCE	WON	36	4	N/A
76	14/03/1908	HN	AWAY	BELFAST	HERBERT WINFIELD	IRELAND	WON	11	5	N/A
77	12/12/1908	TEST	HOME	CARDIFF	BILLY TREW	AUSTRALIA	WON	9	6	N/A
78	16/01/1909	HN	HOME	CARDIFF	BILLY TREW	ENGLAND	WON	8	0	N/A
79	06/02/1909	HN	AWAY	EDINBURGH	BILLY TREW	SCOTLAND	WON	5	3	N/A
80	23/02/1909	TEST	AWAY	PARIS	BILLY TREW	FRANCE	WON	47	5	N/A
81	13/03/1909	HN	HOME	SWANSEA	BILLY TREW	IRELAND	WON	18	5	N/A
82	01/01/1910	SN	HOME	SWANSEA	BILLY TREW	FRANCE	WON	49	14	N/A
83	15/01/1910	SN	AWAY	LONDON	BILLY TREW	ENGLAND	LOST	6	11	N/A

GAME	DATE	TYPE	H/A	CITY	CAPTAIN	OPPONENTS	RESULT	SCORE (FOR)	SCORE (OPP)	COACH
84	05/02/1910	5N	HOME	CARDIFF	BILLY TREW	SCOTLAND	WON	14	0	N/A
85	12/03/1910	5N	AWAY	DUBLIN	REGINALD GIBBS	IRELAND	WON	19	3	N/A
86	21/01/1911	5N	HOME	SWANSEA	BILLY TREW	ENGLAND	WON	15	11	N/A
87	04/02/1911	5N	AWAY	EDINBURGH	BILLY TREW	SCOTLAND	WON	32	10	N/A
88	28/02/1911	5N	AWAY	PARIS	JOHNNIE WILLIAMS	FRANCE	WON	15	0	N/A
89	11/03/1911	5N	HOME	CARDIFF	BILLY TREW	IRELAND	WON	16	0	N/A
90	20/01/1912	5N	AWAY	LONDON	RICHARD OWEN	ENGLAND	LOST	0	8	N/A
91	03/02/1912	5N	HOME	SWANSEA	RICHARD OWEN	SCOTLAND	WON	21	6	N/A
92	09/03/1912	5N	AWAY	BELFAST	JACK BANCROFT	IRELAND	LOST	5	12	N/A
93	25/03/1912	5N	HOME	NEWPORT	TOMMY VILE	FRANCE	WON	14	8	N/A
94	14/12/1912	TEST	HOME	CARDIFF	TOMMY VILE	SOUTH AFRICA	LOST	0	3	N/A
95	18/01/1913	5N	HOME	CARDIFF	TOMMY VILE	ENGLAND	LOST	0	12	N/A
96	01/02/1913	5N	AWAY	EDINBURGH	BILLY TREW	SCOTLAND	WON	8	0	N/A
97	27/02/1913	5N	AWAY	PARIS	BILLY TREW	FRANCE	WON	11	8	N/A
98	08/03/1913	5N	HOME	SWANSEA	JOHN JONES	IRELAND	WON	16	13	N/A
99	07/01/1914	5N	AWAY	LONDON	REV. ALBAN DAVIES	ENGLAND	LOST	9	10	N/A
100	07/02/1914	5N	HOME	CARDIFF	REV. ALBAN DAVIES	SCOTLAND	WON	24	5	N/A
101	02/03/1914	5N	HOME	SWANSEA	REV. ALBAN DAVIES	FRANCE	WON	31	0	N/A
102	14/03/1914	5N	AWAY	BELFAST	REV. ALBAN DAVIES	IRELAND	WON	11	3	N/A
103	21/04/1919	TEST	HOME	SWANSEA	GLYN STEPHENS	NZ ARMY TEAM	LOST	3	6	N/A
104	17/01/1920	5N	HOME	SWANSEA	HARRY UZZELL	ENGLAND	WON	19	5	N/A
105	07/02/1920	5N	AWAY	EDINBURGH	HARRY UZZELL	SCOTLAND	LOST	5	9	N/A
106	17/02/1920	5N	AWAY	PARIS	HARRY UZZELL	FRANCE	WON	6	5	N/A
107	13/03/1920	5N	HOME	CARDIFF	HARRY UZZELL	IRELAND	WON	28	4	N/A
108	15/01/1921	5N	AWAY	LONDON	JACK WETTER	ENGLAND	LOST	3	18	N/A
109	05/02/1921	5N	HOME	SWANSEA	TOMMY VILE	SCOTLAND	LOST	8	14	N/A
110	26/02/1921	5N	HOME	CARDIFF	TOM PARKER	FRANCE	WON	12	4	N/A
111	12/03/1921	5N	AWAY	BELFAST	TOM PARKER	IRELAND	WON	6	0	N/A
112	21/01/1922	5N	HOME	CARDIFF	TOM PARKER	ENGLAND	WON	28	6	N/A
113	04/02/1922	5N	AWAY	EDINBURGH	TOM PARKER	SCOTLAND	DRAW	9	9	N/A
114	11/03/1922	5N	HOME	SWANSEA	TOM PARKER	IRELAND	WON	11	5	N/A
115	22/03/1922	5N	AWAY	PARIS	TOM PARKER	FRANCE	WON	11	3	N/A
116	20/01/1923	5N	AWAY	LONDON	CLEM LEWIS	ENGLAND	LOST	3	7	N/A
117	03/02/1923	5N	HOME	CARDIFF	CLEM LEWIS	SCOTLAND	LOST	8	11	N/A
118	24/02/1923	5N	HOME	SWANSEA	TOM PARKER	FRANCE	WON	16	8	N/A
119	10/03/1923	5N	AWAY	DUBLIN	ALBERT JENKINS	IRELAND	LOST	4	5	N/A
120	19/01/1924	5N	HOME	SWANSEA	JOE REES	ENGLAND	LOST	9	17	N/A
121	02/02/1924	5N	AWAY	EDINBURGH	JACK WHITFIELD	SCOTLAND	LOST	10	35	N/A
122	08/03/1924	5N	HOME	CARDIFF	JACK WETTER	IRELAND	LOST	10	13	N/A
123	27/03/1924	5N	AWAY	PARIS	ROWE HARDING	FRANCE	WON	10	6	N/A
124	29/11/1924	TEST	HOME	SWANSEA	JACK WETTER	NEW ZEALAND	LOST	0	19	N/A
125	17/01/1925	5N	AWAY	LONDON	TOM JOHNSON	ENGLAND	LOST	6	12	N/A

GAME	DATE	TYPE	H/A	CITY	CAPTAIN	OPPONENTS	RESULT	SCORE (FOR)	SCORE (OPP)	COACH
126	07/02/1925	5N	HOME	SWANSEA	STEVE MORRIS	SCOTLAND	LOST	14	24	N/A
127	28/02/1925	5N	HOME	CARDIFF	ARTHUR CORNISH	FRANCE	WON	11	5	N/A
128	14/03/1925	5N	AWAY	BELFAST	IDRIS JONES	IRELAND	LOST	3	19	N/A
129	16/01/1926	5N	HOME	CARDIFF	ROWE HARDING	ENGLAND	DRAW	3	3	N/A
130	06/02/1926	5N	AWAY	EDINBURGH	ARTHUR CORNISH	SCOTLAND	LOST	5	8	N/A
131	13/03/1926	5N	HOME	SWANSEA	ROWE HARDING	IRELAND	WON	11	8	N/A
132	05/04/1926	5N	AWAY	PARIS	WILLIAM DELAHAY	FRANCE	WON	7	5	N/A
133	15/01/1927	5N	AWAY	LONDON	BERNARD TURNBULL	ENGLAND	LOST	9	11	N/A
134	05/02/1927	5N	HOME	CARDIFF	OSSIE MALE	SCOTLAND	LOST	0	5	N/A
135	26/02/1927	5N	HOME	SWANSEA	WICK POWELL	FRANCE	WON	25	7	N/A
136	12/03/1927	5N	AWAY	DUBLIN	WICK POWELL	IRELAND	LOST	9	19	N/A
137	26/11/1927	TEST	HOME	CARDIFF	IVOR JONES	NSW WARATAHS	LOST	8	18	N/A
138	21/01/1928	5N	HOME	SWANSEA	ROWE HARDING	ENGLAND	LOST	8	10	N/A
139	04/02/1928	5N	AWAY	EDINBURGH	OSSIE MALE	SCOTLAND	WON	13	0	N/A
140	10/03/1928	5N	HOME	CARDIFF	ALBERT JENKINS	IRELAND	LOST	10	13	N/A
141	09/04/1928	5N	AWAY	PARIS	OSSIE MALE	FRANCE	LOST	3	8	N/A
142	19/01/1929	5N	AWAY	LONDON	IVOR JONES	ENGLAND	LOST	3	8	N/A
143	02/02/1929	5N	HOME	SWANSEA	GUY MORGAN	SCOTLAND	WON	14	7	N/A
144	23/02/1929	5N	HOME	CARDIFF	GUY MORGAN	FRANCE	WON	8	3	N/A
145	09/03/1929	5N	AWAY	BELFAST	GUY MORGAN	IRELAND	DRAW	5	5	N/A
146	18/01/1930	5N	HOME	CARDIFF	HARRY BOWCOTT	ENGLAND	LOST	3	11	N/A
147	01/02/1930	5N	AWAY	EDINBURGH	IVOR JONES	SCOTLAND	LOST	9	12	N/A
148	08/03/1930	5N	HOME	SWANSEA	JACK BASSETT	IRELAND	WON	12	7	N/A
149	21/04/1930	5N	AWAY	PARIS	GUY MORGAN	FRANCE	WON	11	0	N/A
150	17/01/1931	5N	AWAY	LONDON	JACK BASSETT	ENGLAND	DRAW	11	11	N/A
151	07/02/1931	5N	HOME	CARDIFF	JACK BASSETT	SCOTLAND	WON	13	8	N/A
152	28/02/1931	5N	HOME	SWANSEA	JACK BASSETT	FRANCE	WON	35	3	N/A
153	14/03/1931	5N	AWAY	BELFAST	JACK BASSETT	IRELAND	WON	15	3	N/A
154	05/12/1931	TEST	HOME	SWANSEA	JACK BASSETT	SOUTH AFRICA	LOST	3	8	N/A
155	16/01/1932	5N	HOME	SWANSEA	JACK BASSETT	ENGLAND	WON	12	5	N/A
156	06/02/1932	HN	AWAY	EDINBURGH	JACK BASSETT	SCOTLAND	WON	6	0	N/A
157	12/03/1932	HN	HOME	CARDIFF	JACK BASSETT	IRELAND	LOST	10	12	N/A
158	21/01/1933	HN	AWAY	LONDON	WATCYN THOMAS	ENGLAND	WON	7	3	N/A
159	04/02/1933	HN	HOME	SWANSEA	WATCYN THOMAS	SCOTLAND	LOST	3	11	N/A
160	11/03/1933	HN	AWAY	BELFAST	WATCYN THOMAS	IRELAND	LOST	5	10	N/A
161	20/01/1934	HN	HOME	CARDIFF	JOHN EVANS	ENGLAND	LOST	0	9	N/A
162	03/02/1934	HN	AWAY	EDINBURGH	CLAUD DAVEY	SCOTLAND	WON	13	6	N/A
163	10/03/1934	HN	HOME	SWANSEA	CLAUD DAVEY	IRELAND	WON	13	0	N/A
164	19/01/1935	HN	AWAY	LONDON	CLAUD DAVEY	ENGLAND	DRAW	3	3	N/A
165	02/02/1935	HN	HOME	CARDIFF	CLAUD DAVEY	SCOTLAND	WON	10	6	N/A
166	09/03/1935	HN	AWAY	BELFAST	CLAUD DAVEY	IRELAND	LOST	3	9	N/A
167	21/12/1935	TEST	HOME	CARDIFF	CLAUD DAVEY	NEW ZEALAND	WON	13	12	N/A

GAME	DATE	TYPE	H/A	CITY	CAPTAIN	OPPONENTS	RESULT	SCORE (FOR)	SCORE (OPP)	COACH
168	18/01/1936	HN	HOME	SWANSEA	IDWAL REES	ENGLAND	DRAW	0	0	N/A
169	01/02/1936	HN	AWAY	EDINBURGH	CLAUD DAVEY	SCOTLAND	WON	13	3	N/A
170	14/03/1936	HN	HOME	CARDIFF	IDWAL REES	IRELAND	WON	3	0	N/A
171	16/01/1937	HN	AWAY	LONDON	CLAUD DAVEY	ENGLAND	LOST	3	4	N/A
172	06/02/1937	HN	HOME	SWANSEA	IDWAL REES	SCOTLAND	LOST	6	13	N/A
173	03/04/1937	HN	AWAY	BELFAST	WILF WOOLLER	IRELAND	LOST	3	5	N/A
174	15/01/1938	HN	HOME	CARDIFF	CLIFF JONES	ENGLAND	WON	14	8	N/A
175	05/02/1938	HN	AWAY	EDINBURGH	CLIFF JONES	SCOTLAND	LOST	6	8	N/A
176	12/03/1938	HN	HOME	SWANSEA	CLIFF JONES	IRELAND	WON	11	5	N/A
177	21/01/1939	HN	AWAY	LONDON	WILF WOOLLER	ENGLAND	LOST	0	3	N/A
178	04/02/1939	HN	HOME	CARDIFF	WILF WOOLLER	SCOTLAND	WON	11	3	N/A
179	11/03/1939	HN	AWAY	BELFAST	WILF WOOLLER	IRELAND	WON	7	0	N/A
180	18/01/1947	5N	HOME	CARDIFF	HADYN TANNER	ENGLAND	LOST	6	9	N/A
181	01/02/1947	5N	AWAY	EDINBURGH	HADYN TANNER	SCOTLAND	WON	22	8	N/A
182	22/03/1947	5N	AWAY	PARIS	HADYN TANNER	FRANCE	WON	3	0	N/A
183	29/03/1947	5N	HOME	SWANSEA	HADYN TANNER	IRELAND	WON	6	0	N/A
184	20/12/1947	TEST	HOME	CARDIFF	WILLIAM TAMPLIN	AUSTRALIA	WON	6	0	N/A
185	17/01/1948	5N	AWAY	LONDON	HADYN TANNER	ENGLAND	DRAW	3	3	N/A
186	07/02/1948	5N	HOME	CARDIFF	HAYDN TANNER	SCOTLAND	WON	14	0	N/A
187	21/02/1948	5N	HOME	SWANSEA	HAYDN TANNER	FRANCE	LOST	3	11	N/A
188	13/03/1948	5N	AWAY	BELFAST	HAYDN TANNER	IRELAND	LOST	3	6	N/A
189	15/01/1949	5N	HOME	CARDIFF	HAYDN TANNER	ENGLAND	WON	9	6	N/A
190	05/02/1949	5N	AWAY	EDINBURGH	HAYDN TANNER	SCOTLAND	LOST	5	6	N/A
191	12/03/1949	5N	HOME	SWANSEA	HAYDN TANNER	IRELAND	LOST	0	5	N/A
192	26/03/1949	5N	AWAY	PARIS	HAYDN TANNER	FRANCE	LOST	3	5	N/A
193	21/01/1950	5N	AWAY	LONDON	JOHN GWILLIAM	ENGLAND	WON	11	5	N/A
194	04/02/1950	5N	HOME	SWANSEA	JOHN GWILLIAM	SCOTLAND	WON	12	0	N/A
195	11/03/1950	5N	AWAY	BELFAST	JOHN GWILLIAM	IRELAND	WON	6	3	N/A
196	25/03/1950	5N	HOME	CARDIFF	JOHN GWILLIAM	FRANCE	WON	21	0	N/A
197	20/01/1951	5N	HOME	SWANSEA	JOHN GWILLIAM	ENGLAND	WON	23	5	N/A
198	03/02/1951	5N	AWAY	EDINBURGH	JOHN GWILLIAM	SCOTLAND	LOST	0	19	N/A
199	10/03/1951	5N	HOME	CARDIFF	JOHN GWILLIAM	IRELAND	DRAW	3	3	N/A
200	07/04/1951	5N	AWAY	PARIS	JACK MATTHEWS	FRANCE	LOST	3	8	N/A
201	22/12/1951	TEST	HOME	CARDIFF	JOHN GWILLIAM	SOUTH AFRICA	LOST	3	6	N/A
202	19/01/1952	5N	AWAY	LONDON	JOHN GWILLIAM	ENGLAND	WON	8	6	N/A
203	02/02/1952	5N	HOME	CARDIFF	JOHN GWILLIAM	SCOTLAND	WON	11	0	N/A
204	08/03/1952	5N	AWAY	DUBLIN	JOHN GWILLIAM	IRELAND	WON	14	3	N/A
205	22/03/1952	5N	HOME	SWANSEA	JOHN GWILLIAM	FRANCE	WON	9	5	N/A
206	17/01/1953	5N	HOME	CARDIFF	JOHN GWILLIAM	ENGLAND	LOST	3	8	N/A
207	07/02/1953	5N	AWAY	EDINBURGH	BLEDDYN WILLIAMS	SCOTLAND	WON	12	0	N/A
208	14/03/1953	5N	HOME	SWANSEA	BLEDDYN WILLIAMS	IRELAND	WON	5	3	N/A
209	28/03/1953	5N	AWAY	PARIS	BLEDDYN WILLIAMS	FRANCE	WON	6	3	N/A
210	19/12/1953	TEST	HOME	CARDIFF	BLEDDYN WILLIAMS	NEW ZEALAND	WON	13	8	N/A

GAME	DATE	TYPE	H/A	CITY	CAPTAIN	OPPONENTS	RESULT	SCORE (FOR)	SCORE (OPP)	COACH
211	16/01/1954	5N	AWAY	LONDON	REES STEPHENS	ENGLAND	LOST	6	9	N/A
212	13/03/1954	5N	AWAY	DUBLIN	REES STEPHENS	IRELAND	WON	12	9	N/A
213	27/03/1954	5N	HOME	CARDIFF	REX WILLIS	FRANCE	WON	19	13	N/A
214	10/04/1954	5N	HOME	SWANSEA	KEN JONES	SCOTLAND	WON	15	3	N/A
215	22/01/1955	5N	HOME	CARDIFF	BLEDDYN WILLIAMS	ENGLAND	WON	3	0	N/A
216	05/02/1955	5N	AWAY	EDINBURGH	REX WILLIS	SCOTLAND	LOST	8	14	N/A
217	12/03/1955	5N	HOME	CARDIFF	REES STEPHENS	IRELAND	WON	21	3	N/A
218	26/03/1955	5N	AWAY	PARIS	REES STEPHENS	FRANCE	WON	16	11	N/A
219	21/01/1956	5N	AWAY	LONDON	CLIFF MORGAN	ENGLAND	WON	8	3	N/A
220	04/02/1956	5N	HOME	CARDIFF	CLIFF MORGAN	SCOTLAND	WON	9	3	N/A
221	10/03/1956	5N	AWAY	DUBLIN	CLIFF MORGAN	IRELAND	LOST	3	11	N/A
222	24/03/1956	5N	HOME	CARDIFF	CLIFF MORGAN	FRANCE	WON	5	3	N/A
223	19/01/1957	5N	HOME	CARDIFF	MALCOLM THOMAS	ENGLAND	LOST	0	3	N/A
224	02/02/1957	5N	AWAY	EDINBURGH	MALCOLM THOMAS	SCOTLAND	WON	6	9	N/A
225	09/03/1957	5N	HOME	CARDIFF	REES STEPHENS	IRELAND	WON	6	5	N/A
226	23/03/1957	5N	AWAY	PARIS	REES STEPHENS	FRANCE	WON	19	13	N/A
227	04/01/1958	TEST	HOME	CARDIFF	CLEM THOMAS	AUSTRALIA	WON	9	3	N/A
228	18/01/1958	5N	AWAY	LONDON	CLEM THOMAS	ENGLAND	DRAW	3	3	N/A
229	01/02/1958	5N	HOME	CARDIFF	CLEM THOMAS	SCOTLAND	WON	8	3	N/A
230	15/03/1958	5N	AWAY	DUBLIN	CLEM THOMAS	IRELAND	WON	9	6	N/A
231	29/03/1958	5N	HOME	CARDIFF	CLEM THOMAS	FRANCE	LOST	6	16	N/A
232	17/01/1959	5N	HOME	CARDIFF	CLEM THOMAS	ENGLAND	WON	5	0	N/A
233	07/02/1959	5N	AWAY	EDINBURGH	CLEM THOMAS	SCOTLAND	LOST	5	6	N/A
234	14/03/1959	5N	HOME	CARDIFF	CLEM THOMAS	IRELAND	WON	8	6	N/A
235	04/04/1959	5N	AWAY	PARIS	CLEM THOMAS	FRANCE	LOST	3	11	N/A
236	16/01/1960	5N	AWAY	LONDON	RHYS WILLIAMS	ENGLAND	LOST	6	14	N/A
237	06/02/1960	5N	HOME	CARDIFF	BRYN MEREDITH	SCOTLAND	WON	8	0	N/A
238	12/03/1960	5N	AWAY	DUBLIN	ONLLWYN BRACE	IRELAND	WON	10	9	N/A
239	26/03/1960	5N	HOME	CARDIFF	BRYN MEREDITH	FRANCE	LOST	8	16	N/A
240	03/12/1960	TEST	HOME	CARDIFF	TERRY DAVIES	SOUTH AFRICA	LOST	0	3	N/A
241	21/01/1961	5N	HOME	CARDIFF	TERRY DAVIES	ENGLAND	WON	6	3	N/A
242	11/02/1961	5N	AWAY	EDINBURGH	TERRY DAVIES	SCOTLAND	LOST	0	3	N/A
243	11/03/1961	5N	HOME	CARDIFF	ONLLWYN BRACE	IRELAND	WON	9	0	N/A
244	25/03/1961	5N	AWAY	PARIS	LLOYD WILLIAMS	FRANCE	LOST	6	8	N/A
245	20/01/1962	5N	AWAY	LONDON	LLOYD WILLIAMS	ENGLAND	DRAW	0	0	N/A
246	03/02/1962	5N	HOME	CARDIFF	LLOYD WILLIAMS	SCOTLAND	LOST	3	8	N/A
247	24/03/1962	5N	HOME	CARDIFF	BRYN MEREDITH	FRANCE	WON	3	0	N/A
248	17/11/1962	5N	AWAY	DUBLIN	BRYN MEREDITH	IRELAND	DRAW	3	3	N/A
249	19/01/1963	5N	HOME	CARDIFF	CLIVE ROWLANDS	ENGLAND	LOST	6	13	N/A
250	02/02/1963	5N	AWAY	EDINBURGH	CLIVE ROWLANDS	SCOTLAND	WON	6	0	N/A
251	09/03/1963	5N	HOME	CARDIFF	CLIVE ROWLANDS	IRELAND	LOST	6	14	N/A
252	23/03/1963	5N	AWAY	PARIS	CLIVE ROWLANDS	FRANCE	LOST	3	5	N/A
253	21/12/1963	TEST	HOME	CARDIFF	CLIVE ROWLANDS	NEW ZEALAND	LOST	0	6	N/A

GAME	DATE	TYPE	H/A	CITY	CAPTAIN	OPPONENTS	RESULT	SCORE (FOR)	SCORE (OPP)	COACH
254	18/01/1964	5N	AWAY	LONDON	CLIVE ROWLANDS	ENGLAND	DRAW	6	6	N/A
255	01/02/1964	5N	HOME	CARDIFF	CLIVE ROWLANDS	SCOTLAND	WON	11	3	N/A
256	07/03/1964	5N	AWAY	DUBLIN	CLIVE ROWLANDS	IRELAND	WON	15	6	N/A
257	21/03/1964	5N	HOME	CARDIFF	CLIVE ROWLANDS	FRANCE	DRAW	11	11	N/A
258	23/05/1964	TEST	AWAY	DURBAN	CLIVE ROWLANDS	SOUTH AFRICA	LOST	3	24	N/A
259	16/01/1965	5N	HOME	CARDIFF	CLIVE ROWLANDS	ENGLAND	WON	14	3	N/A
260	06/02/1965	5N	AWAY	EDINBURGH	CLIVE ROWLANDS	SCOTLAND	WON	14	12	N/A
261	13/03/1965	5N	HOME	CARDIFF	CLIVE ROWLANDS	IRELAND	WON	14	8	N/A
262	27/03/1965	5N	AWAY	PARIS	CLIVE ROWLANDS	FRANCE	LOST	13	22	N/A
263	15/01/1966	5N	AWAY	LONDON	ALUN PASK	ENGLAND	WON	11	6	N/A
264	05/02/1966	5N	HOME	CARDIFF	ALUN PASK	SCOTLAND	WON	8	3	N/A
265	12/03/1966	5N	AWAY	DUBLIN	ALUN PASK	IRELAND	LOST	6	9	N/A
266	26/03/1966	5N	HOME	CARDIFF	ALUN PASK	FRANCE	WON	9	8	N/A
267	03/12/1966	TEST	HOME	CARDIFF	ALUN PASK	AUSTRALIA	LOST	11	14	N/A
268	04/02/1967	5N	AWAY	EDINBURGH	ALUN PASK	SCOTLAND	LOST	5	11	N/A
269	11/03/1967	5N	HOME	CARDIFF	DAVID WATKINS	IRELAND	LOST	0	3	N/A
270	01/04/1967	5N	AWAY	PARIS	DAVID WATKINS	FRANCE	LOST	14	20	N/A
271	15/04/1967	5N	HOME	CARDIFF	DAVID WATKINS	ENGLAND	WON	34	21	N/A
272	11/11/1967	TEST	HOME	CARDIFF	NORMAN GALE	NEW ZEALAND	LOST	6	13	DAVID NASH
273	20/01/1968	5N	AWAY	LONDON	NORMAN GALE	ENGLAND	DRAW	11	11	DAVID NASH
274	03/02/1968	5N	HOME	CARDIFF	GARETH EDWARDS	SCOTLAND	WON	5	0	DAVID NASH
275	09/03/1968	5N	AWAY	DUBLIN	JOHN DAWES	IRELAND	LOST	6	9	DAVID NASH
276	23/03/1968	5N	HOME	CARDIFF	GARETH EDWARDS	FRANCE	LOST	9	14	DAVID NASH
277	01/02/1969	5N	AWAY	EDINBURGH	BRIAN PRICE	SCOTLAND	WON	17	3	CLIVE ROWLANDS
278	08/03/1969	5N	HOME	CARDIFF	BRIAN PRICE	IRELAND	WON	24	11	CLIVE ROWLANDS
279	22/03/1969	5N	AWAY	PARIS	BRIAN PRICE	FRANCE	DRAW	8	8	CLIVE ROWLANDS
280	12/04/1969	5N	HOME	CARDIFF	GARETH EDWARDS	ENGLAND	WON	30	9	CLIVE ROWLANDS
281	31/05/1969	TEST (1)	AWAY	CHRISTCHURCH	BRIAN PRICE	NEW ZEALAND	LOST	0	19	CLIVE ROWLANDS
282	14/06/1969	TEST (2)	AWAY	AUCKLAND	BRIAN PRICE	NEW ZEALAND	LOST	12	33	CLIVE ROWLANDS
283	21/06/1969	TEST	AWAY	SYDNEY	BRIAN PRICE	AUSTRALIA	WON	19	16	CLIVE ROWLANDS
284	24/01/1970	TEST	HOME	CARDIFF	GARETH EDWARDS	SOUTH AFRICA	DRAW	6	6	CLIVE ROWLANDS
285	07/02/1970	5N	HOME	CARDIFF	GARETH EDWARDS	SCOTLAND	WON	18	9	CLIVE ROWLANDS
286	28/02/1970	5N	AWAY	LONDON	GARETH EDWARDS	ENGLAND	WON	17	13	CLIVE ROWLANDS
287	14/03/1970	5N	AWAY	DUBLIN	GARETH EDWARDS	IRELAND	LOST	0	14	CLIVE ROWLANDS
288	04/04/1970	5N	HOME	CARDIFF	JOHN DAWES	FRANCE	WON	11	6	CLIVE ROWLANDS
289	16/01/1971	5N	HOME	CARDIFF	JOHN DAWES	ENGLAND	WON	22	6	CLIVE ROWLANDS
290	06/02/1971	5N	AWAY	EDINBURGH	JOHN DAWES	SCOTLAND	WON	19	18	CLIVE ROWLANDS
291	13/03/1971	5N	HOME	CARDIFF	JOHN DAWES	IRELAND	WON	23	9	CLIVE ROWLANDS
292	27/03/1971	5N	AWAY	PARIS	JOHN DAWES	FRANCE	WON	9	5	CLIVE ROWLANDS
293	15/01/1972	5N	AWAY	LONDON	JOHN LLOYD	ENGLAND	WON	12	3	CLIVE ROWLANDS
294	05/02/1972	5N	HOME	CARDIFF	JOHN LLOYD	SCOTLAND	WON	35	12	CLIVE ROWLANDS
295	25/03/1972	5N	HOME	CARDIFF	JOHN LLOYD	FRANCE	WON	20	6	CLIVE ROWLANDS
296	02/12/1972	TEST	HOME	CARDIFF	DELME THOMAS	NEW ZEALAND	LOST	16	19	CLIVE ROWLANDS
297	20/01/1973	5N	HOME	CARDIFF	ARTHUR LEWIS	ENGLAND	WON	25	9	CLIVE ROWLANDS

GAME	DATE	TYPE	H/A	CITY	CAPTAIN	OPPONENTS	RESULT	SCORE (FOR)	SCORE (OPP)	COACH
298	03/02/1973	5N	AWAY	EDINBURGH	ARTHUR LEWIS	SCOTLAND	LOST	9	10	CLIVE ROWLANDS
299	10/03/1973	5N	HOME	CARDIFF	ARTHUR LEWIS	IRELAND	WON	16	12	CLIVE ROWLANDS
300	24/03/1973	5N	AWAY	PARIS	GARETH EDWARDS	FRANCE	LOST	3	12	CLIVE ROWLANDS
301	10/11/1973	TEST	HOME	CARDIFF	GARETH EDWARDS	AUSTRALIA	WON	24	0	CLIVE ROWLANDS
302	19/01/1974	5N	HOME	CARDIFF	GARETH EDWARDS	SCOTLAND	WON	6	0	CLIVE ROWLANDS
303	02/02/1974	5N	AWAY	DUBLIN	GARETH EDWARDS	IRELAND	DRAW	9	9	CLIVE ROWLANDS
304	16/02/1974	5N	HOME	CARDIFF	GARETH EDWARDS	FRANCE	DRAW	16	16	CLIVE ROWLANDS
305	16/03/1974	5N	AWAY	LONDON	GARETH EDWARDS	ENGLAND	LOST	12	16	CLIVE ROWLANDS
306	18/01/1975	5N	AWAY	PARIS	MERVYN DAVIES	FRANCE	WON	25	10	JOHN DAWES
307	15/02/1975	5N	HOME	CARDIFF	MERVYN DAVIES	ENGLAND	WON	20	4	JOHN DAWES
308	01/03/1975	5N	AWAY	EDINBURGH	MERVYN DAVIES	SCOTLAND	LOST	10	12	JOHN DAWES
309	15/03/1975	5N	HOME	CARDIFF	MERVYN DAVIES	IRELAND	WON	32	4	JOHN DAWES
310	20/12/1975	TEST	HOME	CARDIFF	MERVYN DAVIES	AUSTRALIA	WON	28	3	JOHN DAWES
311	17/01/1976	5N	AWAY	LONDON	MERVYN DAVIES	ENGLAND	WON	21	9	JOHN DAWES
312	07/02/1976	5N	HOME	CARDIFF	MERVYN DAVIES	SCOTLAND	WON	28	6	JOHN DAWES
313	21/02/1976	5N	AWAY	DUBLIN	MERVYN DAVIES	IRELAND	WON	34	9	JOHN DAWES
314	06/03/1976	5N	HOME	CARDIFF	MERVYN DAVIES	FRANCE	WON	19	13	JOHN DAWES
315	15/01/1977	5N	HOME	CARDIFF	PHIL BENNETT	IRELAND	WON	25	9	JOHN DAWES
316	05/02/1977	5N	AWAY	PARIS	PHIL BENNETT	FRANCE	LOST	9	16	JOHN DAWES
317	05/03/1977	5N	HOME	CARDIFF	PHIL BENNETT	ENGLAND	WON	14	9	JOHN DAWES
318	19/03/1977	5N	AWAY	EDINBURGH	PHIL BENNETT	SCOTLAND	WON	18	9	JOHN DAWES
319	04/02/1978	5N	AWAY	LONDON	PHIL BENNETT	ENGLAND	WON	9	6	JOHN DAWES
320	18/02/1978	5N	HOME	CARDIFF	PHIL BENNETT	SCOTLAND	WON	22	14	JOHN DAWES
321	04/03/1978	5N	AWAY	DUBLIN	PHIL BENNETT	IRELAND	WON	20	16	JOHN DAWES
322	18/03/1978	5N	HOME	CARDIFF	PHIL BENNETT	FRANCE	WON	16	7	JOHN DAWES
323	11/06/1978	TEST (1)	AWAY	BRISBANE	TERRY COBNER	AUSTRALIA	LOST	8	18	JOHN DAWES
324	17/06/1978	TEST (2)	AWAY	SYDNEY	GERALD DAVIES	AUSTRALIA	LOST	17	19	JOHN DAWES
325	11/11/1978	TEST	HOME	CARDIFF	JPR WILLIAMS	NEW ZEALAND	LOST	12	13	JOHN DAWES
326	20/01/1979	5N	AWAY	EDINBURGH	JPR WILLIAMS	SCOTLAND	WON	19	13	JOHN DAWES
327	03/02/1979	5N	HOME	CARDIFF	JPR WILLIAMS	IRELAND	WON	24	21	JOHN DAWES
328	17/02/1979	5N	AWAY	PARIS	JPR WILLIAMS	FRANCE	LOST	13	14	JOHN DAWES
329	17/03/1979	5N	HOME	CARDIFF	JPR WILLIAMS	ENGLAND	WON	27	3	JOHN DAWES
330	19/01/1980	5N	HOME	CARDIFF	JEFF SQUIRE	FRANCE	WON	18	9	JOHN LLOYD
331	16/02/1980	5N	AWAY	LONDON	JEFF SQUIRE	ENGLAND	LOST	8	9	JOHN LLOYD
332	01/03/1980	5N	HOME	CARDIFF	JEFF SQUIRE	SCOTLAND	WON	17	6	JOHN LLOYD
333	15/03/1980	5N	AWAY	DUBLIN	JEFF SQUIRE	IRELAND	LOST	7	21	JOHN LLOYD
334	01/11/1980	TEST	HOME	CARDIFF	STEVE FENWICK	NEW ZEALAND	LOST	3	23	JOHN LLOYD
335	17/01/1981	5N	HOME	CARDIFF	STEVE FENWICK	ENGLAND	WON	21	19	JOHN LLOYD
336	07/02/1981	5N	AWAY	EDINBURGH	STEVE FENWICK	SCOTLAND	LOST	6	15	JOHN LLOYD
337	21/02/1981	5N	HOME	CARDIFF	JEFF SQUIRE	IRELAND	WON	9	8	JOHN LLOYD
338	07/03/1981	5N	AWAY	PARIS	JEFF SQUIRE	FRANCE	LOST	15	19	JOHN LLOYD
339	05/12/1981	TEST	HOME	CARDIFF	GARETH DAVIES	AUSTRALIA	WON	18	13	JOHN LLOYD
340	23/01/1982	5N	AWAY	DUBLIN	GARETH DAVIES	IRELAND	LOST	12	20	JOHN LLOYD
341	06/02/1982	5N	HOME	CARDIFF	GARETH DAVIES	FRANCE	WON	22	12	JOHN LLOYD

GAME	DATE	TYPE	H/A	CITY	CAPTAIN	OPPONENTS	RESULT	SCORE (FOR)	SCORE (OPP)	COACH
342	06/03/1982	5N	AWAY	LONDON	GARETH DAVIES	ENGLAND	LOST	7	17	JOHN LLOYD
343	20/03/1982	5N	HOME	CARDIFF	GARETH DAVIES	SCOTLAND	LOST	18	34	JOHN LLOYD
344	05/02/1983	5N	HOME	CARDIFF	EDDIE BUTLER	ENGLAND	DRAW	13	13	JOHN BEVAN
345	19/02/1983	5N	AWAY	EDINBURGH	EDDIE BUTLER	SCOTLAND	WON	19	15	JOHN BEVAN
346	05/03/1983	5N	HOME	CARDIFF	EDDIE BUTLER	IRELAND	WON	23	9	JOHN BEVAN
347	19/03/1983	5N	AWAY	PARIS	EDDIE BUTLER	FRANCE	LOST	9	16	JOHN BEVAN
348	12/11/1983	TEST	AWAY	BUCHAREST	EDDIE BUTLER	ROMANIA	LOST	6	24	JOHN BEVAN
349	21/01/1984	5N	HOME	CARDIFF	EDDIE BUTLER	SCOTLAND	LOST	9	15	JOHN BEVAN
350	04/02/1984	5N	AWAY	DUBLIN	MIKE WATKINS	IRELAND	WON	18	9	JOHN BEVAN
351	18/02/1984	5N	HOME	CARDIFF	MIKE WATKINS	FRANCE	LOST	16	21	JOHN BEVAN
352	17/03/1984	5N	AWAY	LONDON	MIKE WATKINS	ENGLAND	WON	24	15	JOHN BEVAN
353	24/11/1984	TEST	HOME	CARDIFF	MIKE WATKINS	AUSTRALIA	LOST	9	28	JOHN BEVAN
354	02/03/1985	5N	AWAY	EDINBURGH	TERRY HOLMES	SCOTLAND	WON	25	21	JOHN BEVAN
355	16/03/1985	5N	HOME	CARDIFF	TERRY HOLMES	IRELAND	LOST	9	21	JOHN BEVAN
356	30/03/1985	5N	AWAY	PARIS	TERRY HOLMES	FRANCE	LOST	3	14	JOHN BEVAN
357	20/04/1985	5N	HOME	CARDIFF	TERRY HOLMES	ENGLAND	WON	24	15	JOHN BEVAN
358	09/11/1985	TEST	HOME	CARDIFF	TERRY HOLMES	FIJI	WON	40	3	JOHN BEVAN
359	18/01/1986	5N	AWAY	LONDON	DAVID PICKERING	ENGLAND	LOST	18	21	TONY GRAY
360	01/02/1986	5N	HOME	CARDIFF	DAVID PICKERING	SCOTLAND	WON	22	15	TONY GRAY
361	15/02/1986	5N	AWAY	DUBLIN	DAVID PICKERING	IRELAND	WON	19	12	TONY GRAY
362	01/03/1986	5N	HOME	CARDIFF	DAVID PICKERING	FRANCE	LOST	15	23	TONY GRAY
363	31/05/1986	TEST	AWAY	SUVA	DAVID PICKERING	FIJI	WON	22	15	TONY GRAY
364	12/06/1986	TEST	AWAY	NUKU'ALOFA	RICHARD MORIARTY	TONGA	WON	15	7	TONY GRAY
365	14/06/1986	TEST	AWAY	APIA	RICHARD MORIARTY	WESTERN SAMOA	WON	32	14	TONY GRAY
366	07/02/1987	5N	AWAY	PARIS	DAVID PICKERING	FRANCE	LOST	9	16	TONY GRAY
367	07/03/1987	5N	HOME	CARDIFF	DAVID PICKERING	ENGLAND	WON	19	12	TONY GRAY
368	21/03/1987	5N	AWAY	EDINBURGH	DAVID PICKERING	SCOTLAND	LOST	15	21	TONY GRAY
369	04/04/1987	5N	HOME	CARDIFF	BILLY JAMES	IRELAND	LOST	11	15	TONY GRAY
370	25/05/1987	WC	NEUT	WELLINGTON	RICHARD MORIARTY	IRELAND	WON	13	6	TONY GRAY
371	29/05/1987	WC	NEUT	PALMERSTON NORTH	RICHARD MORIARTY	TONGA	WON	29	16	TONY GRAY
372	03/06/1987	WC	NEUT	INVERCARGILL	JONATHAN DAVIES	CANADA	WON	40	9	TONY GRAY
373	08/06/1987	WC(QF)	NEUT	BRISBANE	RICHARD MORIARTY	ENGLAND	WON	16	3	TONY GRAY
374	14/06/1987	WC(SF)	NEUT	BRISBANE	RICHARD MORIARTY	NEW ZEALAND	LOST	6	49	TONY GRAY
375	18/06/1987	WC(3/4)	NEUT	ROTORUA	RICHARD MORIARTY	AUSTRALIA	WON	22	21	TONY GRAY
376	07/11/1987	TEST	HOME	CARDIFF	BLEDDYN BOWEN	USA	WON	46	0	TONY GRAY
377	06/02/1988	5N	AWAY	LONDON	BLEDDYN BOWEN	ENGLAND	WON	11	3	TONY GRAY
378	20/02/1988	5N	HOME	CARDIFF	BLEDDYN BOWEN	SCOTLAND	WON	25	20	TONY GRAY
379	05/03/1988	5N	AWAY	DUBLIN	BLEDDYN BOWEN	IRELAND	WON	12	9	TONY GRAY
380	19/03/1988	5N	HOME	CARDIFF	BLEDDYN BOWEN	FRANCE	LOST	9	10	TONY GRAY
381	28/05/1988	TEST (1)	AWAY	CHRISTCHURCH	ROBERT NORSTER	NEW ZEALAND	LOST	3	52	TONY GRAY
382	11/06/1988	TEST (2)	AWAY	AUCKLAND	JONATHAN DAVIES	NEW ZEALAND	LOST	9	54	TONY GRAY
383	12/11/1988	TEST	HOME	CARDIFF	JONATHAN DAVIES	WESTERN SAMOA	WON	28	6	JOHN RYAN
384	10/12/1988	TEST	HOME	CARDIFF	JONATHAN DAVIES	ROMANIA	LOST	9	15	JOHN RYAN
385	21/01/1989	5N	AWAY	EDINBURGH	PAUL THORBURN	SCOTLAND	LOST	7	23	JOHN RYAN

GAME	DATE	TYPE	H/A	CITY	CAPTAIN	OPPONENTS	RESULT	SCORE (FOR)	SCORE (OPP)	COACH
386	04/02/1989	5N	HOME	CARDIFF	PAUL THORBURN	IRELAND	LOST	13	19	JOHN RYAN
387	18/02/1989	5N	AWAY	PARIS	PAUL THORBURN	FRANCE	LOST	12	31	JOHN RYAN
388	18/03/1989	5N	HOME	CARDIFF	PAUL THORBURN	ENGLAND	WON	12	9	JOHN RYAN
389	04/11/1989	TEST	HOME	CARDIFF	ROBERT JONES	NEW ZEALAND	LOST	9	34	JOHN RYAN
390	20/02/1990	5N	HOME	CARDIFF	ROBERT JONES	FRANCE	LOST	19	29	JOHN RYAN
391	17/02/1990	5N	AWAY	LONDON	ROBERT JONES	ENGLAND	LOST	6	34	JOHN RYAN
392	03/03/1990	5N	HOME	CARDIFF	ROBERT JONES	SCOTLAND	LOST	9	13	RON WALDRON
393	24/03/1990	5N	AWAY	DUBLIN	ROBERT JONES	IRELAND	LOST	8	14	RON WALDRON
394	02/06/1990	TEST (1)	AWAY	WINDHOEK	KEVIN PHILLIPS	NAMIBIA	WON	18	9	RON WALDRON
395	09/06/1990	TEST (2)	AWAY	WINDHOEK	PAUL THORBURN	NAMIBIA	WON	34	30	RON WALDRON
396	06/10/1990	TEST	HOME	CARDIFF	PAUL THORBURN	BARBARIANS	LOST	24	31	RON WALDRON
397	19/01/1991	5N	HOME	CARDIFF	PAUL THORBURN	ENGLAND	LOST	6	25	RON WALDRON
398	02/02/1991	5N	AWAY	EDINBURGH	PAUL THORBURN	SCOTLAND	LOST	12	32	RON WALDRON
399	16/02/1991	5N	HOME	CARDIFF	PAUL THORBURN	IRELAND	DRAW	21	21	RON WALDRON
400	02/03/1991	5N	AWAY	PARIS	PAUL THORBURN	FRANCE	LOST	3	36	RON WALDRON
401	22/07/1991	TEST	AWAY	BRISBANE	PAUL THORBURN	AUSTRALIA	LOST	6	63	RON WALDRON
402	04/09/1991	TEST	HOME	CARDIFF	IEUAN EVANS	FRANCE	LOST	9	22	ALAN DAVIES
403	06/10/1991	WC	HOME	CARDIFF	IEUAN EVANS	WESTERN SAMOA	LOST	13	16	ALAN DAVIES
404	09/10/1991	WC	HOME	CARDIFF	IEUAN EVANS	ARGENTINA	WON	16	7	ALAN DAVIES
405	12/10/1991	WC	HOME	CARDIFF	IEUAN EVANS	AUSTRALIA	LOST	3	38	ALAN DAVIES
406	18/01/1992	5N	AWAY	DUBLIN	IEUAN EVANS	IRELAND	WON	16	15	ALAN DAVIES
407	01/02/1992	5N	HOME	CARDIFF	IEUAN EVANS	FRANCE	LOST	9	12	ALAN DAVIES
408	07/03/1992	5N	AWAY	LONDON	IEUAN EVANS	ENGLAND	LOST	0	24	ALAN DAVIES
409	21/03/1992	5N	HOME	CARDIFF	IEUAN EVANS	SCOTLAND	WON	15	12	ALAN DAVIES
410	21/11/1992	TEST	HOME	CARDIFF	IEUAN EVANS	AUSTRALIA	LOST	6	23	ALAN DAVIES
411	06/02/1993	5N	HOME	CARDIFF	IEUAN EVANS	ENGLAND	WON	10	9	ALAN DAVIES
412	20/02/1993	5N	AWAY	EDINBURGH	IEUAN EVANS	SCOTLAND	LOST	0	20	ALAN DAVIES
413	06/03/1993	5N	HOME	CARDIFF	IEUAN EVANS	IRELAND	LOST	14	19	ALAN DAVIES
414	20/03/1993	5N	AWAY	PARIS	IEUAN EVANS	FRANCE	LOST	10	26	ALAN DAVIES
415	22/05/1993	TEST (1)	AWAY	BULAWAYO	GARETH LLEWELLYN	ZIMBABWE	WON	35	14	ALAN DAVIES
416	29/05/1993	TEST (2)	AWAY	HARARE	GARETH LLEWELLYN	ZIMBABWE	WON	42	13	ALAN DAVIES
417	05/06/1993	TEST	AWAY	WINDHOEK	GARETH LLEWELLYN	NAMIBIA	WON	38	23	ALAN DAVIES
418	16/10/1993	TEST	HOME	CARDIFF	IEUAN EVANS	JAPAN	WON	55	5	ALAN DAVIES
419	10/11/1993	TEST	HOME	CARDIFF	IEUAN EVANS	CANADA	LOST	24	26	ALAN DAVIES
420	15/01/1994	5N	AWAY	CARDIFF	IEUAN EVANS	SCOTLAND	WON	29	6	ALAN DAVIES
421	05/02/1994	5N	AWAY	DUBLIN	IEUAN EVANS	IRELAND	WON	17	15	ALAN DAVIES
422	19/02/1994	5N	HOME	CARDIFF	GARETH LLEWELLYN	FRANCE	LOST	24	15	ALAN DAVIES
423	19/03/1994	5N	AWAY	LONDON	IEUAN EVANS	ENGLAND	WON	8	15	ALAN DAVIES
424	17/05/1994	WCQ	AWAY	LISBON	IEUAN EVANS	PORTUGAL	WON	102	11	ALAN DAVIES
425	21/05/1994	WCQ	AWAY	MADRID	IEUAN EVANS	SPAIN	WON	54	0	ALAN DAVIES
426	11/06/1994	TEST	AWAY	MARKHAM	IEUAN EVANS	CANADA	WON	33	15	ALAN DAVIES
427	18/06/1994	TEST	AWAY	SUVA	IEUAN EVANS	FIJI	WON	23	8	ALAN DAVIES
428	22/06/1994	TEST	AWAY	NUKU'ALOFA	IEUAN EVANS	TONGA	WON	18	9	ALAN DAVIES
429	25/06/1994	TEST	AWAY	APIA	IEUAN EVANS	WESTERN SAMOA	LOST	9	34	ALAN DAVIES

GAME	DATE	TYPE	H/A	CITY	CAPTAIN	OPPONENTS	RESULT	SCORE (FOR)	SCORE (OPP)	COACH
430	17/09/1994	WCQ	AWAY	BUCHAREST	IEUAN EVANS	ROMANIA	WON	16	9	ALAN DAVIES
431	12/10/1994	WCQ	HOME	CARDIFF	GARETH LLEWELLYN	ITALY	WON	29	19	ALAN DAVIES
432	26/11/1994	TEST	HOME	CARDIFF	GARETH LLEWELLYN	SOUTH AFRICA	LOST	12	20	ALAN DAVIES
433	21/01/1995	5N	AWAY	PARIS	GARETH LLEWELLYN	FRANCE	LOST	9	21	ALAN DAVIES
434	18/02/1995	5N	HOME	CARDIFF	IEUAN EVANS	ENGLAND	LOST	9	23	ALAN DAVIES
435	04/03/1995	5N	AWAY	EDINBURGH	IEUAN EVANS	SCOTLAND	LOST	13	26	ALAN DAVIES
436	18/03/1995	5N	HOME	CARDIFF	IEUAN EVANS	IRELAND	LOST	12	16	ALAN DAVIES
437	27/05/1995	WC	NEUT	BLOEMFONTEIN	MIKE HALL	JAPAN	WON	57	10	ALEC EVANS
438	31/05/1995	WC	NEUT	JOHANNESBURG	MIKE HALL	NEW ZEALAND	LOST	9	34	ALEC EVANS
439	04/06/1995	WC	NEUT	JOHANNESBURG	MIKE HALL	IRELAND	LOST	23	24	ALEC EVANS
440	02/09/1995	TEST	AWAY	JOHANNESBURG	JONATHAN HUMPHREYS	SOUTH AFRICA	LOST	11	40	ALEC EVANS
441	11/11/1995	TEST	HOME	CARDIFF	JONATHAN HUMPHREYS	FIJI	WON	19	15	KEVIN BOWRING
442	16/01/1996	TEST	HOME	CARDIFF	JONATHAN HUMPHREYS	ITALY	WON	31	26	KEVIN BOWRING
443	03/02/1996	5N	AWAY	LONDON	JONATHAN HUMPHREYS	ENGLAND	LOST	15	21	KEVIN BOWRING
444	17/02/1996	5N	HOME	CARDIFF	JONATHAN HUMPHREYS	SCOTLAND	LOST	14	16	KEVIN BOWRING
445	02/03/1996	5N	AWAY	DUBLIN	JONATHAN HUMPHREYS	IRELAND	LOST	17	30	KEVIN BOWRING
446	16/03/1996	5N	HOME	CARDIFF	JONATHAN HUMPHREYS	FRANCE	WON	16	15	KEVIN BOWRING
447	09/06/1996	TEST (1)	AWAY	BRISBANE	JONATHAN HUMPHREYS	AUSTRALIA	LOST	25	56	KEVIN BOWRING
448	22/06/1996	TEST (2)	AWAY	SYDNEY	JONATHAN HUMPHREYS	AUSTRALIA	LOST	3	42	KEVIN BOWRING
449	24/08/1996	TEST	HOME	CARDIFF	JONATHAN HUMPHREYS	BARBARIANS	WON	31	10	KEVIN BOWRING
450	25/09/1996	TEST	HOME	CARDIFF	NIGEL DAVIES	FRANCE	LOST	33	40	KEVIN BOWRING
451	05/10/1996	TEST	AWAY	ROME	JONATHAN HUMPHREYS	ITALY	WON	31	22	KEVIN BOWRING
452	01/12/1996	TEST	HOME	CARDIFF	JONATHAN HUMPHREYS	AUSTRALIA	LOST	19	28	KEVIN BOWRING
453	15/12/1996	TEST	HOME	CARDIFF	JONATHAN HUMPHREYS	SOUTH AFRICA	LOST	20	37	KEVIN BOWRING
454	11/01/1997	TEST	HOME	CARDIFF	SCOTT GIBBS	USA	WON	34	14	KEVIN BOWRING
455	18/01/1997	5N	AWAY	EDINBURGH	JONATHAN HUMPHREYS	SCOTLAND	WON	34	19	KEVIN BOWRING
456	01/02/1997	5N	HOME	CARDIFF	JONATHAN HUMPHREYS	IRELAND	LOST	25	26	KEVIN BOWRING
457	15/02/1997	5N	AWAY	PARIS	JONATHAN HUMPHREYS	FRANCE	LOST	22	27	KEVIN BOWRING
458	15/03/1997	5N	HOME	CARDIFF	JONATHAN HUMPHREYS	ENGLAND	LOST	13	34	KEVIN BOWRING
459	05/07/1997	TEST (1)	AWAY	WILMINGTON	GWYN JONES	USA	WON	30	20	KEVIN BOWRING
460	12/07/1997	TEST (2)	AWAY	SAN FRANCISCO	GWYN JONES	USA	WON	28	23	KEVIN BOWRING
461	19/07/1997	TEST	AWAY	MARKHAM	PAUL JOHN	CANADA	WON	28	25	KEVIN BOWRING
462	30/08/1997	TEST	HOME	WREXHAM	GWYN JONES	ROMANIA	WON	70	21	KEVIN BOWRING
463	16/11/1997	TEST	HOME	SWANSEA	GWYN JONES	TONGA	WON	46	12	KEVIN BOWRING
464	29/11/1997	TEST	HOME	LONDON	GWYN JONES	NEW ZEALAND	LOST	7	42	KEVIN BOWRING
465	07/02/1998	TEST	HOME	LLANELLI	ROB HOWLEY	ITALY	WON	23	20	KEVIN BOWRING
466	21/02/1998	5N	AWAY	LONDON	ROB HOWLEY	ENGLAND	LOST	26	60	KEVIN BOWRING
467	07/03/1998	5N	HOME	LONDON	ROB HOWLEY	SCOTLAND	WON	19	13	KEVIN BOWRING
468	21/03/1998	5N	AWAY	DUBLIN	ROB HOWLEY	IRELAND	WON	30	21	KEVIN BOWRING
469	05/04/1998	5N	HOME	LONDON	ROB HOWLEY	FRANCE	LOST	0	51	KEVIN BOWRING
470	06/06/1998	TEST	AWAY	HARARE	ROB HOWLEY	ZIMBABWE	WON	49	11	DENNIS JOHN
471	27/06/1998	TEST	AWAY	PRETORIA	KINGSLEY JONES	SOUTH AFRICA	LOST	13	96	DENNIS JOHN
472	14/11/1998	TEST	HOME	LONDON	ROB HOWLEY	SOUTH AFRICA	LOST	20	28	GRAHAM HENRY
473	21/11/1998	TEST	HOME	LLANELLI	ROB HOWLEY	ARGENTINA	WON	43	30	GRAHAM HENRY

GAME	DATE	TYPE	H/A	CITY	CAPTAIN	OPPONENTS	RESULT	SCORE (FOR)	SCORE (OPP)	COACH
474	06/02/1999	5N	AWAY	EDINBURGH	ROB HOWLEY	SCOTLAND	LOST	20	33	GRAHAM HENRY
475	20/02/1999	5N	HOME	LONDON	ROB HOWLEY	IRELAND	LOST	23	29	GRAHAM HENRY
476	06/03/1999	5N	AWAY	PARIS	ROB HOWLEY	FRANCE	WON	34	33	GRAHAM HENRY
477	20/03/1999	TEST	AWAY	TREVISO	ROB HOWLEY	ITALY	WON	60	21	GRAHAM HENRY
478	11/04/1999	5N	HOME	LONDON	ROB HOWLEY	ENGLAND	WON	32	31	GRAHAM HENRY
479	05/06/1999	TEST (1)	AWAY	BUENOS AIRES	ROB HOWLEY	ARGENTINA	WON	36	26	GRAHAM HENRY
480	12/06/1999	TEST (2)	AWAY	BUENOS AIRES	ROB HOWLEY	ARGENTINA	WON	23	16	GRAHAM HENRY
481	26/06/1999	TEST	HOME	CARDIFF	ROB HOWLEY	SOUTH AFRICA	WON	29	19	GRAHAM HENRY
482	21/08/1999	WCW	HOME	CARDIFF	ROB HOWLEY	CANADA	WON	33	19	GRAHAM HENRY
483	28/08/1999	WCW	HOME	CARDIFF	ROB HOWLEY	FRANCE	WON	34	23	GRAHAM HENRY
484	01/10/1999	WC	HOME	CARDIFF	ROB HOWLEY	ARGENTINA	WON	23	18	GRAHAM HENRY
485	09/10/1999	WC	HOME	CARDIFF	ROB HOWLEY	JAPAN	WON	64	15	GRAHAM HENRY
486	14/10/1999	WC	HOME	CARDIFF	ROB HOWLEY	SAMOA	LOST	31	38	GRAHAM HENRY
487	23/10/1999	WC(QF)	HOME	CARDIFF	ROB HOWLEY	AUSTRALIA	LOST	9	24	GRAHAM HENRY
488	05/02/2000	6N	HOME	CARDIFF	DAI YOUNG	FRANCE	LOST	3	36	GRAHAM HENRY
489	19/02/2000	6N	HOME	CARDIFF	DAI YOUNG	ITALY	WON	47	16	GRAHAM HENRY
490	04/03/2000	6N	AWAY	LONDON	DAI YOUNG	ENGLAND	LOST	12	46	GRAHAM HENRY
491	18/03/2000	6N	HOME	CARDIFF	DAI YOUNG	SCOTLAND	WON	26	18	GRAHAM HENRY
492	01/04/2000	6N	AWAY	DUBLIN	DAI YOUNG	IRELAND	WON	23	19	GRAHAM HENRY
493	11/11/2000	TEST	HOME	CARDIFF	MARK TAYLOR	SAMOA	WON	50	6	GRAHAM HENRY
494	18/11/2000	TEST	HOME	CARDIFF	MARK TAYLOR	USA	WON	42	11	GRAHAM HENRY
495	26/11/2000	TEST	HOME	CARDIFF	SCOTT QUINNELL	SOUTH AFRICA	LOST	13	23	GRAHAM HENRY
496	03/02/2001	6N	HOME	CARDIFF	DAI YOUNG	ENGLAND	LOST	15	44	GRAHAM HENRY
497	17/02/2001	6N	AWAY	EDINBURGH	DAI YOUNG	SCOTLAND	DRAW	28	28	GRAHAM HENRY
498	17/03/2001	6N	AWAY	PARIS	DAI YOUNG	FRANCE	WON	43	35	GRAHAM HENRY
499	08/04/2001	6N	AWAY	ROME	DAI YOUNG	ITALY	WON	33	23	GRAHAM HENRY
500	10/06/2001	TEST (1)	AWAY	HIGASHIŌSAKA	ANDY MOORE	JAPAN	WON	64	10	LYNN HOWELLS
501	17/06/2001	TEST (2)	AWAY	TOKYO	ANDY MOORE	JAPAN	WON	53	30	LYNN HOWELLS
502	19/09/2001	TEST	HOME	CARDIFF	DAI YOUNG	ROMANIA	WON	81	9	GRAHAM HENRY
503	13/10/2001	6N	HOME	CARDIFF	DAI YOUNG	IRELAND	LOST	6	36	GRAHAM HENRY
504	10/11/2001	TEST	HOME	CARDIFF	DAI YOUNG	ARGENTINA	LOST	16	30	GRAHAM HENRY
505	17/11/2001	TEST	HOME	CARDIFF	SCOTT QUINNELL	TONGA	WON	51	7	GRAHAM HENRY
506	25/11/2001	TEST	HOME	CARDIFF	SCOTT QUINNELL	AUSTRALIA	LOST	13	21	GRAHAM HENRY
507	03/02/2002	6N	AWAY	DUBLIN	SCOTT QUINNELL	IRELAND	LOST	10	54	GRAHAM HENRY
508	16/02/2002	6N	HOME	CARDIFF	SCOTT QUINNELL	FRANCE	LOST	33	37	STEVE HANSEN
509	02/03/2002	6N	HOME	CARDIFF	SCOTT QUINNELL	ITALY	WON	44	20	STEVE HANSEN
510	23/03/2002	6N	AWAY	LONDON	SCOTT QUINNELL	ENGLAND	LOST	10	50	STEVE HANSEN
511	06/04/2002	6N	HOME	CARDIFF	COLIN CHARVIS	SCOTLAND	LOST	22	27	STEVE HANSEN
512	08/06/2002	TEST (1)	AWAY	BLOEMFONTEIN	COLIN CHARVIS	SOUTH AFRICA	LOST	19	34	STEVE HANSEN
513	15/06/2002	TEST (2)	AWAY	CAPE TOWN	COLIN CHARVIS	SOUTH AFRICA	LOST	8	19	STEVE HANSEN
514	01/11/2002	TEST	HOME	WREXHAM	COLIN CHARVIS	ROMANIA	WON	40	3	STEVE HANSEN
515	09/11/2002	TEST	HOME	CARDIFF	COLIN CHARVIS	FIJI	WON	58	14	STEVE HANSEN
516	16/11/2002	TEST	HOME	CARDIFF	COLIN CHARVIS	CANADA	WON	32	21	STEVE HANSEN
517	23/11/2002	TEST	HOME	CARDIFF	COLIN CHARVIS	NEW ZEALAND	LOST	17	43	STEVE HANSEN

GAME	DATE	TYPE	H/A	CITY	CAPTAIN	OPPONENTS	RESULT	SCORE (FOR)	SCORE (OPP)	COACH
518	15/02/2003	6N	AWAY	ROME	COLIN CHARVIS	ITALY	LOST	22	30	STEVE HANSEN
519	22/02/2003	6N	HOME	CARDIFF	JONATHAN HUMPHREYS	ENGLAND	LOST	9	26	STEVE HANSEN
520	08/03/2003	6N	AWAY	EDINBURGH	MARTYN WILLIAMS	SCOTLAND	LOST	22	30	STEVE HANSEN
521	22/03/2003	6N	HOME	CARDIFF	JONATHAN HUMPHREYS	IRELAND	LOST	24	25	STEVE HANSEN
522	29/03/2003	6N	AWAY	PARIS	MARTYN WILLIAMS	FRANCE	LOST	5	33	STEVE HANSEN
523	14/06/2003	TEST	AWAY	SYDNEY	MARTYN WILLIAMS	AUSTRALIA	LOST	10	30	STEVE HANSEN
524	21/06/2003	TEST	AWAY	HAMILTON	MARTYN WILLIAMS	NEW ZEALAND	LOST	3	55	STEVE HANSEN
525	16/08/2003	WCW	AWAY	DUBLIN	GARETH THOMAS	IRELAND	LOST	12	35	STEVE HANSEN
526	23/08/2003	WCW	HOME	CARDIFF	STEPHEN JONES	ENGLAND	LOST	9	43	STEVE HANSEN
527	27/08/2003	WCW	HOME	WREXHAM	MEFIN DAVIES	ROMANIA	WON	54	8	STEVE HANSEN
528	30/08/2003	WCW	HOME	CARDIFF	COLIN CHARVIS	SCOTLAND	WON	23	9	STEVE HANSEN
529	12/10/2003	WC	NEUT	MELBOURNE	COLIN CHARVIS	CANADA	WON	41	10	STEVE HANSEN
530	19/10/2003	WC	NEUT	CANBERRA	COLIN CHARVIS	TONGA	WON	27	20	STEVE HANSEN
531	25/10/2003	WC	NEUT	CANBERRA	COLIN CHARVIS	ITALY	WON	27	15	STEVE HANSEN
532	02/11/2003	WC	NEUT	SYDNEY	COLIN CHARVIS	NEW ZEALAND	LOST	37	53	STEVE HANSEN
533	09/11/2003	WC (QF)	NEUT	BRISBANE	COLIN CHARVIS	ENGLAND	LOST	17	28	STEVE HANSEN
534	14/02/2004	6N	HOME	CARDIFF	COLIN CHARVIS	SCOTLAND	WON	23	10	STEVE HANSEN
535	22/02/2004	6N	AWAY	DUBLIN	MARTYN WILLIAMS	IRELAND	LOST	15	36	STEVE HANSEN
536	07/03/2004	6N	HOME	CARDIFF	COLIN CHARVIS	FRANCE	LOST	22	29	STEVE HANSEN
537	20/03/2004	6N	AWAY	LONDON	COLIN CHARVIS	ENGLAND	LOST	21	31	STEVE HANSEN
538	27/03/2004	6N	HOME	CARDIFF	COLIN CHARVIS	ITALY	WON	44	10	STEVE HANSEN
539	12/06/2004	TEST (1)	AWAY	TUCUMAN	COLIN CHARVIS	ARGENTINA	LOST	44	50	MIKE RUDDOCK
540	19/06/2004	TEST (2)	AWAY	BUENOS AIRES	COLIN CHARVIS	ARGENTINA	WON	35	20	MIKE RUDDOCK
541	26/06/2004	TEST	AWAY	PRETORIA	COLIN CHARVIS	SOUTH AFRICA	LOST	18	53	MIKE RUDDOCK
542	06/11/2004	TEST	HOME	CARDIFF	GARETH THOMAS	SOUTH AFRICA	LOST	36	38	MIKE RUDDOCK
543	12/11/2004	TEST	HOME	CARDIFF	GARETH THOMAS	ROMANIA	WON	66	7	MIKE RUDDOCK
544	20/11/2004	TEST	HOME	CARDIFF	GARETH THOMAS	NEW ZEALAND	LOST	25	26	MIKE RUDDOCK
545	26/11/2004	TEST	HOME	CARDIFF	COLIN CHARVIS	JAPAN	WON	98	0	MIKE RUDDOCK
546	05/02/2005	6N	HOME	CARDIFF	GARETH THOMAS	ENGLAND	WON	11	9	MIKE RUDDOCK
547	12/02/2005	6N	AWAY	ROME	GARETH THOMAS	ITALY	WON	38	8	MIKE RUDDOCK
548	26/02/2005	6N	AWAY	PARIS	GARETH THOMAS	FRANCE	WON	24	18	MIKE RUDDOCK
549	13/03/2005	6N	AWAY	EDINBURGH	MICHAEL OWEN	SCOTLAND	WON	46	22	MIKE RUDDOCK
550	19/03/2005	6N	HOME	CARDIFF	MICHAEL OWEN	IRELAND	WON	32	20	MIKE RUDDOCK
551	04/06/2005	TEST	AWAY	HARTFORD	MARK TAYLOR	USA	WON	77	3	MIKE RUDDOCK
552	11/06/2005	TEST	AWAY	TORONTO	MARK TAYLOR	CANADA	WON	60	3	MIKE RUDDOCK
553	05/11/2005	TEST	HOME	CARDIFF	GARETH THOMAS	NEW ZEALAND	LOST	3	41	MIKE RUDDOCK
554	11/11/2005	TEST	HOME	CARDIFF	MICHAEL OWEN	FIJI	WON	11	10	MIKE RUDDOCK
555	19/11/2005	TEST	HOME	CARDIFF	GARETH THOMAS	SOUTH AFRICA	LOST	16	33	MIKE RUDDOCK
556	26/11/2005	TEST	HOME	CARDIFF	GARETH THOMAS	AUSTRALIA	WON	24	22	MIKE RUDDOCK
557	04/02/2006	6N	AWAY	LONDON	GARETH THOMAS	ENGLAND	LOST	13	47	MIKE RUDDOCK
558	12/02/2006	6N	HOME	CARDIFF	GARETH THOMAS	SCOTLAND	WON	28	18	MIKE RUDDOCK
559	26/02/2006	6N	AWAY	DUBLIN	MICHAEL OWEN	IRELAND	LOST	5	31	SCOTT JOHNSON
560	11/03/2006	6N	HOME	CARDIFF	MICHAEL OWEN	ITALY	DRAW	18	18	SCOTT JOHNSON
561	18/03/2006	6N	HOME	CARDIFF	MICHAEL OWEN	FRANCE	LOST	16	21	SCOTT JOHNSON

GAME	DATE	TYPE	H/A	CITY	CAPTAIN	OPPONENTS	RESULT	SCORE (FOR)	SCORE (OPP)	COACH
562	11/06/2006	TEST (1)	AWAY	PUERTO MADRYN	DUNCAN JONES	ARGENTINA	LOST	25	27	GARETH JENKINS
563	17/06/2006	TEST (2)	AWAY	BUENOS AIRES	DUNCAN JONES	ARGENTINA	LOST	27	45	GARETH JENKINS
564	04/11/2006	TEST	HOME	CARDIFF	STEPHEN JONES	AUSTRALIA	DRAW	29	29	GARETH JENKINS
565	11/11/2006	TEST	HOME	CARDIFF	DUNCAN JONES	PACIFIC ISLANDERS	WON	38	20	GARETH JENKINS
566	17/11/2006	TEST	HOME	CARDIFF	GARETH THOMAS	CANADA	WON	61	26	GARETH JENKINS
567	25/11/2006	TEST	HOME	CARDIFF	STEPHEN JONES	NEW ZEALAND	LOST	10	45	GARETH JENKINS
568	04/02/2007	6N	HOME	CARDIFF	STEPHEN JONES	IRELAND	LOST	9	19	GARETH JENKINS
569	10/02/2007	6N	AWAY	EDINBURGH	STEPHEN JONES	SCOTLAND	LOST	9	21	GARETH JENKINS
570	24/02/2007	6N	AWAY	PARIS	STEPHEN JONES	FRANCE	LOST	21	32	GARETH JENKINS
571	10/03/2007	6N	AWAY	ROME	STEPHEN JONES	ITALY	LOST	20	23	GARETH JENKINS
572	17/03/2007	6N	HOME	CARDIFF	GARETH THOMAS	ENGLAND	WON	27	18	GARETH JENKINS
573	26/05/2007	TEST (1)	AWAY	SYDNEY	GARETH THOMAS	AUSTRALIA	LOST	23	29	GARETH JENKINS
574	02/06/2007	TEST (2)	AWAY	BRISBANE	GARETH THOMAS	AUSTRALIA	LOST	0	31	GARETH JENKINS
575	04/08/2007	WCW	AWAY	LONDON	GARETH THOMAS	ENGLAND	LOST	5	62	GARETH JENKINS
576	18/08/2007	WCW	HOME	CARDIFF	GARETH THOMAS	ARGENTINA	WON	27	20	GARETH JENKINS
577	26/08/2007	WCW	HOME	CARDIFF	GARETH THOMAS	FRANCE	LOST	7	34	GARETH JENKINS
578	09/09/2007	WC	NEUT	NANTES	DWAYNE PEEL	CANADA	WON	42	17	GARETH JENKINS
579	15/09/2007	WC	HOME	CARDIFF	GARETH THOMAS	AUSTRALIA	LOST	20	32	GARETH JENKINS
580	20/09/2007	WC	HOME	CARDIFF	STEPHEN JONES	JAPAN	WON	72	18	GARETH JENKINS
581	29/09/2007	WC	NEUT	NANTES	GARETH THOMAS	FIJI	LOST	34	38	GARETH JENKINS
582	24/11/2007	TEST	HOME	CARDIFF	GETHIN JENKINS	SOUTH AFRICA	LOST	12	34	NIGEL DAVIES
583	02/02/2008	6N	AWAY	LONDON	RYAN JONES	ENGLAND	WON	26	19	WARREN GATLAND
584	09/02/2008	6N	HOME	CARDIFF	RYAN JONES	SCOTLAND	WON	30	15	WARREN GATLAND
585	23/02/2008	6N	HOME	CARDIFF	RYAN JONES	ITALY	WON	47	8	WARREN GATLAND
586	08/03/2008	6N	AWAY	DUBLIN	RYAN JONES	IRELAND	WON	16	12	WARREN GATLAND
587	15/03/2008	6N	HOME	CARDIFF	RYAN JONES	FRANCE	WON	29	12	WARREN GATLAND
588	07/06/2008	TEST (1)	AWAY	BLOEMFONTEIN	RYAN JONES	SOUTH AFRICA	LOST	17	43	WARREN GATLAND
589	14/06/2008	TEST (2)	AWAY	PRETORIA	RYAN JONES	SOUTH AFRICA	LOST	21	37	WARREN GATLAND
590	08/11/2008	TEST	HOME	CARDIFF	RYAN JONES	SOUTH AFRICA	LOST	15	20	WARREN GATLAND
591	14/11/2008	TEST	HOME	CARDIFF	RYAN JONES	CANADA	WON	34	13	WARREN GATLAND
592	22/11/2008	TEST	HOME	CARDIFF	RYAN JONES	NEW ZEALAND	LOST	9	29	WARREN GATLAND
593	29/11/2008	TEST	HOME	CARDIFF	RYAN JONES	AUSTRALIA	WON	21	18	WARREN GATLAND
594	08/02/2009	6N	AWAY	EDINBURGH	MARTYN WILLIAMS	SCOTLAND	WON	26	13	WARREN GATLAND
595	14/02/2009	6N	HOME	CARDIFF	RYAN JONES	ENGLAND	WON	23	15	WARREN GATLAND
596	27/02/2009	6N	AWAY	PARIS	RYAN JONES	FRANCE	LOST	16	21	WARREN GATLAND
597	14/03/2009	6N	AWAY	ROME	ALUN WYN JONES	ITALY	WON	20	15	WARREN GATLAND
598	21/03/2009	6N	HOME	CARDIFF	RYAN JONES	IRELAND	LOST	15	17	WARREN GATLAND
599	30/05/2009	TEST	AWAY	TORONTO	RYAN JONES	CANADA	WON	32	23	ROBIN McBRYDE
600	06/06/2009	TEST	AWAY	CHICAGO	RYAN JONES	USA	WON	48	15	ROBIN McBRYDE
601	07/11/2009	TEST	HOME	CARDIFF	RYAN JONES	NEW ZEALAND	LOST	12	19	WARREN GATLAND
602	13/11/2009	TEST	HOME	CARDIFF	RYAN JONES	SAMOA	WON	17	13	WARREN GATLAND
603	21/11/2009	TEST	HOME	CARDIFF	RYAN JONES	ARGENTINA	WON	33	16	WARREN GATLAND
604	28/11/2009	TEST	HOME	CARDIFF	GETHIN JENKINS	AUSTRALIA	LOST	12	33	WARREN GATLAND
605	06/02/2010	6N	AWAY	LONDON	RYAN JONES	ENGLAND	LOST	30	17	WARREN GATLAND

GAME	DATE	TYPE	H/A	CITY	CAPTAIN	OPPONENTS	RESULT	SCORE (FOR)	SCORE (OPP)	COACH
606	13/02/2010	6N	HOME	CARDIFF	RYAN JONES	SCOTLAND	WON	31	24	WARREN GATLAND
607	26/02/2010	6N	HOME	CARDIFF	RYAN JONES	FRANCE	LOST	20	26	WARREN GATLAND
608	13/03/2010	6N	AWAY	DUBLIN	MARTYN WILLIAMS	IRELAND	LOST	12	27	WARREN GATLAND
609	20/03/2010	6N	HOME	CARDIFF	RYAN JONES	ITALY	WON	33	10	WARREN GATLAND
610	05/06/2010	TEST	HOME	CARDIFF	RYAN JONES	SOUTH AFRICA	LOST	31	34	WARREN GATLAND
611	19/06/2010	TEST (1)	AWAY	DUNEDIN	RYAN JONES	NEW ZEALAND	LOST	9	42	WARREN GATLAND
612	26/06/2010	TEST (2)	AWAY	HAMILTON	RYAN JONES	NEW ZEALAND	LOST	10	29	WARREN GATLAND
613	06/11/2010	TEST	HOME	CARDIFF	MATTHEW REES	AUSTRALIA	LOST	16	25	WARREN GATLAND
614	13/11/2010	TEST	HOME	CARDIFF	MATTHEW REES	SOUTH AFRICA	LOST	25	29	WARREN GATLAND
615	19/11/2010	TEST	HOME	CARDIFF	RYAN JONES	FIJI	DRAW	16	16	WARREN GATLAND
616	27/11/2010	TEST	HOME	CARDIFF	MATTHEW REES	NEW ZEALAND	LOST	25	37	WARREN GATLAND
617	04/02/2011	6N	HOME	CARDIFF	MATTHEW REES	ENGLAND	LOST	19	26	WARREN GATLAND
618	12/02/2011	6N	AWAY	EDINBURGH	MATTHEW REES	SCOTLAND	WON	24	6	WARREN GATLAND
619	26/02/2011	6N	AWAY	ROME	MATTHEW REES	ITALY	WON	24	16	WARREN GATLAND
620	12/03/2011	6N	HOME	CARDIFF	MATTHEW REES	IRELAND	WON	19	13	WARREN GATLAND
621	19/03/2011	6N	AWAY	PARIS	MATTHEW REES	FRANCE	LOST	9	28	WARREN GATLAND
622	04/06/2011	WCW	HOME	CARDIFF	SAM WARBURTON	BARBARIANS	LOST	28	31	WARREN GATLAND
623	06/08/2011	WCW	AWAY	LONDON	SAM WARBURTON	ENGLAND	LOST	19	23	WARREN GATLAND
624	13/08/2011	WCW	HOME	CARDIFF	SAM WARBURTON	ENGLAND	WON	19	9	WARREN GATLAND
625	20/08/2011	WCW	HOME	CARDIFF	MARTYN WILLIAMS	ARGENTINA	WON	28	13	WARREN GATLAND
626	11/09/2011	WC	NEUT	WELLINGTON	SAM WARBURTON	SOUTH AFRICA	LOST	16	17	WARREN GATLAND
627	18/09/2011	WC	NEUT	HAMILTON	SAM WARBURTON	SAMOA	WON	17	10	WARREN GATLAND
628	26/09/2011	WC	NEUT	NEW PLYMOUTH	SAM WARBURTON	NAMIBIA	WON	81	7	WARREN GATLAND
629	02/10/2011	WC	NEUT	AUCKLAND	SAM WARBURTON	FIJI	WON	66	0	WARREN GATLAND
630	08/10/2011	WC(QF)	NEUT	WELLINGTON	SAM WARBURTON	IRELAND	WON	22	10	WARREN GATLAND
631	15/10/2011	WC(SF)	NEUT	AUCKLAND	SAM WARBURTON	FRANCE	LOST	8	9	WARREN GATLAND
632	21/10/2011	WC(3/4)	NEUT	AUCKLAND	GETHIN JENKINS	AUSTRALIA	LOST	18	21	WARREN GATLAND
633	03/12/2011	TEST	HOME	CARDIFF	SAM WARBURTON	AUSTRALIA	LOST	18	24	WARREN GATLAND
634	05/02/2012	6N	AWAY	DUBLIN	SAM WARBURTON	IRELAND	WON	23	21	WARREN GATLAND
635	12/02/2012	6N	HOME	CARDIFF	RYAN JONES	SCOTLAND	WON	27	13	WARREN GATLAND
636	25/02/2012	6N	AWAY	LONDON	SAM WARBURTON	ENGLAND	WON	19	12	WARREN GATLAND
637	10/03/2012	6N	HOME	CARDIFF	GETHIN JENKINS	ITALY	WON	24	3	WARREN GATLAND
638	17/03/2012	6N	HOME	CARDIFF	SAM WARBURTON	FRANCE	WON	16	9	WARREN GATLAND
639	02/06/2012	TEST	HOME	CARDIFF	MATTHEW REES	BARBARIANS	WON	30	21	ROBERT HOWLEY
640	09/06/2012	TEST (1)	AWAY	BRISBANE	SAM WARBURTON	AUSTRALIA	LOST	19	27	ROBERT HOWLEY
641	16/06/2012	TEST (2)	AWAY	MELBOURNE	SAM WARBURTON	AUSTRALIA	LOST	23	25	ROBERT HOWLEY
642	23/06/2012	TEST (3)	AWAY	SYDNEY	SAM WARBURTON	AUSTRALIA	LOST	19	20	ROBERT HOWLEY
643	10/11/2012	TEST	HOME	CARDIFF	SAM WARBURTON	ARGENTINA	LOST	12	26	ROBERT HOWLEY
644	16/11/2012	TEST	HOME	CARDIFF	RYAN JONES	SAMOA	LOST	19	26	ROBERT HOWLEY
645	24/11/2012	TEST	HOME	CARDIFF	SAM WARBURTON	NEW ZEALAND	LOST	10	33	WARREN GATLAND
646	01/12/2012	TEST	HOME	CARDIFF	SAM WARBURTON	AUSTRALIA	LOST	12	14	WARREN GATLAND
647	02/02/2013	6N	HOME	CARDIFF	SAM WARBURTON	IRELAND	LOST	22	30	ROBERT HOWLEY
648	09/02/2013	6N	AWAY	PARIS	RYAN JONES	FRANCE	WON	16	6	ROBERT HOWLEY
649	23/02/2013	6N	AWAY	ROME	RYAN JONES	ITALY	WON	26	9	ROBERT HOWLEY

GAME	DATE	TYPE	H/A	CITY	CAPTAIN	OPPONENTS	RESULT	SCORE (FOR)	SCORE (OPP)	COACH
650	09/03/2013	6N	AWAY	EDINBURGH	RYAN JONES	SCOTLAND	WON	28	18	ROBERT HOWLEY
651	16/03/2013	6N	HOME	CARDIFF	GETHIN JENKINS	ENGLAND	WON	30	3	ROBERT HOWLEY
652	08/06/2013	TEST (1)	AWAY	OSAKA	BRADLEY DAVIES	JAPAN	WON	22	18	ROBIN McBRYDE
653	15/06/2013	TEST (2)	AWAY	TOKYO	BRADLEY DAVIES	JAPAN	LOST	8	23	ROBIN McBRYDE
654	09/11/2013	TEST	HOME	CARDIFF	SAM WARBURTON	SOUTH AFRICA	LOST	15	24	WARREN GATLAND
655	16/11/2013	TEST	HOME	CARDIFF	SAM WARBURTON	ARGENTINA	WON	40	6	WARREN GATLAND
656	22/11/2013	TEST	HOME	CARDIFF	RYAN JONES	TONGA	WON	17	7	WARREN GATLAND
657	30/11/2013	TEST	HOME	CARDIFF	SAM WARBURTON	AUSTRALIA	LOST	26	30	WARREN GATLAND
658	01/02/2014	6N	HOME	CARDIFF	ALUN WYN JONES	ITALY	WON	23	15	WARREN GATLAND
659	08/02/2014	6N	AWAY	DUBLIN	SAM WARBURTON	IRELAND	LOST	3	26	WARREN GATLAND
660	21/02/2014	6N	HOME	CARDIFF	SAM WARBURTON	FRANCE	WON	27	6	WARREN GATLAND
661	09/03/2014	6N	AWAY	LONDON	SAM WARBURTON	ENGLAND	LOST	18	29	WARREN GATLAND
662	15/03/2014	6N	HOME	CARDIFF	SAM WARBURTON	SCOTLAND	WON	51	3	WARREN GATLAND
663	14/06/2014	TEST (1)	AWAY	DURBAN	ALUN WYN JONES	SOUTH AFRICA	LOST	16	38	WARREN GATLAND
664	21/06/2014	TEST (2)	AWAY	NELSPRUIT	ALUN WYN JONES	SOUTH AFRICA	LOST	30	31	WARREN GATLAND
665	08/11/2014	TEST	HOME	CARDIFF	SAM WARBURTON	AUSTRALIA	LOST	28	33	WARREN GATLAND
666	15/11/2014	TEST	HOME	CARDIFF	GETHIN JENKINS	FIJI	WON	17	13	WARREN GATLAND
667	22/11/2014	TEST	HOME	CARDIFF	SAM WARBURTON	NEW ZEALAND	LOST	16	34	WARREN GATLAND
668	29/11/2014	TEST	HOME	CARDIFF	SAM WARBURTON	SOUTH AFRICA	WON	12	6	WARREN GATLAND
669	06/02/2015	6N	HOME	CARDIFF	SAM WARBURTON	ENGLAND	LOST	16	21	WARREN GATLAND
670	15/02/2015	6N	AWAY	EDINBURGH	SAM WARBURTON	SCOTLAND	WON	26	23	WARREN GATLAND
671	28/02/2015	6N	AWAY	PARIS	SAM WARBURTON	FRANCE	WON	20	13	WARREN GATLAND
672	14/03/2015	6N	HOME	CARDIFF	SAM WARBURTON	IRELAND	WON	23	16	WARREN GATLAND
673	21/03/2015	6N	AWAY	ROME	SCOTT WILLIAMS	ITALY	WON	61	20	WARREN GATLAND
674	08/08/2015	WCW	HOME	CARDIFF	SAM WARBURTON	IRELAND	LOST	21	35	WARREN GATLAND
675	29/08/2015	WCW	AWAY	DUBLIN	ALUN WYN JONES	IRELAND	WON	16	10	WARREN GATLAND
676	05/09/2015	WCW	HOME	CARDIFF	SAM WARBURTON	ITALY	WON	23	19	WARREN GATLAND
677	20/09/2015	WC	HOME	CARDIFF	SAM WARBURTON	URUGUAY	WON	54	9	WARREN GATLAND
678	26/09/2015	WC	AWAY	LONDON	SAM WARBURTON	ENGLAND	WON	28	25	WARREN GATLAND
679	01/10/2015	WC	HOME	CARDIFF	SAM WARBURTON	FIJI	WON	23	13	WARREN GATLAND
680	10/10/2015	WC	AWAY	LONDON	SAM WARBURTON	AUSTRALIA	LOST	6	15	WARREN GATLAND
681	17/10/2015	WC(QF)	NEUT	LONDON	SAM WARBURTON	SOUTH AFRICA	LOST	19	23	WARREN GATLAND
682	07/02/2016	6N	AWAY	DUBLIN	SAM WARBURTON	IRELAND	DRAW	16	16	WARREN GATLAND
683	13/02/2016	6N	HOME	CARDIFF	SAM WARBURTON	SCOTLAND	WON	27	23	WARREN GATLAND
684	26/02/2016	6N	HOME	CARDIFF	SAM WARBURTON	FRANCE	WON	19	10	WARREN GATLAND
685	12/03/2016	6N	AWAY	LONDON	SAM WARBURTON	ENGLAND	LOST	21	25	WARREN GATLAND
686	19/03/2016	6N	HOME	CARDIFF	DAN LYDIATE	ITALY	WON	67	14	WARREN GATLAND
687	29/05/2016	TEST	AWAY	LONDON	DAN LYDIATE	ENGLAND	LOST	13	27	WARREN GATLAND
688	11/06/2016	TEST (1)	AWAY	AUCKLAND	SAM WARBURTON	NEW ZEALAND	LOST	21	39	WARREN GATLAND
689	18/06/2016	TEST (2)	AWAY	WELLINGTON	SAM WARBURTON	NEW ZEALAND	LOST	22	36	WARREN GATLAND
690	25/06/2016	TEST (3)	AWAY	DUNEDIN	SAM WARBURTON	NEW ZEALAND	LOST	6	46	WARREN GATLAND
691	05/11/2016	TEST	HOME	CARDIFF	GETHIN JENKINS	AUSTRALIA	LOST	8	32	ROBERT HOWLEY
692	12/11/2016	TEST	HOME	CARDIFF	GETHIN JENKINS	ARGENTINA	WON	24	20	ROBERT HOWLEY
693	19/11/2016	TEST	HOME	CARDIFF	SAM WARBURTON	JAPAN	WON	33	30	ROBERT HOWLEY

GAME	DATE	TYPE	H/A	CITY	CAPTAIN	OPPONENTS	RESULT	SCORE (FOR)	SCORE (OPP)	COACH
694	26/11/2016	TEST	HOME	CARDIFF	GETHIN JENKINS	SOUTH AFRICA	WON	27	13	ROBERT HOWLEY
695	05/02/2017	6N	AWAY	ROME	ALUN WYN JONES	ITALY	WON	33	7	ROBERT HOWLEY
696	11/02/2017	6N	HOME	CARDIFF	ALUN WYN JONES	ENGLAND	LOST	16	21	ROBERT HOWLEY
697	25/02/2017	6N	AWAY	EDINBURGH	ALUN WYN JONES	SCOTLAND	LOST	13	29	ROBERT HOWLEY
698	10/03/2017	6N	HOME	CARDIFF	ALUN WYN JONES	IRELAND	WON	22	9	ROBERT HOWLEY
699	18/03/2017	6N	AWAY	PARIS	ALUN WYN JONES	FRANCE	LOST	18	20	ROBERT HOWLEY
700	16/06/2017	TEST	NEUT	AUCKLAND	JAMIE ROBERTS	TONGA	WON	24	6	ROBIN McBRYDE
701	23/06/2017	TEST	AWAY	APIA	JAMIE ROBERTS	SAMOA	WON	19	17	ROBIN McBRYDE
702	11/11/2017	TEST	HOME	CARDIFF	ALUN WYN JONES	AUSTRALIA	LOST	21	29	WARREN GATLAND
703	18/11/2017	TEST	HOME	CARDIFF	DAN LYDIATE	GEORGIA	WON	13	6	WARREN GATLAND
704	25/11/2017	TEST	HOME	CARDIFF	ALUN WYN JONES	NEW ZEALAND	LOST	18	33	WARREN GATLAND
705	02/12/2017	TEST	HOME	CARDIFF	ALUN WYN JONES	SOUTH AFRICA	WON	24	22	WARREN GATLAND
706	03/02/2018	6N	HOME	CARDIFF	ALUN WYN JONES	SCOTLAND	WON	34	7	WARREN GATLAND
707	10/02/2018	6N	AWAY	LONDON	ALUN WYN JONES	ENGLAND	LOST	6	12	WARREN GATLAND
708	24/02/2018	6N	AWAY	DUBLIN	ALUN WYN JONES	IRELAND	LOST	27	37	WARREN GATLAND
709	11/03/2018	6N	HOME	CARDIFF	TAULUPE FALETAU	ITALY	WON	38	14	WARREN GATLAND
710	17/03/2018	6N	HOME	CARDIFF	ALUN WYN JONES	FRANCE	WON	14	13	WARREN GATLAND
711	02/06/2018	TEST	NEUT	WASHINGTON DC	ELLIS JENKINS	SOUTH AFRICA	WON	22	20	WARREN GATLAND
712	09/06/2018	TEST (1)	AWAY	SAN JUAN	CORY HILL	ARGENTINA	WON	23	10	WARREN GATLAND
713	16/06/2018	TEST (2)	AWAY	SANTA FE	CORY HILL	ARGENTINA	WON	30	12	WARREN GATLAND
714	03/11/2018	TEST	HOME	CARDIFF	ALUN WYN JONES	SCOTLAND	WON	21	10	WARREN GATLAND
715	10/11/2018	TEST	HOME	CARDIFF	ALUN WYN JONES	AUSTRALIA	WON	9	6	WARREN GATLAND
716	17/11/2018	TEST	HOME	CARDIFF	ELLIS JENKINS	TONGA	WON	74	24	WARREN GATLAND
717	24/11/2018	TEST	HOME	CARDIFF	ALUN WYN JONES	SOUTH AFRICA	WON	20	11	WARREN GATLAND
718	01/02/2019	6N	AWAY	PARIS	ALUN WYN JONES	FRANCE	WON	24	19	WARREN GATLAND
719	09/02/2019	6N	AWAY	ROME	JONATHAN DAVIES	ITALY	WON	26	15	WARREN GATLAND
720	23/02/2019	6N	HOME	CARDIFF	ALUN WYN JONES	ENGLAND	WON	21	13	WARREN GATLAND
721	09/03/2019	6N	AWAY	EDINBURGH	ALUN WYN JONES	SCOTLAND	WON	18	11	WARREN GATLAND
722	16/03/2019	6N	HOME	CARDIFF	ALUN WYN JONES	IRELAND	WON	25	7	WARREN GATLAND
723	11/08/2019	WCW	AWAY	LONDON	ALUN WYN JONES	ENGLAND	LOST	19	33	WARREN GATLAND
724	17/08/2019	WCW	HOME	CARDIFF	ALUN WYN JONES	ENGLAND	WON	13	6	WARREN GATLAND
725	31/08/2019	WCW	HOME	CARDIFF	JOSH NAVIDI	IRELAND	LOST	17	22	WARREN GATLAND
726	07/09/2019	WCW	AWAY	DUBLIN	ALUN WYN JONES	IRELAND	LOST	10	19	WARREN GATLAND
727	23/09/2019	WC	NEUT	TOYOTA	ALUN WYN JONES	GEORGIA	WON	43	14	WARREN GATLAND
728	29/09/2019	WC	NEUT	TOKYO	ALUN WYN JONES	AUSTRALIA	WON	29	25	WARREN GATLAND
729	09/10/2019	WC	NEUT	OITA	ALUN WYN JONES	FIJI	WON	29	17	WARREN GATLAND
730	13/10/2019	WC	NEUT	KUMAMOTO	JUSTIN TIPURIC	URUGUAY	WON	35	13	WARREN GATLAND
731	20/10/2019	WC(QF)	NEUT	OITA	ALUN WYN JONES	FRANCE	WON	20	19	WARREN GATLAND
732	27/10/2019	WC (SF)	NEUT	YOKOHAMA	ALUN WYN JONES	SOUTH AFRICA	LOST	16	19	WARREN GATLAND
733	01/11/2019	WC(3/4)	NEUT	TOKYO	ALUN WYN JONES	NEW ZEALAND	LOST	17	40	WARREN GATLAND
734	01/02/2020	6N	HOME	CARDIFF	ALUN WYN JONES	ITALY	WON	42	0	WAYNE PIVAC
735	08/02/2020	6N	AWAY	DUBLIN	ALUN WYN JONES	IRELAND	LOST	14	24	WAYNE PIVAC
736	22/02/2020	6N	HOME	CARDIFF	ALUN WYN JONES	FRANCE	LOST	23	27	WAYNE PIVAC
737	07/03/2020	6N	AWAY	LONDON	ALUN WYN JONES	ENGLAND	LOST	30	33	WAYNE PIVAC

GAME	DATE	TYPE	H/A	CITY	CAPTAIN	OPPONENTS	RESULT	SCORE (FOR)	SCORE (OPP)	COACH
738	24/10/2020	TEST	AWAY	PARIS	ALUN WYN JONES	FRANCE	LOST	21	38	WAYNE PIVAC
739	31/10/2020	6N	HOME	LLANELLI	ALUN WYN JONES	SCOTLAND	LOST	10	14	WAYNE PIVAC
740	13/11/2020	AUTC	AWAY	DUBLIN	ALUN WYN JONES	IRELAND	LOST	9	32	WAYNE PIVAC
741	21/11/2020	AUTC	HOME	LLANELLI	JUSTIN TIPURIC	GEORGIA	WON	18	0	WAYNE PIVAC
742	28/11/2020	AUTC	HOME	LLANELLI	ALUN WYN JONES	ENGLAND	LOST	13	24	WAYNE PIVAC
743	05/12/2020	AUTC	HOME	LLANELLI	ALUN WYN JONES	ITALY	WON	38	18	WAYNE PIVAC
744	07/02/2021	6N	HOME	CARDIFF	ALUN WYN JONES	IRELAND	WON	21	16	WAYNE PIVAC
745	13/02/2021	6N	AWAY	EDINBURGH	ALUN WYN JONES	SCOTLAND	WON	25	24	WAYNE PIVAC
746	27/02/2021	6N	HOME	CARDIFF	ALUN WYN JONES	ENGLAND	WON	40	24	WAYNE PIVAC
747	13/03/2021	6N	AWAY	ROME	ALUN WYN JONES	ITALY	WON	48	7	WAYNE PIVAC
748	20/03/2021	6N	AWAY	PARIS	ALUN WYN JONES	FRANCE	LOST	30	32	WAYNE PIVAC
749	03/07/2021	TEST	HOME	CARDIFF	JONATHAN DAVIES	CANADA	WON	68	12	WAYNE PIVAC
750	10/07/2021	TEST (1)	HOME	CARDIFF	JONATHAN DAVIES	ARGENTINA	DRAW	20	20	WAYNE PIVAC
751	17/07/2021	TEST (2)	HOME	CARDIFF	JONATHAN DAVIES	ARGENTINA	LOST	11	33	WAYNE PIVAC
752	30/10/2021	TEST	HOME	CARDIFF	ALUN WYN JONES	NEW ZEALAND	LOST	16	54	WAYNE PIVAC
753	06/11/2021	TEST	HOME	CARDIFF	JONATHAN DAVIES	SOUTH AFRICA	LOST	18	23	WAYNE PIVAC
754	14/11/2021	TEST	HOME	CARDIFF	ELLIS JENKINS	FIJI	WON	38	23	WAYNE PIVAC
755	20/11/2021	TEST	HOME	CARDIFF	ELLIS JENKINS	AUSTRALIA	WON	29	28	WAYNE PIVAC

SELECT BIBLIOGRAPHY

BOOKS

History of Welsh International Rugby (1999) – John Billot (Roman Way Books)

Seeing Red – Twelve Tumultuous Years in Welsh Rugby (2008) – Alun Carter with Nick Bishop (Mainstream Publishing)

The Wales Rugby Miscellany (2008) – Rob Cole and Stuart Farmer (Vision Sports Publishing)

Cardiff Rugby Club – History and Statistics 1876–1975 (1975) – D.E. Davies (Cardiff Athletic Club)

Welsh International Matches 1881–2011 (2011) – Howard Evans (Y Lolfa)

The International Rugby Championship 1883–1983 (1984) – Terry Godwin (Willow Books)

The Phoenix Book of International Rugby (1987) – John Griffiths (Phoenix House)

Behind the Dragon (2019) – Ross Harries (Polaris Publishing)

1905 Originals (2005) – Bob Howitt and Dianne Haworth (Harper Sports)

The Priceless Gift – 125 Years of Welsh Rugby Captains (2005) – Steve Lewis (Mainstream Press)

Prince Gwyn: Gwyn Nicholls and the First Golden Era of Welsh Rugby (1999) – David Parry-Jones (Seren)

Taff's Acre – A History and Celebration of Cardiff Arms Park (1984) – Edited by David Parry-Jones (Willow Books)

A Game for Hooligans – The History of Rugby Union (2006) – Huw Richards (Mainstream Publishing)

The Illustrated History of Welsh Rugby (1980) – J.B.G. Thomas (Pelham)

The Men in Scarlet (1972) – J.B.G. Thomas (Pelham)

Rugby-Playing Man (1977) – Watcyn Thomas (Pelham)

A Century of Welsh Rugby Players (1979) – Wayne Thomas (Ansells Ltd)

Fields of Praise (1980) – David Smith and Gareth Williams (University of Wales Press)

1905 and All That (1991) – Gareth Williams (Gomer Press)

ANNUALS

Rothmans Rugby Union Yearbook (Multiple editions referenced) (Queen Anne Press)

Welsh Brewers Rugby Annual for Wales/Worthington Rugby Annual for Wales/Buy as You View Rugby Annual for Wales (Multiple editions referenced from 1969 to 2003)

WEBSITES

BBC, Cardiff Rugby Museum, *The Daily Telegraph*, ESPN Scrum.com, Gloucester Rugby Heritage, *The Guardian*, People's Collection Wales, *The Times*, Swansea RFC, Wales Online, Wikipedia, Welsh Newspapers Online (The National Library of Wales), WRU official website.

ACKNOWLEDGEMENTS

Just as all number eights must recognise the work those in front of them perform for every try they grab from the back of a scrum, so every author must acknowledge the support of others when nursing a book into the world.

My eternal gratitude to Peter Burns and all at Polaris Publishing for believing in this book and helping me to fulfil a lifelong rugby and writing ambition. I send both thanks and huge admiration to this book's chief illustrator, Raluca Moldovan. She has been a loyal and inspiring collaborator who believed in the project when it was nothing more than an acorn of an idea in my head. Raluca, all the midnight oil you've burned cooked up a perfect visual feast. Here's to many more projects together. Similarly, Josel Nicolas's creativity, enthusiasm and art continues to inspire me and I'm honoured to have had him, and Ched De Gala work on this title. My niece, Carys Feehan, is at the start of what I know will be a hugely successful career in the art world. I'm immensely proud to have her weave a sprinkle of her magic for the cover of the book too. Last but not least on the artistic front, Anne Cakebread's painstaking recreation of every Welsh shirt ever worn by the Test side (under my obsessive eye) must be applauded. Bravo!

Charlie Campbell, Richard Beard, Carolyn Hodges, Rob Cole, John Griffiths, Lloyd Roderick, Hugh Godwin, David McGahan, Toby Trotman, Phil Atkinson and Dave Dow (Swansea RFC) have all in some way inspired, advised, helped or corrected me along the way. Thanks also to Richard Williams and Gloucester Rugby Heritage for help with the 1900 Welsh team photo. I wish to offer my thanks and admiration to Ian Greensill and Katie Field for their patience and professionalism in editing, proofing and improving my copy.

Finally, I cannot express adequately the debt I owe to my family. Firstly, my father has not only been an inspiration to me on the field as a player himself (one of my happiest memories was getting to play a game with him for Barry Plastics before he retired), but, along with my mother, he opened up the world of rugby to me. Dad somehow always managed to get international tickets for me and my sister growing up, providing countless cherished memories – even if the matches themselves, as detailed in this very book, were frequently horror shows.

My father's tireless work in checking the stats for this book went beyond the call of paternal duty and I am indebted to him once again. Any errors that may remain are my own. Love also to my mother for taking me to see my first Cardiff games and for buying me John Griffiths's superb book *The Phoenix Book of International Rugby* when I was a young child – a book that started my love of rugby history. My cousin, Marc Stafford, has worked wonders over the years with technical support for theeastterrace. com. Without the exposure that website gave me, I would not have had so many opportunities to write professionally on this great game. Thank you, Marc.

To my two children, Michael and Helena – you are an inspiration. I hope, when you are older, this book will in some small way further connect you to your ancestral homeland. Finally, to my wife Helena, I offer immeasurable thanks. I will never forget your support over the years and your willingness to let me lose myself in 19th-century match reports when things needed fixing, domestic chores needed doing or enthusiastic children needed entertaining. I hope I did you proud.

James Stafford

ABOUT THE AUTHOR AND ILLUSTRATORS

James Stafford

James is founder of cult rugby website *The East Terrace* and has written on sport for a wide range of newspapers, websites and magazines. In 2017, his collection of short webcomics, *The Sorrowful Putto of Prague*, was published to critical acclaim in the Czech Republic. James broke various limbs and ruined multiple muscles, ligaments and nerves playing rugby for Barry Plastics, Old Belvedere, London Japanese and Nyrsko. Born in Cardiff and raised in Barry, he now lives in Prague.

Twitter/Instagram: @jpstafford
Website: www.theeastterrace.com

Raluca Moldovan

Raluca is a book, comics and commercial illustrator based in Constanța, Romania. Her previous published work includes *The Sorrowful Putto of Prague* (also by James Stafford).

Instagram: @_raloux

Carys Feehan

Carys Feehan, who provided the book's cover art, is a Welsh animation student currently studying in California. Born and raised in Hong Kong, her Welsh heritage has consistently inspired her art work in painting, illustration and filmmaking.

Instagram: @burnthelampposts
Website: www.carysfeehan.weebly.com

Josel Nicolas

Josel, who provided the player illustrations in each chapter, is a Filipino comics editor, artist and writer. He has been making comics since 2006 and previously collaborated with James Stafford on *The Sorrowful Putto of Prague* comics.

Instagram: *@joselnicolasart*
Contact: *josel.nicolas@gmail.com*

Ched De Gala

Ched, who worked on the player illustrations in each chapter, is a freelance Filipino comics artist who enjoys sports.

Instagram: *@ang.sa.tin*
Latest work available at Penlab.Ink

Anne Cakebread

Anne Cakebread is a freelance illustrator with over 20 years' experience in publishing and TV, including cover art and illustrations for numerous books and magazines. She also illustrated sets and props for Boomerang on S4C's award-winning ABC. Anne grew up and went to school in Radyr, Cardiff and now lives with her partner, two whippets and lurcher in St Dogmaels. She runs an art gallery in Cardigan.

Website: *www.cakebreadillustrations.com*